Sonnet Sequences and Social Distinction in Renaissance England

Why were sonnet sequences popular in Renaissance England? In this study, Christopher Warley suggests that sonneteers created a vocabulary to describe, and to invent, new forms of social distinction before an explicit language of social class existed. The tensions inherent in the genre – between lyric and narrative, between sonnet and sequence – offered writers a means of reconceptualizing the relation between individuals and society, a way to try to come to grips with the broad social transformations taking place at the end of the sixteenth century. By stressing the struggle over social classification, the book revises studies that have tied the influence of sonnet sequences either to courtly love or to Renaissance individualism. Drawing on Marxist aesthetic theory, it offers detailed examinations of sequences by Lok, Sidney, Spenser, Shakespeare, Wroth, and Milton. It will be valuable to readers interested in Renaissance and genre studies, and post-Marxist theories of class.

CHRISTOPHER WARLEY is Assistant Professor in the Department of English, Oakland University, Michigan.

Cambridge Studies in Renaissance Literature and Culture

Since the 1970s there has been a broad and vital reinterpretation of the nature of literary texts, a move away from formalism to a sense of literature as an aspect of social, economic, political, and cultural history. While the earliest New Historicist work was criticized for a narrow and anecdotal view of history, it also served as an important stimulus for post-structuralist, feminist, Marxist, and psychoanalytical work, which in turn has increasingly informed and redirected it. Recent writing on the nature of representation, the historical construction of gender and of the concept of identity itself, on theatre as a political and economic phenomenon and on the ideologies of art generally, reveals the breadth of the field. Cambridge Studies in Renaissance Literature and Culture is designed to offer historically oriented studies of Renaissance literature and theatre which make use of the insights afforded by theoretical perspectives. The view of history envisioned is above all a view of our history, a reading of the Renaissance for and from our own time.

Recent titles include

A complete list of books in the series is given at the end of the volume

Sonnet Sequences and Social Distinction in Renaissance England

Christopher Warley
Oakland University, Michigan

 CAMBRIDGE
UNIVERSITY PRESS

CAMBRIDGE UNIVERSITY PRESS

Cambridge, New York, Melbourne, Madrid, Cape Town, Singapore, São Paulo

Cambridge University Press
The Edinburgh Building, Cambridge CB2 2RU, UK

Published in the United States of America by Cambridge University Press, New York

www.cambridge.org
Information on this title: www.cambridge.org/9780521842549

First published 2005

Printed in the United Kingdom at the University Press, Cambridge

A catalogue record for this book is available from the British Library

Library of Congress Cataloguing in Publication data

Warley, Christopher, 1969–
    Sonnet sequences and social distinction in Renaissance England / Christopher Warley.
        p. cm. – (Cambridge studies in Renaissance literature and culture ; [49])
    Series numbering inferred from publisher's listing.
    Includes bibliographical references and index.
    ISBN 0-521-84254-9
    1. Sonnets, English–History and criticism.   2. English poetry–Early modern,
    1500-1700–History and criticism.   3. Literature and society–English–History–16th
    century.   4. Literature and society–England–History–17th century.   5. Social classes in
    literature.   6. Renaissance–England.   7. Cycles (Literature) I. Title. II. Series.

PR509.S7W37 2005
821'.0420903–dc22   200405876

ISBN-13 978-0-521-84254-9   - hardback
ISBN-10 0-521-84254-9   - hardback

For R. N. C.

Contents

Preface

"Self-consciousness exists in and for itself when, and by the fact that, it so exists for another": Hegel's famous first phrase from section 178 of *The Phenomenology of Spirit*, upon which so much twentieth-century critical theory rests, would not have exactly seemed news to Renaissance love poets, who had been writing their own version of a master-slave dialectic in the poetry that dominated Europe for hundreds of years. I have no evidence that Hegel actually paid any attention to sonnet sequences, but his understanding of the interpenetration of subject and object has, for me, an obvious precedent in the dynamics of Renaissance sonnet sequences. The "subject and object problem," what Ernst Cassirer called the "striving" basic to the platonic and neo-platonic doctrine of *eros*, formed the background in one way or another of most Renaissance love poetry. Thanks to Joel Fineman's *Shakespeare's Perjured Eye*, the location of sonnets in such a philosophical trajectory is largely secure. What is less clear is the story of the participation of sonnet sequences in the production of specific social positions. If Renaissance sonneteers would recognize Hegel's argument, they would have also found familiar Marx's critique of Hegel – that subjects and objects are always actual relations between people, not ideas; and that their relation ineluctably involves social oppression. For Marx, the movement between subject and object also sets in motion a historical narrative, the move from feudalism to capitalism, of one set of social positions for another. This was a struggle every Renaissance sonneteer knew intimately.

This book is an effort to understand the participation of sonnet sequences in this transition, a transition which consists not only of a shift in economic systems but also a shift in conceptions of social distinction. It is a transformation made possible by, among many other things, the gradual articulation of new forms of social distinction in Renaissance sonnet sequences. My basic argument is that sonnet sequences became popular in England in and around the 1590s because they provided a form to describe social positions for which no explicit vocabulary existed. I insist throughout that one cannot talk about Renaissance sonnet sequences without talking about social distinction; it is probably worth stressing that it does not follow that one cannot talk about social distinction in the Renaissance without talking about sonnet sequences.

I am fortunate to have had lots of friends and colleagues willing to put up with this book. Special thanks go to Roland Greene, whose sympathy and support I can never requite; and Emily Bartels, who patiently and enthusiastically advised the dissertation version. Jacqueline Miller and Ann Coiro were best of advisers on interminable early drafts, and Stephen Orgel's reading of the final manuscript effortlessly clarified things that had seemed opaque to me. I am lucky to know Elizabeth Hanson, Lori Newcomb, and Curtis Perry, who, within the sometimes bruising world of academe, remind me that thinking about the Renaissance can actually be worthwhile, and even fun. I am grateful to Vicki Cooper, Rebecca Jones, and Joanna Breeze at Cambridge for making my life with the manuscript much easier. Endless thanks to an anonymous reader for Cambridge, Jenny Andersen, Rob Anderson, Leeds Barrol, Marshall Brown, Anne Coldiron, Jonathan Goldberg, Richard Halpern, Margaret Hannay, Chris Martin, Mark Netzloff, William Oram, and Anne Prescott, who all made vital comments on individual chapters. I am especially grateful to Anne Prescott and Leeds Barrol, whose Folger seminars were crucial shaping influences. Mark Netzloff's invitation to the Early Modern Group at Wisconsin-Milwaukee made possible some vital last-minute revisions. Thanks to the librarians at the Folger, Oakland, Rutgers, Michigan, Penn, and Princeton for their generous assistance. I have learned a lot from conversations with Barbara Correll, Valerie Forman, Barbara Fuchs, Bill Galperin, Myra Jehlen, Ron Levao, Bridget Lyons, Michael McKeon, David Lee Miller, Larry Scanlon, Gordon Schochet, Jim Siemon, Henry Turner, and Dan Vitkus. Thanks to my colleagues at Oakland University for making the department such an amiable place to work. Extra thanks to the fabulous staffs at Tuscany Cafe in Philadelphia and Java Hutt in Birmingham where, escaping from very small apartments, I wrote much of this book. Extra special thanks to students at Rutgers and Oakland whose skepticism, resistance, and energy can't be valued highly enough. I am lucky to have a group of fabulous friends who sort of understand why anyone would want to write such a thing: Erik Dussere, Jason Gieger, David Toise, Jonathan Nashel, Rebecca Brittenham, Joseph Chaves, Matt Guterl, and Annie Gilson. Finally, Rosanne Currarino, the nicest person on the planet, read every syllable, patiently endured my rants, and gently corrected my prose and my pride.

Earlier versions of some chapters appeared previously as "'The English straine': Drayton's *Ideas*, 1594–1619," in *Material Culture and Cultural*

Materialisms in the Middle Ages and the Renaissance, ed. Curtis Perry (Brepols, 2001), 177–202; "'An English box': Calvinism and Class in Anne Lok's *A Meditation of a Penitent Sinner*," *Spenser Studies* XV (2001): 205–41; and "'So plenty makes me poore': Ireland, Capitalism, and Class in Spenser's *Amoretti and Epithalamion*," *ELH* 69.3 (2002): 567–98.

1   Sonnet sequences and social distinction

Why must we worry over so simple a thing as preface-making?[1]

The individual or collective classification struggles aimed at transforming the categories of perception and appreciation of the social world and, through this, the social world itself, are indeed a forgotten dimension of the class struggle.[2]

Who so shall duly consider the whole Progresse of mans estate from life to death, shall finde it gentle Reader, to be nothing else but a verse pilgrimage through this earth to another world.[3]

One of the remarkable features of Drayton's 1619 folio *Poems* is the persistent voice of Drayton the pedantic literary historian. At the beginning of each section, a note lectures readers about the poem that follows. The preface to *The Barrons Warres* contains an elaborate discussion (complete with diagrams) of the rhyme-scheme of the stanzas, and Drayton goes on to cite as models "*Homers Iliads*, and *Ulysiads*," "*Virgils Æneis, Statius Thebaies, Silius* worke of the Carthaginian warre, *Illyricus Argonauticks, Vida's Christeies*," and Spenser. At the beginning of the *Odes*, Drayton launches into a two-page defense of his use of the term "ode" ("yet Criticism it selfe cannot say, that the Name is wrongfully vsurped"), citing as models Pindar, Anacreon, Horace, Petrarch, Chaucer, and "Colin Clout." Drayton justifies his use of "heroicall" in *Englands Heroicall Epistles* (from Ovid), of "legend" in *The Legend of Robert, Dvke of Normandy, Matilda the Faire, Pierce Gaveston . . . [and] Thomas Cromwell* ("*so called of the Latine Gerund,* Legendum, *and signifying . . . things specially worthy to be read, was anciently used in an Ecclesiasticall sense, and restrained therein to things written in Prose, touching the Lives of Saints*"). Likewise, he defends his use of an animal in *The Owle* ("*As the Princes of the* Greekes *and* Latines, *the first of the Frogs Warre, the latter of a poore Gnat*") and finally of "pastoral" in *Pastorals Contayning Eglogues, With the Man in the Moone* (from Theocritus, Virgil, and, of course, Spenser again).

    Idea, however, receives no such attention. Rather than a learned discussion of models ("from Petrarch, the *Pléiade*, Sidney, and Spenser"),

1

the only prefatory material to *Idea* is the sonnet "To the Reader of these Sonnets":

> INTO *these Loves, who but for Passion lookes,*
> *At this first sight, here let him lay them by,*
> *And seeke else-where, in turning other Bookes,*
> *Which better may his labour satisfie.*
> *No farre-fetch'd Sigh shall ever wound my Brest,*
> *Love from mine Eye a Teare shall never wring,*
> *Nor in* Ah-mees *my whyning Sonnets drest,*
> *(A Libertine) fanstastickly I sing:*
> *My Verse is the true image of my Mind,*
> *Ever in motion, still desiring change;*
> *And as thus to Varietie inclin'd,*
> *So in all Humors sportively I range:*
> *My Muse is rightly of the* English *straine,*
> *That cannot long one Fashion intertaine.*[4]

While the sonnet alludes to "other Bookes" where one seeking "Passion" might be better served, those books are never cataloged. Instead, the speaker tries sharply to distinguish himself from a vague sense of "*Ah-mees* in whyning Sonnets drest" by emphasizing that "My Muse is rightly of the *English* straine, / That cannot long one Fashion intertaine." The sonnet certainly invokes a loose tradition within and against which it is set, but read against the detailed, almost prolix, standard of Drayton's other introductions, "Into these Loves" sounds notably brief and vague. Despite Drayton's evident obsession with delineating the poets and the works upon which his own are based, the exact genre of *Idea* and the contours of "the English straine" are never made explicit. Indeed, Drayton's gestures toward "other Bookes" might suggest a nervousness about his new and (merely) fashionable poetry. What did Drayton think he was writing? What models does he follow? What genre is *Idea*?

This book tries to answer these questions by reconsidering, in broad poetic and social perspectives, what works like *Idea* are and what it meant to write them in Renaissance England. I call these works *sonnet sequences*, which is not a term Drayton or any other English Renaissance writer uses.[5] I employ it, somewhat anachronistically, in order to explain what Drayton was writing, but I also use it to understand why he did not, and could not, write a preface to *Idea*. Unlike epic and romance, which were well-defined forms with distinct classical precedents that maintained definite social positions in the Renaissance, sonnet sequences were always hazy in both their form and their social implications.[6] They were, in Petrarch's famous phrase, "rime sparse," scattered rhymes, whose coherence is notoriously difficult to pin down. Sonnet sequences have classical influences (Ovid and Catullus most prominently), but there are no classical precedents.[7] As Bakhtin remarks about the novel, Renaissance sonnet sequences develop "in the full light of the historical day." Like novels, the "forces that define" sonnet sequences "as a genre are at work before our very eyes."[8] The absence of a preface to *Idea* is consequently more than a purely literary or linguistic problem: it is also a social problem. The cultural importance of sonnet sequences from 1560–1619 occurs, I will argue, because they provided writers with a unique form to describe, and to invent, new social positions before there existed an explicit vocabulary to define them. There is no preface to *Idea*, and no name in the period for the sort of work it is, because the social position that could create such a name is in the process of differentiating itself. My interest in reading these works lies in this emergent sense of social distinction embedded in a tacit sense of form. As a result, I am not interested in defining sonnet sequences in any systematic way.[9] Rather than supplying the missing preface to *Idea*, I want instead to describe the implications of its conspicuous absence. Sonnet sequences articulate an emergent way of making social distinctions for which no explicit terms existed in Renaissance England, and I will call this nascent process *class*. By the term class I do not mean distinct groups or "classes"; instead, throughout the book class names a unique process of social differentiation. Sequences are not, of course, the only location where such a procedure appears, but, as their massive literary influence suggests, they are a vital one.

The dynamics of this implicit sense of form are tied up in the couplet of Drayton's introductory sonnet: "My Muse is rightly of the *English* straine, / That cannot long one Fashion intertaine." "[S]traine" here is a structural, virtually generic, term; it means an order, a class, a lineage – a specific means of organizing the playful changes of "Fashion." The genre of the poem might reasonably be called, in this sense, "the English straine" itself, because "English straine" names the order into which the sonnet fits ("is rightly of"). But "straine" also means tension and discontinuity. The playful paradox of the sonnet, of course, is that whatever organizing principle operates in the poem is centrally defined by its fashionableness, by its mutability and changeableness – exactly the opposite, in some sense, of an organizing principle. "Straine" means both order and absence of order; it suggests a virtually random, isolated poem as well as a more coherent work and a tradition within which that poem fits, a presence and its deconstruction. If the sonnet is distinguished by its position within "the *English* straine," it is also distinguished by its changeableness, by its resistance to being "positioned" at all.

The social implications of this formal argument are apparent in the word "Fashion." "Fashion" signifies not only a momentary cultural taste of which Drayton's speaker is a dedicated follower. "Fashion" also implies a social rank, a sort or kind. When Hermione protests in *The Winter's Tale*, for example, that she has been "denied" the "child-bed privilege" "which 'longs / To women of all fashion," she means a "privilege" belonging to women of all social rank.[10] Her complaint is that her social status has not assisted her at all, that she is denied "privileges" enjoyed by all women; moreover, she seems to stress that all women *have* a fashion, that they do not exist apart from a specific rank. The speaker's claim in Drayton's sonnet that he is "rightly of the *English* straine / That cannot long one fashion intertaine" consequently indicates that he occupies a specific point in social space. To be of "the *English* straine" is to exist in a particular "Fashion," a particular social position. Drayton's speaker is remarkable, of course, because his "Fashion" calls social rank and social order itself into question. "The *English* straine . . . cannot long one *Fashion* intertaine": his strain cannot long maintain a particular social rank or a specific social order. Instead, Drayton's "straine" "*inter*taine[s]": it obtains or gets a distinct social position between ("inter") more permanently maintained social positions or "Fashions." What is changeable or fashionable in *Idea* is not only poetic taste but the social distinction produced and reflected by that taste: the fashion of fashion. We might consequently call the performance of Drayton's speaker an instance of what Stephen Greenblatt terms "self-fashioning," but it is a "Fashion" that calls into question the stability of the very social order into which this poetic self places itself.[11] Drayton's speaker both claims a social rank and calls into question the means by which social rank might be understood at all: "Fashion" itself becomes merely "fashionable."

At the same time, the contradictions tied up in Drayton's fashionable strain themselves reflect broader social processes. Drayton's speaker does not only insert himself into a preexisting order; his desire to do so enacts a structuring process – a social order which orders the speaker. To paraphrase Bourdieu, distinctions distinguish the distinguisher; fashion fashions the fashioner.[12] Drayton's speaker claims to be "rightly of the *English* straine" because "the *English* straine" has already, in a sense, created his desire to be rightly of it. Such an argument need not mean that Drayton's speaker is merely contained within a larger social formation, helplessly interpellated by the ideological apparatus of "the *English* straine" or a mere effect of power, two by now notorious critical turns.[13] Instead, the subtle breakdown in social order apparent in Drayton's strain, its ability to "intertaine" Fashion, is also a manifestation of a broader shift in social categories, a social struggle over how to classify and organize social space.[14] What *is* "the social order" in this sonnet? What is "the *English* straine" that inscribes itself through the speaker's desire?[15] The paradox of the sonnet is a social position which emerges out of a change in social positioning, that emerges out of social incommensurability. The work actively participates in the struggle to conceptualize, and to produce, poetic and social order in early seventeenth-century England. This process of production signals, in Christopher Pye's words, "that any cultural phenomenon exists always in relation to a necessarily forced and unstable totalization of the social domain as such."[16] Drayton's "*English* straine" is a struggle over what the social order is and should be.[17]

The 1619 *Idea* stands at the end of a moment in which sonnet sequences maintained a remarkable cultural influence. Sonnet sequences were popular in England for about thirty years, from the 1580s to the 1610s. Depending on how one counts, there were about twenty written, but their influence was felt everywhere, ranging from parody (Donne insisted that only a fool couldn't write a sonnet; Jonson went to some length to explain why he wrote "not of love") to hegemonic dominance (Queen Elizabeth's tendency to use the language of sonnets to conduct foreign policy).[18] Nevertheless, the primary source of the influence of sonnet sequences, I will argue, is their participation in social struggle, their conceptual discontinuity. I want to describe the dynamics of Drayton's "straine" without stabilizing it to the point where it becomes definitive and systematic because it is the social and poetic instability of sequences which made them culturally influential. My operating assumption is that sonnet sequences throughout the period tend to articulate a series of social and linguistic contradictions. On the one hand, these works generally imagine an idealized social order – Lok's Calvinist God, Sidney's nobility, Spenser's Irish landlord, Shakespeare's young man. This idealized order inscribes itself in the desires of the speakers in the sequences; what they desire is, in a general sense, this ideal order. On the other hand, the vocabulary and conceptual apparatus used to reinforce that order tends paradoxically to undermine it. In an effort to be "rightly of" a particular social order, sonnet speakers instead articulate a new form of social distinction. When Shakespeare's speaker uses a distinct economic vocabulary to praise the young man ("increase," the last word of the first line of the first sonnet, means among other things financial interest), that vocabulary itself becomes associated with the dark lady – the conceptual antithesis of the young man. The distinction the work tries to confer on the young man threatens to collapse as a result of the very vocabulary used to create that distinction.

Likewise, when Spenser's speaker in the *Amoretti* fantasizes about becoming a quasi-feudal landlord, that social imaginary is undermined when he describes both his land and his lady as capital – a new form of property which tends to replace "lords" of land with "owners" of land. Sonnet sequences articulate new forms of social authority, consequently, but they do so without the cooperation, or possibly even the awareness, of their speakers.[19]

The forms of social distinction that emerge in these sequences are consequently an unintended consequence of their internally contradicted desires. As Joel Fineman argues in *Shakespeare's Perjured Eye*, the presence of the dark lady in Shakespeare's *Sonnets*, as one who "is both fair and foul at once," "situate[s] the poetics of ideal visionary presence in a retrospective past, marking it as something which exists 'now' only as an imaginary ideal *after which* the poet lusts . . . Representation carries with it its regretting difference from that which it presents, provoking a desire for that which, as representation, it necessarily absents."[20] While Fineman sees this "perjur'd eye" as an "invention" of Shakespeare's *Sonnets*, I see this internally contradicted desire as a general feature of all sonnet sequences in the period. More importantly, I see this desire as a *social* desire, a yearning for an idealized social order that, in turn, articulates the social position of the speaker. Rather than Fineman's term "poetic subjectivity," an abstraction which tends to obscure the social specificity of desire under the rule of what Fineman calls the "languageness of language," we should instead speak of *social distinction*. Bourdieu's phrase maintains the emphasis on the "regretting difference" of Fineman's subject, but it addresses itself to the social position of such utterance, what Marx (whom Fineman curiously never mentions) might call the real conditions of such difference. The social struggle in these sequences lies in the (preposterously failing) efforts of the speakers to impose one system of classification – a Calvinist God, a feudal lord – by utilizing a set of terms which introduces a different system of classification – say, mercantilism. This struggle, in and of itself, demarcates the social positions of these sonnet speakers, and this process is what Drayton calls "the *English* straine," an emergent form of social distinction.

These are not the usual questions posed about sonnet sequences. Indeed, for well over a hundred years, the name of the genre of *Idea*, and the models that Drayton follows, have seemed pretty obvious. In what has become an orthodox literary history, *Idea* is ordinarily seen as a work following the model of Petrarch's *Rime Sparse* and subsequent continental poets that is composed out of conventional, often hyperbolic language expressing the complaint of a male lover directed at a cruel yet remote mistress.[21] In this now traditional account, Drayton's *Idea* sits (a bit belatedly) at the end of the great moment of Petrarchism in England, the "vogue for sonneteering." This vogue occurred in the 1590s in the wake of the publication of Sidney's *Astrophil and Stella* in 1591, and it drew upon and expressed many of the core ideas of the cult of Queen Elizabeth. Sonnet sequences were popular and culturally significant, the argument runs, because a prominent, learned noble had written one and because they struck a chord with Elizabeth's political penchant for depicting herself as a love object. The association with the prestige of humanist continental learning and the power of the English court likewise encouraged the influence of these poems on other genres, readily apparent in works from *Romeo and Juliet* to Book III of *The Faerie Queene*. Something like this definition has held since about the mid-nineteenth century. Since the 1960s, this account has been partially amended, so that now the conventional language of Petrarchism is generally understood as also facilitating more political concerns, especially the ideological construction of the Elizabethan court, Tudor absolutism, Renaissance patriarchy, and nascent imperialism. Over the last twenty-five years, the idea that Renaissance sonnet sequences are not simply about love but also about politics broadly conceived has itself become nearly as entrenched as the concept of their "conventional" language.[22]

There have always been well-known difficulties with these explanations, but recent scholarship has begun to push them to the breaking point. First, if the vogue for sonnets was closely tied to the cult of Elizabeth, how come this vogue did not occur until twenty-five years after she came to power? Tying sonnets to the queen likewise assumes a cultural centrality to the court that much recent historical work has substantially called into question.[23] Steven May has shown that very few Elizabethan poets could count as "courtiers," and even fewer writers of sonnet sequences could.[24] If court remained a crucial influence upon any poet, it was certainly not the only one. Second, if Petrarchism was a highly conventional language, why are the works under that name often so different? As William Kennedy has shown, there were many "Petrarchs" in Renaissance Europe "authorizing" a wide variety of political, religious, and gender configurations; out of the many commentaries on the *Rime Sparse* "emerges a Petrarch who could be anything and everything to all readers."[25] Suggesting that English sonneteers are somehow "late" on the Renaissance literary scene, that they stand at the end of an exhausted epideictic tradition, posits a homogeneity to Petrarchism that exists only in theory, a true path through Petrarchism that no one ever actually took. It assumes that

Petrarchism is, in Roland Greene's critique, "one thing," a literary form with a clear set of ideological implications.[26] Indeed, the critical compulsion to trace the origins of sequences to the unified corpus of Petrarch perhaps betrays a critical suspicion that these works might be thoroughly *un*conventional and that they are continually on the verge of deconstructing themselves. Third, if Petrarchism was so central to the formation of Renaissance patriarchy, why is the use of gender in these works so notoriously slippery – from conspicuously female authors, to dominating queens, to effeminate, if not emasculated, male speakers? As Diana Henderson argues, the gender dynamics of Petrarchism in the period do not play out an "injustice" so much as they dramatize a number of competing interests. Lynn Enterline similarly emphasizes that the "narrow focus on the Petrarchan *blason*" inaugurated by the work of Nancy Vickers has produced "a too monolithic view of subjectivity and masculinity (or of gender more generally) and a too pessimistic view of the regulatory force of [Petrarch's] rhetorical practice."[27] Such criticism has consequently begun to undermine the concept of an eternal "masculine domination" in these works by examining the "historical mechanisms and institutions" which abstract specific gender relations from their historical moment in order to make these relations appear universal.[28]

In light of such revisions, it is no longer critically viable simply to label *Idea* and other sonnet sequences as "Petrarchan" and then proceed to catalogue the various ideologies purportedly expressed by a homogenous tradition. As I argue in chapter two, the use of "conventions" to read Renaissance sonnet sequences was effectively invented in the nineteenth century and actually reiterates nineteenth-century conceptions of class. I do not at all mean to imply, of course, that a tradition of sonneteering did not exist in the Renaissance or that there were no "Petrarchan tropes": these things obviously existed. Drayton and the other writers I study are clearly operating within well-defined, though largely tacit, parameters, and it is impossible that any contemporary reader would pick up the 1619 folio, turn to *Idea*, and have no idea what it was. The term "sonnet" itself, though flexible, tended to indicate a poem of a particular length with a particular rhyme scheme (though, as we will see, the sharp differentiation of rhyme scheme according to author and nationality – especially Italian versus English, Petrarch versus Shakespeare – is also largely a nineteenth-century phenomenon). Throughout, I am interested in precisely this pervasive yet tacit understanding of the form. At the same time, however, the conspicuous lack of a preface for *Idea* is inescapable in such an otherwise scholarly volume; likewise, the mutability of the term "sonnet" to mean anything from a strictly defined poetic form to any love poem at all reiterates the opaque unity of these works. As Greene argues, lyric was "a widely adaptable literary technology in the early modern period, offering an outlet to any number of formed views and inchoate reactions";[29] putting sonnets into a broader work, a sequence of sonnets, tends in the period to exacerbate this adaptability, not resolve it into a coherent, systemic, and ideologically stable meaning. Filling in the blank at the start of *Idea* with a static conception of "Petrarchism" consequently misses everything that is dynamic about Drayton's work and sequences in general: Drayton both knows perfectly well what he is writing, and he has no name for it – that is, at some level he does not know what he is writing even though he has a feel for how it ought to look. Like other sonneteers, Drayton participates in a series of social contradictions of which he is only partially aware but to which he intuitively responds. Rather than a homogeneous poetic tradition, sonnet sequences mediate between a wide range of cultural events: English Calvinism (Lok), colonial activity in Ireland (Spenser), mercantilism and the new language of economics (Shakespeare), the book trade and absolutism (Drayton), and the reinvention of a masculine, aristocratic imaginary (Sidney). Sonnet sequences are intimately connected to all these issues (and many others as well, of course) because they provide a form within which writers could begin to describe the implications of these events and discourses, a vocabulary with which a new sort of social distinction, class, could in part be invented. The distance between a devout Calvinist like Anne Lok and a public playwright like William Shakespeare is consequently not so great as it might initially seem.[30] What ties them together are not simply the technical similarities of their works (fourteen-line poems gathered together) but the broader cultural implications of the incommensurability of the form itself: the social distinction that begins to emerge in poetic form.

There is, of course, a long critical tradition of formal analysis of these works, and it has tended to center on the complex relation between "sonnet" and "sequence," between the desires and language of particular sonnets and the broader organizations within which those desires exist. The terms usually deployed to describe this problem are "lyric" and "narrative," by which critics have tended to mean either a sense of a sonnet sequence as an internally directed, lyric performance or a sense of it as an externally directly mimesis, usually an attempt to represent a performance or character.[31] Conceived in a lyric mode, for example, Drayton's "English straine" is an isolated, ephemeral moment, resisting, if not transcending, any broader organizing principle. Here is the fragility, the temporal effervescence, the inwardness, that critics since the Romantics have celebrated as lyric's most important defining feature.[32]

On the other hand, conceived as a narrative, Drayton's sonnet is an introduction to a more coherent story, the tale of his passion and his love, a familiar (the usual term is "conventional") complaint that firmly establishes the position of the sonnet in a narrative trajectory and (usually) a social hierarchy. Whatever lyric brilliance flashes forth is contained in the broader conceptual organization of the story of the speaker's woe.[33]

At a phenomenological level, this tension probably always exists in any lyric utterance. I depend on this formal tradition in my account of sequences, and in particular on those readers (Mazzota, Vickers, Freccero, Greene) who have stressed the dialectical relation between lyric and narrative in these works. But I also build on this tradition by stressing the historical specificity of these formal relations: while a phenomenological reading can always identify these formal structures, what those structures signal socially changes dramatically over time. Writing in 1880 to D. G. Rossetti, T. H. Hall Caine makes clear that he imagines sonnets and sequences as very different things. He remarks about Shakespeare's *Sonnets* that "although every fully authenticated sonnet has something about [it] of the charm peculiar to Shakespeare whenever the personality of the creator is seen behind the veil of the creation, I doubt if there are not very many poor things in the series when judged of *as sonnets*, not as *parts of a poem*."[34] In contrast, for Drayton, and for all English Renaissance sonneteers, such distinctions remain much less clear. Rather than resolving this formal tension in favor of lyric or narrative, for these writers the relation between "sonnet" and "sequence," between lyric and narrative, remains, in the end, undecidable. If such aporia is, as Derrida demonstrates, a necessary effect of language, the *focus* upon that undecidability, whether in Derridean criticism or Renaissance sonnet sequences, is historically specific. As Bourdieu argues about Derrida's celebrated reading of Kant, the emphasis on incommensurability manifests a specific social position (marking, in Derrida's work, not the end of philosophy but the rebirth of the philosopher).[35] What then are the social effects of Renaissance writers such as Drayton adopting a form and highlighting its undecidability, a form that conspicuously fails to enforce a transcendent or metaphysical grounding of meaning, a work to which one cannot write a preface? Or, to put the matter slightly differently, why would a form that stresses the unrequitedness of desire and the undecidability of its own generic contours become popular?

It is within these parameters that I view the relation between sonnet and sequence as an issue of what Fredric Jameson famously calls the "ideology of form." The relation between lyric and narrative in sequences is "an ideological act in its own right, with the function of inventing imaginary or formal 'solutions' to unresolvable social contradictions."[36] While Jamesonian critiques have typically stressed the "solutions" available in the closure of narrative forms – romances, novels, epics – such "solutions" need not mean that, at a narrative level, anything actually gets solved (through a marriage, or the founding of a nation, to take the two most obvious examples). Instead, Jameson's understanding of "form" derives from a tradition that begins with Marx's analysis of the form of commodities and continues through Freud's analysis of the form of dream-thoughts.[37] Slavoj Žižek succinctly summarizes this tradition of reading the social import of form:

the point [in both Marxist and Freudian analysis] is to avoid the properly fetishistic fascination of the "content" supposedly hidden behind the form: the "secret" to be unveiled through analysis is not the content hidden by the form (the form of commodities, the form of dreams) but, on the contrary, *the "secret" of the form itself* . . . the real problem is not to penetrate to the "hidden kernel" of the commodity [or the latent dream-thoughts] . . . but to explain why [for example] work assumed the form of the value of a commodity, why it can affirm its social character only in the commodity-form of its product.[38]

Rather than viewing sonnet sequences as a mystery to be solved – into what terms should we translate the desire of a sonnet speaker in order to understand what's "really" going on? – the social implications of these works lie in the fact of their peculiar, opaque form itself. What social authority, what organizing principle, emerges in Drayton's strains? What "social character" is affirmed in the emphasis on the undecidable relation between sonnet and sequence? The historical "secret" of Shakespeare's *Sonnets*, for instance, does not lie in knowing who the young man or the dark lady "really" are; neither does it consist of showing that the work is really a political allegory of patronage relationships or courtly ambition. Instead, the historical problem of the work (and all sonnet sequences) is its form itself – the fact that the speaker's desire for a noble youth and a dark lady exists in this particular way. The form corresponds to the conceptual structures by which the work produces itself and which cannot otherwise be given a definite representation.

But form is more than the embodiment of social contradictions: it is a crucial participant in social struggle as well, a primary locus for political and social agency. Jameson's formulation has the advantage of emphasizing the instrumentality of literary form – that it is not only the reflection of broader social structures but an active participant in these real social problems, a force which creates social structures, rather than merely reflecting or transgressing them. Such a conception of the agency of form has been developed along different lines in poststructural emphases on performativity and embodiment – most obviously, in the work of Judith Butler[39] – but the connections between performativity and form receive an especially full development in the work of Bourdieu.[40] While his reception in the Anglophone world has tended to emphasize his purported structural determinism, Bourdieu's work, with its emphasis on structures of difference, seems to me in many respects quite close to Derrida (though it is a comparison both, to the best of my knowledge, tend to resist).[41] What I wish mostly to adopt from Bourdieu, aside from some specific theoretical arguments, is a critical posture that sees class as a vital issue moving beyond questions of representation or economic determination, and which fully participates in a poststructural critical project. More specifically, what interests me about Bourdieu is his ability to describe "class" relations without reducing them to a single determinant (most famously, economic relations) and without essentializing the identity of a group by confusing a theoretical class, put in place by a researcher or literary historian, with an actually existing group.[42] Instead, Bourdieu's work theorizes a world of constant differentiation, of "social distinction," in his signature phrase: every taste, every moment of self-description, every act, reflects the distribution and redistribution of various forms of capital and situates an agent in a particular social position. But at the same time, Bourdieu is equally concerned to stress the agency within this differential – what he terms, in the second head note to this chapter, "class struggle." The phrase "social distinction" names both these processes: the continual situating of individuals, independently of their will, within a social structure; but also the participation of individuals in the transformation of "the categories of perception." Bourdieu is able to argue both of these positions simultaneously in part because his conception of "structure" is different from otherwise similar theorists. Instead of an "episteme" (Foucault) or a "totality" (Lukács), Bourdieu stresses the continual struggle to categorize, to organize conceptually, "social space." Unlike a definite structure, social space "is defined by the mutual exclusion, or *distinction*, of the positions which constitute it, that is, as a structure of juxtaposition of social positions." Bourdieu's conception of distinction is thus for me a sort of social *différance*, "the difference written into the very structure of the social space,"[43] that has real, objective, social effects.

Bourdieu's analysis is particularly helpful for reading sonnet sequences because in the "strain" between lyric and narrative, between sonnet and sequence, we see a continual struggle over the construction of social space. "Lyric" and "narrative" are themselves specific means of classifying. Sonnet sequences are historically interesting because the social order they manifest is always partial and is constantly undermined – neither lyric nor narrative ever finally succeeds in imposing itself completely in these works. But such incompleteness has definite social implications nonetheless. We might call the capital that accrues in Renaissance sonnet sequences the social distinction of distinction, of difference: undecidability and unrequitedness signal the distinctiveness of these works.

It is this social distinction, the question of the socially incommensurable, which I will call throughout "class." Sonnet sequences participate in the broadest historical sense in the emergence of class as a conceptual category. They are producers of what Mary Poovey describes as "the discursive matrix that preexisted and made possible the Marxist category of class" and participants in what Bourdieu calls the "mysterious alchemy" by which a "group in struggle" emerges.[44] The Renaissance may be fairly defined as the moment in which the long-term shift from status to class was at its most categorically confused. Somehow, a social order based on a broad system of "resemblances" changed into a social order based on a system of differences; the cosmos embodied in one's "status" transforms into a differentiated world based upon one's class.[45] Sonnet sequences participate in this long-term transformation, what Marxist historiography traditionally has called the transition from feudalism to capitalism. There has been no shortage of controversy over how (or even whether) such a transition occurred. In a renovation of the transition debate, Robert Brenner sharply challenges traditional accounts of a "bourgeois commercial revolution," accounts which he associates with the varying theories of Adam Smith, Ferdinand Braudel, and Immanuel Wallerstein, among others. In various versions of the revolution thesis, the bourgeoisie free from the inhibiting clutches of feudalism, a commercial impulse through colonialism, primitive accumulation, a protestant work ethic, and so on. The most glaring problem with such a theory, suggests Brenner, is that it must posit the existence of the bourgeoisie as a class; its circular logic accounts "for the origins of capitalism by the action of capitalists functioning in a capitalist manner."[46] This essentialized middle class consequently (and notoriously) seems perennially "rising," while capitalism becomes naturalized as nothing more than uninhibited commercialism, an innate urge to trade. Instead, Brenner suggests that the emergence of capitalism and its unique social relations ought to be seen as an "unintended consequence" of feudalism.[47] Capitalism for Brenner emerges as medieval lords and peasants try to reinforce feudal property relations. These groups are eventually forced, through the logic of their property relations, to create and to participate in market-dominated valuations of land, especially through market rents; change emerges as a result of the contradictions within feudal social relations themselves.

By emphasizing the internally contradictory desires of sonnet speakers, their paradoxical urges to distinguish themselves, I loosely place this study in the trajectory Brenner outlines. Following Brenner, I am interested in how new social positions in the period are generated out of the logic of previous social relations; following Bourdieu, I see this generation as the product of a continuous process of social differentiation. Instead of associating sonnet sequences with a "middle class" (or with the aristocracy or court), I want to describe how the process of social differentiation in these works helps to form the very idea of class as a unique process of social distinction.[48] The social distinction which sonnet sequences help to concretize is unintentional; the speakers of Sidney, Spenser, and Shakespeare, for instance, want to reinforce an aristocratic social imaginary, not start a revolution. If from our perspective this strain might seem teleological, the inevitable first step in the emergence of a bourgeois class consciousness, it should also seem bewildering. After all, the world these works help to create does not really conform very much to the social ideal they set out to imagine: a Calvinist paradise (Lok), a stable nobility (Sidney), a feudal manor (Spenser), or a homosocial utopia (Shakespeare).

If form is the primary means by which these distinctions become focused, gender is a primary discourse by which this transition is conceptualized. Several recent studies have argued that gender differentiation becomes one of the ways that writers in the Renaissance begin to challenge the system of social status – an authority broadly based upon institutions and blood relations – and begin to imagine a different way of conceptualizing social position. A modern understanding of gender emerges, as Michael McKeon argues, in tandem with the emergence of class.[49] Katherine Eggert similarly suggests that "*female authority itself* is the leitmotif around which issues of experimentation in literary form emerge and cluster . . . femininity, for the Renaissance, is a state of mind: a mind that is similarly disorderly, unstable, unwilling to remain within acceptable bounds or to focus upon acceptable aims."[50] In sonnet sequences, gender more generally is "unstable" in the sense that it is a central differentiating feature of the social positions of speakers. We should not confuse this position with its later counterparts. Writing about the conditions of women in Victorian England, and specifically about the emergence of new divorce laws, Poovey suggests that in the nineteenth century "assumptions about gender were more intractable . . . than assumptions about class." "[T]he issue of equality for all classes," for instance in divorce proceedings, "could be safely discussed precisely – and only – because the naturalness of the sexual double standard was a foregone conclusion."[51] The system of sexual differentiation inaugurated in the eighteenth century – the sharp biologically empirical distinction between men and women detailed by Thomas Laqueur and others[52] – provides a social stability which makes possible a discussion of class mobility because the social impact of class mobility is necessarily tempered by the intractability of a sex/gender system. Throughout this study, I assume that something like the inverse holds true in Renaissance sonnet sequences. The stability of institutional authority – nobles, the Church, the monarchy – makes possible the discussion of gender mobility (for instance, the feminization of male sonnet speakers) because the social impact of such gender mobility is limited by the stability of these institutions. Over the course of the book, I argue that the use of gender in sequences gradually changes. From Lok to Shakespeare, gender slippage, and especially femininity, tends to signal, if not set in motion, a wide variety of social contradictions. After Drayton, the gender of a "class" position becomes more explicitly masculine as the sharply differentiated sex/gender system Poovey and others describe begins to concretize – for example, in Wroth's *Pamphilia to Amphilanthus*. Likewise, Milton's sonnets provide a useful model for nineteenth-century writers like Wordsworth in part because the conspicuously public authority of Milton's speaker (his class position) is also conspicuously male.

Let me end this introductory chapter with a preface. In "To the Christian Reader," the prefatory epistle to his 1593 sonnet sequence *Svndry Christian Passions Contained in two hundred Sonnets . . .* , Henry Lok, son of Anne Lok, struggles with the vast theoretical difficulty of describing historical change. Lok initially seeks to justify his use of the form of the sonnet and his organization of them into a conceptual whole. But rather than, as it were, writing a preface for Drayton's *Idea* – rather than abstracting the idea of a sequence, turning it into an object of knowledge – Lok appeals to his own work's capacity to represent life: "represent" it not as mimesis but as form. "Who so shall duly consider the whole Progresse of mans estate from life to death, shall finde it gentle Reader, to be nothing else but a verse pilgrimage through this earth to another world." For Lok, life in England in the 1590s for people like himself is not "like" a sonnet sequence – it is a sonnet sequence, a "verse pilgrimage." Throughout his preface he defends this construction of existence, this categorization of social space, by working to "satisfie" his readers "first in the cause of my writing [the sonnets] in verse, then of the confused placing of them without speciall titles":

for my deducing these passions into Sonnets, it answereth (as I suppose) best for the shortnesse, to the nature of passions, and common [burden] of men, who are either not long touched with so good motions, or by their worldly affaires not permitted to continue much reading; as for the cause of my so preposterous placing of them and devision onely into two sorts, I confesse indeed I am perswaded their disorder doth best fit the nature of mankind, who commonly is delighted with contraries, and exercised with extreames, and also as they were by God ministred to my minde, to set down by sundry accidents in my private estate and feeling[.][53]

Lok's concern that he does not have "speciall titles" for individual sonnets clearly alludes to collections like Tottel's *Miscellany* (which I discuss in relation to Henry's mother Anne) that added titles to individual sonnets to provide a context for reading them. He worries that his lack of titles threatens to produce interpretive chaos. He emphasizes, however, that the very "disorder" of his sonnets "doth best fit the nature of mankind." In their apparent randomness, set down as they occur to him, the sonnets themselves reflect an order, a "nature," the will of God as he "ministred" to Lok's "minde." It is, however, a "preposterous" order, in Patricia Parker's phrase literally "behind for before, back for front, second for first, end or sequel for beginning." In Shakespeare, suggests Parker, the term "preposterous functions as a marker of the disruption of orders based on linearity, sequence, and place" – orders both linguistic and social.[54] Lok's "preposterous placing" similarly disrupts order, but in that disruption it also seeks to create a new order, "another world." If on the one hand Lok invites us to view his work as unordered and haphazard, such "sundry accidents" themselves constitute a "Progresse," a "pilgrimage." Indeed, "sundry accidents" as a phrase recalls the title of the work, *Svndry Christian Passions Contained in two hundred Sonnets*, which implies Lok's sense of social structure and the mediating role of his sequence in it. "Svndry," according the *OED*, in this period means both "separately, apart" and "of a single object." Lok's work, like "the whole Progresse of mans estate from life to death," is both separate – randomly occurring sonnets – and "of a single object" – constituting an integral whole. Like Drayton's "straine," Lok's term "svndry" simultaneously posits and undermines order.

But what order? In one sense, Lok sets his work against the apparent randomness of life, for the sonnets are "wisnesses of the impediments most stopping [him] in [his] Christian pilgrimage" and are consequently not "altogether unprofitable for others to imitate." At the same time, it is the fact that he inhabits such randomness, both as an abstract essence of existence ("the nature of passions, and common [burden] of men") and as a set of material practices (men are "by their worldly affaires not permitted to continue much reading") which provokes him to desire the narrative organization of a pilgrimage or progress. This contradictory existence is embodied in the division of the sequence into "two equall parts," as the title page terms it, or "onely into two sorts," as the introduction suggests: either "Meditations, Humiliations, and Praiers," as in the first part; or "Comfort, Ioy, and Thanksgiuing," as in the second part. While Lok tries to place his sonnets "onely into two sorts," his language betrays an inability to set himself, his work, and Elizabethan society generally into only two sorts of people.[55] Lok's emphasis on the movement from "mans *estate*" to his "private *estate*" suggests not simply religious concerns but unstable categories of social distinction. If man's estate has a "Progresse," is it similar to the "Progress" of a Queen through her lands, a process by which social and political order is created and enforced? What does it mean for Lok, both the son of a mercer and sometime member of James VI's court,[56] to compare his own Christian pilgrimage to a royal progress? Does the monarchy maintain a cultural hegemony by which it becomes the pattern for all subjects to imagine themselves, regardless of their social standing? Or does Lok's use of "progress" to describe "mans estate" suggest that the monarch's authority is rather subordinate to the very randomness Lok's sequence tries, in part, to overcome? Likewise, why in a religious work that tries to make universal claims about the conditions of human existence should Lok concern himself with the social rank of his readers? Imagining himself and his sonnets as a "private estate" points to a shifting conception of social order from ideas about the three estates to something else – something apparently of particular concern to a "*gentle* Reader." Somehow, the participation of an undefined sense of a "private estate" articulated in this "verse pilgrimage" will produce "another world" – a world whose social order remains nevertheless unclear. Rather than stabilizing the world in which he lives, or reflecting a static social order of sorts of people, Lok's use of "estate" reiterates a sense of social change and an uncomfortable groping about for conceptual categories with which to explain his existence. What "mans estate" and "private estate" *mean* is in part what Lok's work attempts to figure out. For Lok, the form of the sonnet sequence itself, in all its sundriness, becomes the means by which he measures the change from "mans estate" to "another world." But his work is also the means he uses to enact the change of estates and to concretize his own authority which is, he emphasizes, "not . . . altogether unprofitable for others to imitate." What, then, is this "profit" to be acquired in "another world"?

Lok's preface, as Derrida might remark, reiterates its own difference, rather than securing the meaning of the work. But these are linguistic differences, as Bourdieu might stress, that are also social distinctions. In the chapters that follow, I will be concerned to describe as precisely as possible these poetic struggles with an eye toward the social form they help to create. But I also proceed with an emphasis on the different desires of these particular speakers, for the world they help to make is very much an unintended consequence. Speakers of sonnets never imagined themselves as part of a bourgeois vanguard, nor did they imagine themselves as merely a tool of the workings of late-feudal monarchical power. How they did imagine themselves, what it was they desired, and what the social effects of these desires were – these are the problems tied up in Drayton's "English straine," in Lok's "another world," and these are the problems I seek to address in this book.

2 Post-romantic lyric: class and the critical apparatus of sonnet conventions

All translations into languages that are the heirs and depositaries of Western metaphysics thus produce on the *pharmakon* an *effect of analysis* that violently destroys it, reduces it to one of its simple elements by interpreting it, paradoxically enough, in the light of the ulterior developments it itself has made possible.[1]

[A]ll isolated or discrete cultural analysis always involves a buried or repressed theory of historical periodization.[2]

Any historical study of Renaissance sonnet sequences must begin in the nineteenth century. Though obviously neither sonnets nor sonnet sequences were literally invented in the nineteenth century, the extensive, explicit, theoretical scrutiny of them begun with the Romantics has fundamentally shaped understandings of both sequences and the Renaissance ever since. The term "sonnet sequence" was thought up by Dante Gabriel Rossetti in 1880, and at least sixteen sonnet anthologies, dozens of articles and essays, and over two hundred and sixty sonnet sequences appeared through the century.[3] The renewed interest in the sonnet eventually resulted in the critical apparatus still ordinarily used today to describe sonnet sequences: the familiar vocabulary of sonnet "conventions," of Petrarchism and its attendant ideology. This critical apparatus has become so pervasive as to seem self-evident; what could possibly be more obvious than Petrarchan cliches? As the concise introduction to Sidney's *Astrophil and Stella* in the seventh edition *Norton Anthology of English Literature* puts it,

[Sidney used] well established conventions, borrowed from Petrarch and his many Italian, French, and Spanish imitators. These conventions bequeathed a loose framework of plot, marking the stages of a love relationship from its starting point in the lover's attraction to the lady's beauty through various trials, sufferings, conflicts, and occasional encouragements to a conclusion in which nothing is resolved.[4]

These remarks seem so straight-forward that I have felt the need to write an entire chapter to explain why they are not. Rather than simply borrowings "bequeathed" by Renaissance continental predecessors, this chapter argues that such "conventions" are largely a symptom of the critical apparatus created to understand sonnets in the nineteenth century. More specifically, it argues that invisibly coupled to the vocabulary of sonnet conventions is a theory of social class. Renaissance writers undoubtedly had a clear sense of a common poetics of "unrequitedness," and they freely copied and translated one another. The critical language used to understand that poetic currency, in contrast, is a nineteenth-century phenomenon. Sidney obviously borrowed from Petrarch, but the explanation of that borrowing as "conventional" occurs in nineteenth-century essays, anthologies, and sonnet sequences.[5] As Lawrence Manley argues, after Romanticism conceptions of convention shift dramatically. From antiquity through the Renaissance, "convention" typically means social custom, and it is contrasted to "universal nature," to permanent, unchanging truths. At the end of the eighteenth century, Manley shows that this understanding is replaced by a "*romantic* opposition between convention and the individual."[6] The sonnet apparatus, with its emphasis on conventionality, is a product of this new opposition between unique individuality and conventional social structures. This opposition has definite implications for the imagination of social classes. When the evaluation of sonnets and sonnet sequences becomes the object of systematic understanding after the Romantics, they become forms of cultural capital; when they become cultural capital, sonnet sequences help create an aristocracy of culture that uses its poetic taste to distinguish itself.[7]

A study of social position in *Renaissance* sonnet sequences, consequently, must try to understand more precisely the relation between the cultural capital that sonnet sequences offered nineteenth-century writers and readers, the rereading (even invention) of Renaissance sonnet sequences that the production of such sonnet capital entailed, and the shaping effect such capital had on twentieth-century criticism of Renaissance sequences. If we want to read Drayton's "straine" that I outlined in the first chapter, we must begin by unpacking what Derrida terms the "effect of analysis," the ossified series of either/or questions that has constituted sonnet criticism since the Romantics. More specifically, we should begin with the procedure Bourdieu terms "structuring structures," the reflexive process of examining the categories that make "sonnet sequences" objects available for literary-historical study as well as the practice of that examination itself. As Loïc J. D. Wacquant puts it, "[w]hat has to be constantly scrutinized and *neutralized, in the very act of construction of the object*, is the collective scientific unconscious embedded in theories, problems, and (especially national) categories of scholarly judgment . . . It is not the individual unconscious of the researcher but the epistemological unconscious of his discipline that must be unearthed." Such an admittedly "quasi-mono-maniacal insistence on the necessity of the reflexive return" means, for a study of sonnet sequences, examining the nineteenth-century apparatus and "scrutinizing" the "collective scientific unconscious" embedded in this critical vocabulary.[8]

What does this apparatus consist of? Nineteenth-century criticism produced two intimately related criteria for judging sonnet sequences, one formal, and one social. First, sonnet sequences became defined by a central opposition between *conventional* writing and *original* writing, between uninspired, rote productions and Romantic conceptions of true poetic sentiment. This opposition is an instance of what I will term a *post-romantic* conception of lyric in which lyric becomes defined as a poem that sets in motion two incompatible modes of understanding. Second, the sonnet apparatus participates in what Ellen Meiksins Wood terms "The Bourgeois Paradigm," a conception of historical development that imagines the aristocracy and the bourgeoisie as transhistorical antago-nists in a fight for social supremacy: the bourgeoisie become synonymous with "capitalism," while the aristocracy become synonymous with "feudalism."[9] This paradigm is itself, however, a central component of a specific social position, what Bourdieu calls an aristocracy of culture, created in the nineteenth century that sought new means to legitimate its social authority beyond the rule of noble blood lines.[10] Post-romantic lyric and the Bourgeois Paradigm are connected because the formal opposition between conventional and original sonnets sets in motion the opposition between aristocratic and bourgeois, though which term is aligned with which flip-flops over time – sometimes "original" sonnets are aristocratic, sometimes they are bourgeois.

Post-romantic lyric is, in the language of its most powerful explicator Paul de Man, a "modern" lyric that deploys two incommensurable modes of understanding. Modern lyric consists of both "representation" and "allegory," a mimetic and a non-representational language, and these two languages are "blind" to their mutual dependence:

All representational poetry is always also allegorical, whether it be aware of it or not, and the allegorical power of the language undermines and obscures the specific literal meaning of a representation open to understanding. But all allegorical poetry must contain a representational element that invites and allows for understanding, only to discover that the understanding it reaches is necessarily in error . . . The structure of modernity reveals the paradoxical nature of a structure that makes lyric poetry into an enigma which never stops asking for the unreachable answer to its own riddle.[11]

This paradoxical relation in lyric between representation and allegory is, for de Man, an "enigma" of language, a basic condition of any "modern" lyric because it is an expression of the "structure of modernity" itself. De Man's description of lyric accounts for the pervasive contrast between lyric and narrative in sonnet criticism I described in the first chapter. Renaissance sonnet-"lyrics" have generally been read as either "representation" (for example, "mirrors" of a Tudor regime) or "allegory," internally consistent lamps of autonomous selfhood (for example, expressions of unmediated individual passion).[12] These two readings, however, depend upon the exclusion of one another for their definitional stability. New Historicism's emphasis that, in Arthur Marotti's paradigmatic formulation, "love is not love" in sonnet sequences but court politics depends upon the exclusion of the true, personal love that earlier generations saw as the most important feature of sequences: in the nineteenth century, personal love in sonnets was, by definition, removed from the mundane world of politics.[13] In contrast to these oppositions, de Man's rhetorical reading makes the very instability between these terms the defining feature of "modern lyric."

This largely formal paradox has nevertheless distinct social implications. De Man's "rhetorical reading" is, after all, itself an imposition of a historically specific social position. His effort to see the relation between representation and allegory as an "enigma" conflates a specific social disposition with a universal paradox, a law of "modern" language.[14] In contrast, Theodor Adorno's reading of lyric emphasizes the historical specificity of such a paradox itself. On a purely formal level, Adorno's description of the relation between "lyric and society" is effectively compatible with de Man's account: an allegorical mode, what Adorno terms lyric's "principle of individuation," is contrasted with a "representative" mode, what Adorno terms "society." Adorno, however, views the relation between these two less as a linguistic paradox than as a specific historical dialectic, a characteristic of commodification under industrial capitalism: "The lyric spirit's idiosyncratic opposition to the superior world of material things is a form of reaction to the reification of the world, to the domination of human beings by commodification that has developed since the beginning of the modern area, since the industrial revolution became the dominant force in life."[15] While de Man views the paradox of lyric as "caused by . . . the absolute ambivalence of a language,"[16] Adorno insists that such ambivalence should be viewed as a paradigmatic embodiment of an industrial-capitalist logic: lyric's allegory, its "individuation," is also an "idiosyncratic opposition" to a representative mode, "commodification under industrial capitalism." Rather than a rhetoric, the contradiction basic to lyric embodies "an inherently antagonist world": "the social interpretation of lyric . . . must discover how the entirety of a society, conceived as an internally contradictory unity, is manifested in the work of art."[17] What Adorno finds crucial about lyric, and art in general, is its ability to articulate its own historical moment in its very form – its capacity to embody, and render critically visible, the dynamic, historically specific dialectic that constitutes bourgeois thought itself.

This chapter argues that the opposition of original/conventional that defines sonnet sequences after Romanticism functions like de Man's lyric paradox: original and conventional are incommensurable languages blind to their mutual dependence. In turn, originality's "resistance" to convention is, as Adorno emphasizes, an expression of the dialectic central to industrial capitalism and bourgeois thought: it sets in motion Wood's Bourgeois Paradigm. Dialectically examining the form of post-romantic lyric consequently exposes the aristocracy of culture that the apparatus of sonnet conventions silently puts in place. If we do not examine this apparatus, we are doomed to reiterate the oppositions that it puts in play. Sonnet sequences will always seem original or conventional, aristocratic or bourgeois, and criticism will remain blind in de Man's sense to the interdependence of these categories.[18] As we will see, even revisionary twentieth-century efforts at historicizing Renaissance sonnets largely follow post-romantic ideas. By defining sonnet sequences as conventional or original, twentieth-century criticism compulsively repeats the theory of social class first created in the nineteenth century.

At the same time, the point of examining nineteenth-century construc-tions of sonnets and sonnet sequences in a study of Renaissance sonnets is not merely a matter of bracketing off nineteenth-century influence, of demystifying the universal categories of nineteenth-century criticism. The term "sonnet sequence" ineluctably involves us in the very processes we wish to examine. "The Renaissance sonnet sequence" can never exist as a pure object, free of the bias of examining it through nineteenth-century spectacles, because the post-romantic language of convention makes sonnet sequences, and in part class, *visible* in the Renaissance (I also hope it is apparent that I like the critics I discuss here). Indeed, I retain the term "sonnet sequence" throughout this book in order to emphasize this process of historical mediation. The vocabulary of the nineteenth and twentieth centuries, with its internal contradiction, is the condition that makes possible any reading of Renaissance sonnet sequences, what Derrida describes, in relation to philosophy, as the "precondition of discourse."[19] We need to examine the nineteenth-century sonnet apparatus, in short, because without it Renaissance sonnet sequences, and in part Renaissance conceptions of class, would not be readable at all.

The Dialectic of Romanticism

By the end of the seventeenth century, Renaissance sonnet sequences, a dominant form at the Elizabethan fin-de-siècle, had largely dropped from the British literary landscape, and for much of the eighteenth century, no one liked them much at all. As Dr. Johnson infamously remarked in his "Life of Milton," the best that could be said of Milton's sonnets is "that they are not bad," and he insisted that "[t]he fabrick of a sonnet, however adapted to the Italian language, has never succeeded in ours."[20] Instead, eighteenth-century excavations of the British literary past in anthologies like Thomas Percy's *Reliques of Ancient English Poetry* (1765), Thomas Warton's *History of English Poetry* (1774–81), Henry Headley's *Select Beauties of Ancient English Poetry, with remarks* (1787), and Robert Anderson's *Works of the British Poets* (1792–95) established a literary canon out of the "major" works of Spenser, Shakespeare, and Milton. These volumes, as Jonathan Kramnick argues, effectively established a British poetic trinity. Though writers like Warton were occasionally interested in Shakespeare's "lyric strength," that lyricism emerged from the plays, not the sonnets.[21] It was not until the later half of the eighteenth century that sonnets reemerged on the literary scene as, in Charlotte Smith's words, "no improper vehicle for a single sentiment."[22] In the Preface and "Introductory Dissertation" to his 1803 anthology of sonnets *Petrarca: A Selection of Sonnets from Various Authors*, George Henderson argues that "[t]he abundant proofs of the capability of the Sonnet to give expression to tender or melancholy sensations, places it very properly on a respectable footing in the rank of elegiac poetry." The sonnet as a form "is not unfitly adapted to give stronger and more feeling utterance to a pathetic thought."[23] Likewise, Coleridge early in his literary career emphasized the use of the sonnet for affect. "The Sonnet," according to Coleridge, "is a small poem in which some lonely feeling is developed," and the best examples are those "in which moral Sentiments, Affections, or Feelings, are deduced from, and associated with, the scenery of Nature . . . They create a sweet and indissoluble union between the intellectual and the material world."[24]

For Henderson such sentiment in the sonnet is a new improvement largely absent from Renaissance sonnets in English. Though he sometimes praises Wyatt, Sidney, Spenser, Shakespeare, Daniel, and especially Surrey (whose sonnets express "tenderness and simplicity"), Henderson generally finds little of poetic merit in any works in English before Drummond's sonnets appeared in 1616:

Before [Drummond's] time, it must be acknowledged, with very few exceptions, our Sonnets seem entirely deficient of the qualities which his so eminently possess, correctness of expression and harmony of structure. Indeed, it will in too many instances be found, that our early Sonnets abound with sentiments so hyperbolically uttered, and resemblances so extravagantly and uncouthly drawn, as must necessarily render them disgusting to any but a rude or uncultivated taste.[25]

In "Introduction to the Sonnet," Coleridge voices similar opinions of Petrarch, claiming to be unable "to discover either sense, nature, or poetic fancy in Petrarch's poems; they appear to me all one cold glitter of heavy conceits and metaphysical abstractions."[26] For early Romantics, Renaissance sonnets in English (and sometimes Petrarch himself) remain either too hyperbolic for their sentiment to be tasteful or too abstract for there to be sufficient sentiment at all.

In these early instances of Romantic poetic reflection, the opposition of contemporary sentiment to the rude abstractions of Renaissance sonnets sets in motion a dialectic fundamental to Romantic thought. As Anne Janowitz argues, "we should consider romanticism to be the literary form of a struggle taking place on many levels of society between the claims of individualism and the claims of communitarianism; that is, those claims that respond to identity as an always already existing voluntaristic self, and those that figure identity as emerging from a fabric of social narratives, with their attendant goals and expectations."[27] Emerging within this dialectic, the sentimentality of early romantic sonneteers tends to veer between public feeling and private passion. If the context by which a sonnet should be judged is the emotional and interior life of the writer, as Adela Pinch suggests, such interior affectivity always becomes caught up in an exterior, public world: "On the one hand, [contemporary writers] assert that feelings are personal, that they have origins in an individual's experience and are authenticated by their individuality. On the other hand they reveal that feelings may be impersonal; that one's feelings may really be someone else's; that feelings may be purely conventional, or have no discernible origins."[28] The Romantic celebration of individual feeling emerges always in relation to a backdrop of "impersonal" or "purely conventional" feelings that threaten to undermine the very authenticity which writers celebrated, even as the impersonal makes the personal possible at all. In this light, John Guillory's remarks on Gray's *Elegy* are readily applicable to the romantic sonnet; they generate out of their very quotableness "a reception-scenario characterized by the reader's pleased recognition that 'this is my truth,' while at the same time concealing the fact that this pleasure is founded upon the subliminal recognition that 'this is my language.' "[29] The reaction that emerges from sonnets – this is my sentiment – might be seen then as a prime instance of Wordsworth's notorious dictum that "every Author . . . has had the task of *creating* the taste by which he is to be enjoyed."[30]

Within this dialectic Renaissance sonnets play a crucial role, and one which has had nearly permanent effects on the ways they have been read ever since. In Henderson's anthology, English Renaissance sonnets function as an impersonal background, the potential repudiation of genuine emotion, upon which contemporary sentimentality is erected. This unsentimental view of English Renaissance sonneteers is para-doxically made possible by Henderson's obsession with Petrarch: "when I named the present volume PETRARCA, I was influenced but by one motive – that of veneration – of respect for the Genius and Name of HIM."[31] Against this vision of Petrarch, Henderson finds English Renaissance sonnets "disgusting": Petrarch is a poetic genius; English sonneteers are derivative if highly learned. A decade after Henderson's anthology, Capel Lofft similarly celebrates Petrarch's "perpetual Claim . . . on Posterity" as a poet of "Taste" and "refin'd Sensibility," but he too finds little to celebrate in English sonneteers. He quotes from Simmons' biography of Milton that "in the Childhood, as it may be call'd, of the English Muse [the sonnet] was made the vehicle of his love by the tender, the gallant, the accomplisht, and the ill-fated SURREY. In the succeeding Generation the SONNET was constructed, *though not with rigid accuracy*, by SYDNEY, SPENSER, SHAKESPEARE: and still more happily by DRUMMOND" (my italics).[32] English sonneteers (again with the notable exception of Surrey and Drummond) are inaccurate, unsentimental copiers. The dialectic of a romantic construction of emotional life finds an antithesis in the Petrarch *ism* of English Renaissance sonnets.

Setting up English Renaissance sonnets as the Other of romantic sensibility necessitates, however, a tacit understanding of similarity between the two. The use of the form of the sonnet itself posits a resemblance between the Renaissance and Romantic period: the English Renaissance seems to possess the very sentiment romantic writers and editors wish to claim for themselves. A primary way of negotiating this implicit identification was nationalism, celebrating English sonnets against their continental counterparts. Critical arguments about the allegedly essential differences between the "Italian" and "English" sonnet forms, arguments which have plagued undergraduates for years, originate in these nineteenth-century debates.[33] English and Italian sonnets were differentiated in terms of rhyme schemes and in terms of tone.[34] Within these arguments, Petrarch is alternately invoked as either a towering poet or as the name of an influence against which English sonnets, English taste, and English nationalism must be erected. Such nationalism is clearly implicated in the broader nineteenth-century project of the British colonial empire, staking out in the sonnet a figurative territory which is, on a global scale, far from any scanty plot of ground. One of the fundamental points of discussion for nineteenth-century commentators is whether or not the English sonnet is, as T. H. Hall Caine put it, "a bastard outcome of the Italian." Caine vociferously argues that "[d]own to Spenser . . . no deliberate effort appears to have been made to naturalize any specific form of the Italian sonnet," and he concludes that "[w]hat may with unerring accuracy be ascribed to Milton is a desire to vindicate the *English* sonnet in England."[35] Such nationalism bequeaths a double legacy to the study of Petrarch in England: Petrarch simultaneously represents that which Romanticism most celebrates in the sonnet as well as a lingering foreigner whose influence always threatens to corrupt the purity of English and British nationalism. In relation to English sonnets, consequently, it is rarely clear – even today – whether the charge of "Petrarchism" leveled against an English writer is a compliment or an insult.

It is within this paradoxical Petrarchism that nineteenth-century commentators separate Shakespeare's *Sonnets* from his contemporaries. Though even as late as 1803 Henderson could view Shakespeare's *Sonnets* as just as "uncouthly draw" as any English Renaissance sequence, by 1820 the gradual and increasingly familiar process of transforming Shakespeare, in Gary Taylor's words, "from the public dramatic poet of the Restoration and eighteenth century into a private lyric poet who could be embraced, celebrated, and appropriated by the Romantics"[36] was largely complete. From the Johnson-Steevens 1778 edition of Shakespeare's works, to Malone's decision to attach the 1609 quarto of Shakespeare's *Sonnets* to his 1780 supplement to Johnson-Steevens, to Malone's inclusion of the *Sonnets* in his 1790 edition,[37] Shakespeare-the-sonneteer became increasingly distanced from his contemporaries. This distancing, of course, did not escape the dialectic of Romanticism. Pinch and Margreta de Grazia note that the quotation of Shakespeare's sonnets as the expression of true inner emotion was decidedly contradictory: "if romantic readers of Shakespearean sonnets would have understood the tears of sonnet 64 as Shakespeare's own tears – the habit of quotation having personalized his words – the period's addiction to quotation had also made Shakespeare's words and feelings everybody's."[38] Likewise, when Keats turns to Shakespeare's *Sonnets* as a primary poetic model, that appropriation exhibits a dynamic similar to Keats' other notorious turn to Renaissance literature, "On First Looking Into Chapman's Homer." What Pinch calls the "circulation of feeling" makes it difficult to decide whether Keats is colonizing Shakespeare or Shakespeare is colonizing Keats, which of the two is Cortez, which the Indian.

Within a dozen years of Keats' sonnets, however, a vocabulary emerges to make these sorts of distinctions clearer: non-Shakespearean

English Renaissance sonnets are *conventional*. Only with the emphasis upon individual sentiment as a distinctive sign of individual poetic genius does "conventional" become a poetic insult. The first instance of "conventional" recorded in the *OED* meaning "Characterized by convention; in accordance with accepted artificial standards of conduct or taste; not natural, original, or spontaneous" is Thomas Carlyle's *Sartor Resartus* (1833–34). Likewise, the first instance of "convention" meaning "In a bad sense: Accepted usage become artificial and formal, and felt to be repressive of the natural in conduct or art" is Tennyson's *The Princess* (1847).[39] The dialectic of conventional and original emerges in early Victorian reactions to romantic theories of poetry. At this moment, when conventional and original become systematic, explicit poetic criteria, post-romantic lyrics in their fully paradoxical form can be said to appear.

Distinctions between conventional and original, however, signal not simply differences in literary quality; they also signal social differences. For nineteenth-century writers, original does not only mean artistically better: it means socially better. Nowhere is the intimate connection between literary and social senses of convention clearer than in the treatment of Shakespeare's *Sonnets*. The intricate relation between the conventionality of Renaissance sonnets and the originality of Shakespeare becomes more or less settled by the end of the century, and it is given its definitive form by Sidney Lee. Lee's work outlines a clear conception of the conventions which govern Renaissance sonnets. In this vein, Lee's *A Life of William Shakespeare* (1898) initially dismisses the romanticization of Shakespeare's *Sonnets* by insisting that the "typical collection of Elizabethan sonnets was a mosaic of plagiarisms, a medley of imitative studies." The representation of the dark lady, for instance, results from "the exacting conventions of the sonnetteering contagion, and not [Shakespeare's] experiences or emotions."[40] Lee emphasizes that the *Sonnets* were probably written early in Shakespeare's career, and that they thus stand in contrast to the original, mature genius of the later plays. In his two-volume anthology *Elizabethan Sonnets* (1904), Lee likewise presses this argument. His anthology, still the only collection of English Renaissance sonnet sequences,[41] extracts sequences out of the swamp of material in Arber's *English Garner*, which had reproduced them amidst almost random pieces of poetry, military accounts, histories, and so on. Unlike most nineteenth-century anthologies, Lee reproduces Elizabethan sonnet sequences (more or less) in their entirety, rather than choosing the "best" sonnets. The very fact that he does not excerpt the poems points to his assumptions about them: Renaissance sonnets are not "disgusting" because their emotion is unrealized; they are *conventional* works whose sheer repetitiveness – and lack of originality – is only apparent when they are examined *in toto*.[42] In his introduction, Lee reacts to a hundred years of sonnet criticism when he remarks that "[o]ne is accustomed to regard the literary energy of sixteenth-century England as mainly a national movement, as an outburst of original thought which owed little to foreign influence or suggestion." Instead, he emphasizes that "the Elizabethan lyric in nearly all its varied shapes of song and sonnet was, to a very large extent, directly borrowed from foreign lands . . . The English renderings are as a rule too literal borrowings to be reckoned, in a justly critical estimate, among wholly original compositions."[43]

The emphasis on convention nevertheless betrays an emphasis on originality as the dominant measure of poetic quality. After all, what is conspicuous in Elizabethan sonnets for Lee is their *lack* of originality; they are inferior poetic products because they do not measure up to the earlier romantic poetic ideology which he is partially reacting against. Lee's poetic criteria, then, are not anti-romantic so much as post-romantic, a shift of emphasis but not a basic change in the criteria for poetic evaluation. In this light, the introduction to *Elizabethan Sonnets* nuances Lee's earlier assessment of Shakespeare's *Sonnets* in his biography. On the one hand, he stresses again that sequences should not by and large be read as poems expressing genuine emotion; but on the other hand, he wishes to claim that out of this poetic morass emerges Shakespeare's poetic genius. This contradiction appears most sharply in Lee's decision *not* to include Shakespeare in his anthology. As Lee argues at the start of his introduction to *Elizabethan Sonnets*,

[t]hese volumes, which offer the reader fifteen collections of sonnets, bring together a substantial part of the vast sonnet-literature which was produced in elizabethan [*sic*] England. One conspicuous contribution to that literature is indeed omitted. Shakespeare's sonnets find no place here. Their exclusion is well justified. In the first place, unlike the work of his contemporaries in the same field, Shakespeare's sonnets are readily accessible elsewhere. In the second place, Shakespeare's sonnets possess an incomparable poetic merit and a psychological interest which entitle them to a place apart from other examples of the like branch of literary effort. At the same time, every serious student of Shakespeare's sonnets will find it to his advantage to study them in conjunction with the inferior work of his contemporaries. Not merely will his appreciation of their aesthetic quality be thereby quickened, but he will understand the contemporary circumstances of literary history which brought them into being. A comparative investigation alone renders it possible to estimate the extent to which Shakespeare's sonnets were coloured by the conventions and conceits of professional sonneteers of the period.[44]

The issue of the exceptionalism of Shakespeare's *Sonnets*, begun in the 1780s, solidified by Keats, is here given its largely definitive modern shape. In terms of the basic trajectory of the argument, there is little difference, for instance, between Lee's account of Shakespeare and Joel Fineman's sense of an exhausted tradition of epideictic poetry; in both cases, Shakespeare resists the tradition from which he emerges.[45] Lee describes the extrication of Shakespeare's "psychological interest" from the slough of inferior poetic production. That poetic production is associated with "professional sonneteers," their "conventions and conceits," and one studies them in order to understand better the "incomparable poetic merit" of Shakespeare's "place apart."

The *social* contours of this argument become apparent when we place some critical pressure on Lee's disassociation of Shakespeare from "professional sonneteers." Shakespeare's "unconventional" sonnets distinguish him specifically from hack writers who possess no true poetic feeling, no true originality. In the final sentence of the introduction, Lee argues that "[o]nly when the Elizabethan sonnet is studied comparatively with the sonnet of France and Italy are the elements of its composition revealed. When the analysis is completed, Shakespeare's sonnets, despite their exalted poetic quality, will be acknowledged to owe a very large debt to the vast sonneteering literature of sixteenth-century Europe on which they set a glorious crown."[46] Shakespeare's sonnets set a "glorious crown" upon the otherwise conventional "vast sonneteering literature." This "crown" distances Shakespeare from the teeming multitude of sonnet conventions by marking his superior taste, his conspicuously English distance from foreign influence, and his aristocratic, even monarchical, rule over the professional masses. And yet Lee's poetic sensibility permits him to recognize that Shakespeare only becomes distinct "despite" his similarity to other sonneteers. In the word "despite" lies the contradiction fundamental to post-romantic conceptions of lyric: Shakespeare's originality is visible only by contrast to the conventionality of his contemporaries.

Seeking to distinguish true, original artistry from professional production was, of course, a central occupation of Victorian criticism. It is apparent in William Morris' championing of the arts and crafts movement, which stressed the simple and pure design of the true artisan in direct reaction to the emergence of mass-produced goods; in Ruskin's celebration (mediated through his view of the Renaissance) of pure aestheticism; in Matthew Arnold's sense of "sweetness and light" set off from a multitude doing as it likes; and in the general artistic decadence of Oscar Wilde, whose conception of aestheticism was famously filtered through Shakespeare's *Sonnets* in *The Portrait of Mr. W. H.*[47] It is likewise apparent in the nineteenth-century obsession with the sonnet. One writer remarked in *The Dublin Review* in 1876 that "the increasing attention bestowed on the history and structure of the Sonnet [is] an indication of the growth of a higher and healthier poetical taste."[48] As Jennifer Wagner suggests, "[t]he [nineteenth-century] obsession with sonnets and with *collecting* them . . . is material evidence of an aestheticist ideology permeating the literary culture and narrowing literary interests into an abstract idealism of form." While Wagner sees this formal compulsion as a general withdrawal from the public sphere,[49] Linda Dowling insists that such aesthetic criteria are inherently public themselves. For earlier Victorians like Ruskin and Morris, pure aestheticism signaled "liberal or even utopian reform"; by the time of Oscar Wilde, aesthetic taste was a virtually aristocratic, that is minority, vision set against the fragmented social life of industrial capitalism:

At the heart of the vision of aesthetic democracy inspiring Ruskin and Morris, one still evident in Wilde's musings on mankind and utopia, lies an ideal of aristocratic sensibility unrecognized as such . . . as the hidden source of value in moral and aesthetic terms. On a purely logical or semantic level, the collapse that had threatened aesthetic democracy from the very beginning is the loss or emptying out of meaning that occurs in any context where "noble" or "aristocratic" is no longer permitted to function in relation to a set of terms – the ignoble, the vulgar, the base – in opposition to which it had originally assumed its meaning.[50]

Dowling locates the source of this paradox in the origins of Whig theories of democratic rule, specifically in the theory of "moral sense" put forward in Shaftesbury's *Characteristics of Men, Manners, Opinions, Times, Etc.* (1711).[51] This distinction between aristocratic taste and the teeming, undifferentiated masses becomes a cornerstone of what Bourdieu terms "the aristocracy of culture." For Bourdieu, "taste" is a primary manifestation of cultural capital; taste fulfills "a social function of legitimating social differences" which is different from the "symbolic capital that is socially and even legally guaranteed" by the name "noble."[52] Reading, collecting, and criticizing sonnets legitimates the "aristocratic" taste of nineteenth-century bourgeois writers, and this taste helps to create, in the fully paradoxical sense Dowling sets out, what Wood terms the Bourgeois Paradigm: the bourgeoisie distinguish and legitimate themselves as a class by continually defining themselves *against* the aristocracy as a status and *as* an aristocracy in terms of taste.

Seen within the emergence of an aristocracy of culture, Lee's conventional, Elizabethan "professional sonneteers" are like machines making overly ornate Victorian furniture. Against this quasi-industrial manufacturing appears "a higher and healthier poetical taste" – the "crown" of Shakespeare. It is consequently crucial that Lee emphasizes in the close of his introduction that Shakespeare, "*despite*" his poetic genius, owes a "debt" to "professional sonneteers" because Shakespeare is conspicuously not noble. For Lee, Shakespeare's genius, his originality, does not in any way serve to reinforce the interests of an aristocratic ruling class. Instead, Shakespeare's *Sonnets* participate in the production of an aristocracy of culture – those who collect "psychological interest" – which at the very same time labels Shakespeare as *not* aristocratic but as bourgeois.

Lee's crowning of Shakespeare's *Sonnets* occurs within a more general connection between sonnets and cultural capital, for the bourgeois aristocracy of culture stands behind and sets in motion the nineteenth-century rejuvenation of the sonnet. Writing in 1887, William Sharp reacted with surprise and horror "that even now there are many well-read people who have no idea of what a sonnet is than that it is a short poem."[53] How could one learn about sonnets and acquire the taste to determine which ones were good? One might turn to David M. Main's *A Treasury of English Sonnets* (1880), an anthology specifically aimed at students. Main's book includes two hundred and thirty-eight pages of notes for two hundred and thirty-four pages of sonnets, commentary and examples that shape "students" and make them capable of distinguishing true poetry from mere dreck.[54] The problem of identifying the best sonnets likewise underlies the creation of the term "sonnet sequence" itself, a phrase created by D. G. Rossetti as a potential title for T. H. Hall Caine's anthology of sonnets. Writing to Caine to propose titles for the anthology, Rossetti suggested "A Sonnet Sequence from Elder to Modern Work, with 50 (?) hitherto unprinted Sonnets by living writers."[55] Caine didn't use "sonnet sequence" (he named his anthology *Sonnets of Three Centuries*), but Rossetti did – for the 1881 revision of *House of Life: A Sonnet Sequence*. For Rossetti and Caine, the question of the anthology's title signaled a general problem of how to classify the poems – what sonnets to include, how to order them, how to lay them out on the page to demonstrate rhyme schemes, and, of course, what to call the book. The other potential titles thrown about – "The Sonnet Castaly"; "The English Sonnet Muse from Elizabeth's reign to Victoria's" – suggest very different conceptions of the anthology. It might be a reflection of a single, transhistorical spring ("Castaly") or it might imply a connection between that "muse" and the political organization of a female monarch. Rossetti later had doubts about "sequence" because it wouldn't make sense if the newest poems were put first. This discussion over the title of the anthology was crucial because it expressed the ordering structure, the taste, within which the "best" sonnets could become visible. "I shouldn't like the book to be called simply Selected and Original Sonnets," remarked Caine.[56] Like romantic sentiment, the sonnets in Caine's anthology always threaten to express the "general" and public taste, rather than existing as, in Rossetti's famous phrase, a "moment's monument." One contradiction Caine and Rossetti struggled with in trying to come up with a title, in short, is that sonnets in the anthology must be "aristocratic," the best, in order to express their bourgeois taste.[57]

Similarly, Charles Tomlinson's *The Sonnet* (1874) draws upon an increasingly concrete sense of a national literature to construct a class structure intimately related to poetic form. While "one of Petrarch's sonnets, recited or sung to an Italian multitude, would excite enthusiasm," in England, claims Tomlinson, "[o]ur most popular poetry is the song or ballad" such as verses by Burns. In England at least, poetry, and sonnets in particular, distinguish the upper class from the lower:

The Italian poet, captured by banditti, who saved himself and his party from spoliation by reciting his verses, would have no chance with English highwaymen, any more than our best English poet under similar conditions. The gondolier of Venice, who, singing a stanza of Tasso, was responded to by brother gondoliers in succeeding stanzas, has no equivalent among English boatmen. But if one of the latter were to open out with – "And did you not hear of a jolly young waterman?" he would be not only keenly appreciated, but responded to by all his mates. I have heard French and Italian mechanics sing trios and quartets in harmony while engaged in their work. I have never heard English mechanics make such an attempt . . . [58]

For Tomlinson, Italy (and to a lesser extent France) acts as an effectively imaginary locale where high and low art intermingle, where the lower classes know and love high art. Such is not the case in England, where Tomlinson's knowledge of sonnets sets him conspicuously apart from "mechanics" and other potential "banditti" from whom he is otherwise at a loss how to save himself. Tomlinson can thus desire an imaginary land (here called Italy) where art is part of a democratic impulse, embraced by everyone from bandits to mechanics to gondoliers, while at the same time using that very vision of democracy to situate himself socially above English mechanics too rude to appreciate a good sonnet.

The production of an aristocracy of culture is similarly at work in the notorious scandal of Shakespeare's *Sonnets*, a work that has proven at times to have too much "psychological interest" for some people. As Peter Stallybrass argues, "the drive towards unity of character (Shakespeare's character, the characters of the Sonnets) produced more and more dramatic consequences at the level of sexual identity. The Sonnets, previously a marginal aspect of Shakespeare's corpus, became [in the nineteenth century] a crucial site on which 'sexual identity' was invented and contested." The concern with sexual "normality" in Shakespeare's *Sonnets* is, as Stallybrass suggests, a "hysterical symptom" provoked because the *Sonnets* conspicuously do not adhere to the default heterosexuality of the aristocracy of culture. The increasing obsession with the biography of poets, for instance, is facilitated by situating the "I" of a sonnet in relation to an idealized domestic sphere defined by the constancy of the female object. Questions of the "real" identity of the female object (who is Astrophil's Stella? who is the dark lady?) further the project of heterosexualizing and domesticating the "interior" life of Renaissance poets. Yet it is equally crucial to recognize that such maneuvers *also* obscure the creation of the class position tied to domestic heterosexuality. Shakespeare's *Sonnets* could (and do) provoke drama in terms of sexual identity, but the very fact of the allegedly "exceptional" nature of Shakespeare's sequence – that it contains a male object of desire – *reinforces* the class structure which it simultaneously challenges at the level of sexuality. Shakespeare's sequence becomes "anti-Petrarchan" and "unconventional" because it contains male-male desire; and yet this desire enforces the exceptionality of the sonnets and their participation in the production of a distinct class structure. Only Shakespeare's *Sonnets*, after all, threw off almost totally the Petrarchan clothes in which the early Romantics saw other Renaissance sequences, and ironically the male object of desire in the *Sonnets* in part facilitates this process. The "revolting" sexuality in Shakespeare's work distances him from the conventional, and in Henderson's terms "disgusting," productions of his contemporaries. Stallybrass' final sense that "we need now to reconstruct the cultural history of Shakespeare . . . to understand how the imaginary terrain of our own bodies came into being" reiterates, even as it critiques, Shakespeare's "exceptionality."[59] "[O]ur own bodies" here means bourgeois bodies, not anyone's body. The history of sexuality also participates in the construction of distinct social positions; it too is a historically determined taste.

Other English Renaissance sonneteers were of course not always read as clichéd and conventional. In his *English Garner*, for instance, Edward Arber spends pages extricating the biographical details allegedly behind Sidney's *Astrophil and Stella*, something which he does for virtually no other poet in the eight-volume collection.[60] An emphasis on Sidney's biography is likewise apparent in lectures on Shakespeare and Elizabethan poetry given by the American poet Sidney Lanier in 1879 at Johns Hopkins. The passage is worth quoting at length for the clarity of its expression of the close identifications between inner emotion, sexual orientation, domestic space, and class position:

[*Astrophil and Stella*] is really a record of [Sidney's] passion for Lady Rich . . .
Sidney fell in love with her while they were both free; but, for some reason not
now known, she was forced to marry Lord Rich, a man who seems to have been
in every way unsuitable to her. After his beloved was thus snatched from him
Sidney's affection for her appears to have acquired double vehemence: and most
of these sonnets are outbursts of his soul, written to her during this tragic period
when he was in all the agonies of a death-struggle with a passion which you can
easily see must have torn such a soul as his above all of lesser strength. It was like
binding him to two wild horses and then lashing them in different directions. The
very nobility of his nature, on the one hand, made him cling to her with all the
desperate constancy of a soul that could not love lightly; while the same nobility
continually tortured him with the consciousness that his love was wrong, that its
object belonged to another, and that its best success could only end in inward
baseness and outward disgrace. Now all the phases of this passion lie bare to our
eyes in these sonnets.[61]

Sidney here sounds like nothing so much as a character out of a
nineteenth-century novel, torn between his love for a woman and his
dedication to the institution of heterosexual, bourgeois marriage. For
Lanier, Sidney's passion marks "the nobility of his nature," but his
"nobility" in turn also denies that passion as transgressing monogamy
and domesticity, those foundations of a tasteful life: Lady Rich, after all,
is married. Though his nobility of passion marks an aristocratic taste, his
unwillingness to violate marriage situates him firmly within bourgeois
norms. He is, consequently, bound to "two wild horses" headed in
"different directions," an aristocratic passion that violates marriage, and
a bourgeois sensibility that restrains his passion. Here is the very
conceptual contradiction between aristocracy and bourgeoisie that
Dowling suggests sits at the core of Whig life. Sidney's potentially
adulterous relationship is an exception to "conventionalism" not unlike
Shakespeare's male-male desire, and if it cannot be fully reconciled to
bourgeois ideals of heterosexual, monogamous marriage as a primary
social foundation, it can nevertheless also be used to reinforce the very
ideal it seems to subvert. Sidney's potential "inward baseness" is replaced
by a noble outward passion, an originality which refuses to violate the
threshold of heterosexual marriage and the class structure it facilitates.

Such representations of Sidney nevertheless are largely exceptions
within the broad Victorian critical estimation of English Renaissance
sonnets. More characteristic is Martha Foote Crowe's delicate introduction to her 1896 collection *Elizabethan Sonnet-Cycles*. Crowe follows
Romantic precedent by insisting that the sonnet is "the most perfect
vehicle that has ever been devised for the expression of a single
importunate emotion," that despite the formal departures from the
Petrarchan model of Wyatt and Surrey "one rule seemed to be uniformly

obeyed – that the poem should be the expression of a single, simple emotion." She tempers this sentimental judgment, however, by noting that the "melody and descant" of sonnets "were not, in some ears at least, without monotony," citing as examples Daniel, Constable, Lodge, Drayton, Fletcher, Brooke, Percy, and two anonymous sequences. This observation is finally brought back to Keatsian ideals: "but the glints of a loftier ideal shining now and then among the conventions, lift the cycle above the level of mere ear-pleasing rhythms and fantastical imageries. Moreover, the sonnet-cycles on the whole show an independence and spontaneousness of poetic energy, a delight in the pure joy of making, a *naiveté*, that richly frame the picture of the golden world they present."[62] "Now and then" Renaissance sonneteers besides Shakespeare shine "among the conventions." Otherwise, they are monotonous. Originality and conventionality, Englishness and Petrarchism, bourgeois and aristocratic: these are the post-romantic criteria by which English Renaissance sonnets are viewed.

Criticism, Convention, and the Shape of the Renaissance

Twentieth-century readings of the social position of Renaissance sonnet sequences emerge out of this post-romantic conception of lyric, its attendant paradoxical aestheticism, and the aristocracy of culture both set in motion. Within this use of convention to map the social space of Renaissance England lies a solution to the initially curious lack of interest in sonnet sequences and Petrarchism generally by T. S. Eliot and his followers. Even as "the sonnet" became a primary testing ground for new critical practice, with the obvious exception of Shakespeare, sonnet sequences received surprisingly little attention from early New Criticism, which generally preferred the "metaphysical" poets. Instead, much of the criticism of sequences of the first half of the twentieth century – for example, books by L. C. John, Lu Emily Pearson, and Janet Scott – might be thought of as old historicist, concerned with nuancing and extending Lee's sense of the conventionality of these works rather than demonstrating their internal consistency.[63] The reason for this new critical neglect probably lies in the association of conventionality with mass production. As Guillory suggests, New Criticism might be thought of as an institutionalization of the quasi-religious association of sensibility set against the degrading vulgarity of modernity and mass-production that Eliot and Leavis saw as the primary function of art within "the tradition."[64] Logically speaking, if one were looking for an association of sensibility, one could do worse than turn to sonnets, whose very conventionality expresses a unification of thought and feeling.

Instead, set up as vulgar, mass produced items by Lee and his inheritors, New Criticism finds one of its primary poets of the period in a writer allegedly reacting *against* such conventionalized production: Donne. Here lies the origin of a generation worth of studies worried about whether Donne is or is not "Petrarchan." Donne stands for an association of sensibility in his own time against the "mass production" of the Elizabethans – the merely fashionable, merely transitory, "vogue" for sonneteering.[65]

Those mid-century works that do actually consider sonnet sequences – in particular, works by J. W. Lever, Hallett Smith, C. S. Lewis, and J. B. Leishman – tend to rearticulate the historical constructions of Sidney Lee: that Petrarchism in England is the vulgar prehistory out of which, and against which, the genius of Shakespeare emerged. Lever's *The Elizabethan Love Sonnet* takes up the nineteenth-century concern with nationalism and race (how Italian are English sonnets?) by turning Shakespeare, the middle-class Englishman with aristocratic poetic taste, into a racialized, archetypical "vates" :

The English genius speaks through Shakespeare's sonnets as surely as the Italian genius speaks through the sonnets of Petrarch. The English imagination operates in Shakespeare's great compound metaphors, reaching down to a dark core of elemental conflict, while Petrarch's metaphors diffuse an Italian vision of the radiant integrity of spirit and nature . . . the English spirit is triumphantly ascendant in the figure of the Friend, the doomed yet immortal victim and conqueror of Time . . . in the Friend – whichever Elizabethan nobleman provided his living counterpart, whatever Renaissance or Christian virtues he embodied – we may recognize the archetypal, all too human *monndryhten* of northern epic and lay, such a fated hero as was Beowulf or Sigemund or the lost lord of *The Wanderer*, in whose patronage the poet found his sole source of joy upon earth and whose love surpassed the love of women.[66]

Victorian nationalism is converted into racial archetypes; the "originality" of Shakespeare reaches back through an ethnically pure, homosocial past to Beowulf, the foundation of an English national literature, an English ethnic identity, and English bourgeois originality. Nevertheless, the Nordic whiteness of Lever's Shakespeare only becomes possible against the backdrop of the "typical," rather than "archetypical," rendering of "the Italian genius" into English by Shakespeare's predecessors. Earlier in his conclusion, Lever stresses that the genius of Shakespeare lies in moving beyond conventions, for as far as Lever is concerned the late Elizabethan sonnet was "vitiated" by "its failure to evolve a new and arresting central theme which could replace the obsolete conventions of courtly love."[67]

Lever's nationalist contrast between the respective genius of Petrarch and Shakespeare nevertheless maintains a similarity between them, a connection codified by J. B. Leishman's *Themes and Variations in Shakespeare's Sonnets*. Nowhere is the interplay of poetic taste and class distinction more finely tuned than in Leishman's analysis. Partially forsaking national boundaries, Leishman views Shakespeare as participating in a long-term poetic project originating with Petrarch. Reacting against "the commonplace that there are certain obvious differences between Shakespeare's Sonnets and those of all his predecessors and contemporaries," Leishman retraces Sidney Lee's emphasis on Shakespeare's debt, but he does it with a more nuanced, new-critical eye. He stresses that "nowhere else is comparison so possible and so profitable, in no other portion of his work can Shakespeare be so appropriately 'committed with his peers'" as in the *Sonnets*. Poetic distinctions remain social distinctions, however. The only poets really worthy of the name of Shakespeare's "peer" turn out to be continental sonneteers. As Leishman remarks at the beginning of his section on "Shakespeare and his English predecessors," "[t]o turn from the great European poets we have been considering to the sonnets of Shakespeare's English contemporaries is to enter a region of comparative provinciality and amateurishness." This amateurishness takes on distinct class over-tones, as Leishman's consideration of Drayton's "Whilst thus my pen strives to eternize thee" suggests: "I must confess that I find in this sonnet of Drayton's a mixture of peevishness and boasting – quite different from the occasionally splendid, if shocking, arrogance of Ronsard – which seems slightly absurd and produces an impression of something like parody ('Ere am I, wearin' meself out to make you immortal')." Shakespeare shares Ronsard's quasi-aristocratic splendidness, while Drayton and other English sonneteers seem painful, lower-class poetasters with bad accents. When, for instance, he does praise other English writers, it is almost invariably because they sound momentarily more "Shake-spearean." It is nevertheless a testament to both the dialectical quality of Shakespearean exceptionalism and Leishman's capacity as a close-reader that he also notes that "[i]t may well have been from Shakespeare that Drayton learnt to speak of his own poetry in a manner appropriate to a 'servant.' "[68]

These mid-century critical works also articulate the means by which they will be largely inverted by the next generation of critics. From the perspective of late-Victorian England, there is little new in Hallett Smith's insistence that sixteenth-century English poetry does not express "the private experience and biography of the poet" but rather that "the appropriate context for poetry is a series of ideals, values, commonplaces, or conventions." This argument, after all, is the basis upon which the genius of Shakespeare is erected by Lee. What is significantly different in Smith's book is an increasing valorization of that very sense of conventionality, newly rendered as artifice. This valorization had begun to appear twenty years earlier in reformulations of Lee by Janet Scott and Lu Emily Pearson, but Smith ties it closely to new critical principles of poetic craft. In his reading of *Astrophil and Stella*, for instance, Smith quite explicitly rejects "the old position, stated most forcibly by Sir Sidney Lee . . . that Sidney's sonnets [are] highly derivative and that these professions of originality [are] in themselves conventional." Instead, Smith carefully distinguishes between "Sidney" and "Astrophil" in order to emphasize that "it is clear that the most complex rhetorical and dramatic resources are utilized in the sonnets by Sidney." Smith emphasizes that "Sidney . . . uses very considerable art" to show that the conventions themselves, dismissed by Lee as the vulgar mass-productions of "professional writers," are instead worthy of the name of poetry. When Smith insists at the start of his chapter on sonnets that "[w]hat seems Elizabethan to us is the method and manner of Petrarch,"[69] he now seems to mean it as a compliment.

C. S. Lewis similarly celebrates the legitimacy of convention, with Daniel and Lodge as prime examples. He rejects Lee's dichotomy between originality and convention by stressing the originality in uses of convention: "Some, like Sir Sidney Lee, demand originality and consider a poem to be somehow discounted if you can find a foreign original. Others may want high seriousness, or irony, or social awareness." Instead, Lewis emphasizes that Lodge and Daniel (and most other Elizabethan sonneteers) offer a secular litany, a series of conventions that give voice to – one might say interpellate – readers and would-be lovers:

The sonneteers wrote not to tell their own love stories, not to express whatever in their own loves was local and peculiar, but to give us others, the inarticulate lovers, a voice. The reader was to seek in a sonnet not what the poet felt but what he himself felt, what all men felt. A good sonnet . . . was like a good public prayer: the test is whether the congregation can 'join' and make it their own, not whether it provides interesting materials for the spiritual biography of the compiler.[70]

The conventional language of sonnets becomes not mass-produced goods but the public language for the expression of inner passion; rather than expressing the originality of an author, it makes the individuality of a *reader* possible. Lewis' rendering of sequences rearticulates the post-romantic lyric dialectic – public language forms private passion such that it is no longer clear how to distinguish the two. It is on this basis that

Lewis views Shakespeare's *Sonnets* as "the highest and purest achievement of the Golden way of writing," even though he stresses that the sequence "differs in character as well as in excellence from those of the other Elizabethans."[71] Shakespeare is both conventional and exceptional, the perfect blend of originality Lewis sees emerging out of conventionality itself.

Sonnet criticism of the last forty years has been largely concerned with working out the historical implications of this renewed acceptance of the validity of conventional writing. Indeed, if one were to look, in terms of Renaissance studies of Petrarchism, for a date marking the beginning of New Historicism's account of Renaissance England, one could do worse than 1961 – the date G. K. Hunter's *John Lyly* was published. Hunter's book announces itself as a powerful criticism of Whig literary history – that is, the sort of history written by Lee – and Hunter memorably turns not only to Lyly's court-centered humanism but also to the conventionality of Petrarchism to mount his attack: "the court of Elizabeth was neither natural nor free. Its ritual was artificial to the last degree, despotic and repetitive. The sovereign was a painted idol rather than a person; the codes of manners it encouraged were exotic, Petrarchan and Italianate."[72] For Hunter this "exotic" language still facilitates a "moral content" not dissimilar to that emphasized by literary-historians like Lee; though he rejects the explicit narrative of Whig history, in other words, Hunter's new critical methodology retains the values basic to Whig history. But order emerges not, as it had for Victorian writers, through the "central urge towards modern freedom and naturalness" in the expression of Elizabethan heroes like Drake or Marlowe or Shakespeare but through the "artificial" – that is, conventional – world of court. Rather than great Elizabethan individuals, Hunter instead finds the center of gravity in the period in the complexities of Elizabethan court life – a life defined largely through exotic Petrarchan conventions. In terms of the historical situation of sonnet sequences, the changes embodied by Hunter could not be more dramatic. Conventionality, no longer the sign of "professional writers" and a vulgar, mass-produced sensibility, is transformed into a sign of *nobility and court*. In other words, the class association of convention is thoroughly inverted. The courtly power of a writer lies not in his *resistance* to Petrarchan conventions but rather in his *manipulation* of them.

The connection between the manipulation of convention and the aristocracy becomes, after Hunter, a central feature of readings of Petrarchan poetry. Here lies a primary origin of new historicist renderings of "court" and "sonnet conventions" in Renaissance England. Criticism of sonnet sequences operating within Hunter's parameters concentrated its attention on Sidney, and to a lesser extent Spenser, as somehow representative of all of Elizabethan courtly society. The alleged conventionality of *Astrophil and Stella* facilitates the imagination of Sidney as the paradigmatic Elizabethan courtier. Between 1958 and 1968 six book-length studies of Sidney appeared, and Hunter's voice is audible in Arthur Marotti's seminal argument that Elizabethan sonnet sequences are not about love but about courtly ambition, where again Sidney stands as the central example.[73] The effect of these readings is not a rejection of the post-romantic lyricism and Whig history embedded in the very term "convention" but rather an *inversion* of it; the bourgeoisie and the aristocracy remain historical antagonists, but the emphasis is shifted from the rising middle class to the continuing dominance of the aristocracy, a "lineage of absolutism."[74]

In one of the more closely argued new historicist renderings of a sonnet sequence, Ann Rosalind Jones and Peter Stallybrass suggest that Sidney's *Astrophil and Stella* becomes representative of the power dynamics of Elizabethan absolutism by collapsing the distinction between the "private" sphere of love and the "public" sphere of courts. As a result, "the logic of his poems coincides with political rhetoric in ways that raise the question of whether the lover-poet is in control of the situation – or whether he is constructed by it."[75] If the sequence looks like court, the court, in turn, ends up looking like a sonnet sequence: Queen Elizabeth herself becomes a living Petrarchan mistress. Convention, "the logic of [Sidney's] poems," acts here as what Fredric Jameson, in his seminal critique of New Historicism, calls a repressed homological structure or theory. For Jameson, New Historicism differs from previous "immanent" modes of analysis because it prolongs "the procedure of 'homology'" but "eschews homology's theory and abandons the concept of 'structure.'" New Historicism thus draws on Lévi-Straussian structuralism – an abstract structure permits the reading of distinct phenomenon as homologous – but in turn rejects the overt theorization of that structural principle itself.[76] The use of convention by Jones and Stallybrass operates, in Jameson's terms, as a "pretext" that facilitates the creation of a single critical "montage" of Astrophil and Sidney, poetry and politics, and Elizabethan courtly society generally.[77] This tacit structuring force of convention permits them to compare what would initially appear to be distinct phenomena – "private" love and "public" politics – and to place them within a general montage of the Elizabethan court. As Jones and Stallybrass put it, "[o]ne can identify a set of homologies between lover/beloved, suitor/patron and courtier/prince." At the same time, a definition of what precisely "convention" means, that is, a theorization of the structuring homology, remains nevertheless quite restricted. Throughout the essay, Jones and Stallybrass make general assertions about the sonnet sequence (it "emphasizes two kinds of artifice"; it "is based on a formula by which the man is subjected to his lady while, at the same time, the situation enables him to pour forth his eloquence in an attempt to influence her")[78], and they gesture at the "power" and "symbolic violence" sequences contain. Conventionality itself, however – the vocabulary that enables the identification of sonnet and court – remains largely unremarked upon.

The result of this procedure is an emphasis on power itself – what Jones and Stallybrass call "the dominant social practices of [Sidney's] time"[79] – as a totalizing yet elusive force. Any profession of "true love" by Astrophil is immediately contained (even provoked) by the discursive totality of court. The language of convention itself eliminates the possibility of Astrophil's "personal" love for Stella because the very terms he uses to describe himself are located within the conventional language of court culture. Because Jones and Stallybrass reject Whig history, middle-class desire (a private love) and the "subversion" it facilitates are impossible. This familiar new historical impasse between "subversion" and "containment" (is Astrophil subverting Elizabeth or contained by her?) consequently might be read as an extension of Woods' "Bourgeois Paradigm": the bourgeoisie (true love, an inner life, a private sphere) is set as the antagonistic (if ultimately unrealizable) social opposition to "court" and the "monarchy," that is, to the aristocracy. This social contradiction is likewise set in motion by de Man's lyric paradox: Astrophil's allegorical mode, his personal love, is blindly dependent upon a representative mode – the depiction of Elizabethan court life in the sequence. Despite being far removed from the nineteenth-century taste which gave rise to this opposition, the adherence to the language of convention by Jones and Stallybrass tacitly necessitates an adherence to a nineteenth-century language of class. Astrophil is original or conventional, bourgeois or aristocratic; he has a private life of love or a public life of political ambition.

The cultural analysis of sonnet sequences, then, always involves a theory of class inherited from the nineteenth century – the Bourgeois Paradigm – because that theory is imbedded in the critical apparatus – convention – used to read sequences. Even revisionary criticism like that of Jones and Stallybrass ends up reiterating the class structure embedded in nineteenth-century conceptions of "Petrarchism." The strongest new historical criticism of sonnets tends to keep this post-romantic lyric paradox in play, but the social world of the Renaissance always ends up defined by this contradiction. Patricia Fumerton, for example, insists that because Elizabethan sonnet sequences are "wholly conventional," they articulate "an essential instability in the notions of 'private' and 'public' and in the relations between them."[80] This "essential instability" should be seen as a result of the social implications of the critical imposition of a formal rhetoric derived from the nineteenth century, de Man's modern lyric paradox. More recent efforts to read race and imperialism in sequences likewise tend to repeat the oppositions embedded in convention.[81] Far from historicizing Renaissance poems, "conventional" readings of sonnet sequences – from the sentiment of the Romantic rejuvenation of the sonnet, to the Victorian diagnosis of the sonnet contagion, to the new historicist construction of containment – continually shuffle the same set of historical options, the same criteria for constructing social space. Jameson's sense that "all isolated or discrete cultural analysis always involves a buried or repressed theory of historical periodization," one head note to this chapter, becomes clear in the habit of viewing the possibilities of social position in Renaissance sonnet sequences through post-romantic conceptions of lyric and through post-romantic conceptions of social class. As long as criticism of Renaissance sonnet sequences comprehends them in terms of formal conventions, the paradox of post-romantic lyric and its attendant class structure is inescapable.

This chapter has tried to stress that the way out of this impasse cannot lie in just bracketing off nineteenth-century and "humanist" constructions of class and form to get a touch of the real Renaissance. Instead, I agree with Roland Greene's suggestion that "the Western lyric sequence" is a single, "post-Petrarchan" form, and with Joel Fineman's sense that these works set in motion an "epoch of subjectivity." "[T]here is at least the possibility," writes Fineman, "that modernist – and, for that matter, postmodernist – theories of the self are not so much a theoretical account or explanation of subjectivity as they are the conclusion of the literary subjectivity initially invented in the Renaissance."[82] The conceptualization of such an epoch enables Fineman to see Shakespeare's *Sonnets* as prefiguring, say, Lacan's reading of Merleau-Ponty's reading of Sartre's reading of Husserl; it also facilitates Greene's understanding of a fundamental connection between Petrarch, Sidney, Taylor, Whitman, Yeats, Neruda, and Adán.

What if we think of this epoch as not only demarcating an account of a poetic subject but also as inaugurating a new mode of social distinction? What if this mode creates, among other things, the Bourgeois Paradigm and the aristocracy of culture, an "epoch of class"? Such questions are, for me at least, the preconditions of a historical reading of Renaissance sonnet sequences. They are a way of beginning to explain why sequences were interesting to Renaissance writers and why they may be interesting today. I don't want to overstress this Grand Historical Frame: my primary interest in what follows lies in trying to figure out how to *read* these often enigmatic works. Nevertheless, it is probably worth remarking that one reason we should still read these four-hundred-year-old poems – and surely some justification is required – is their capacity to embody the stirrings of a historical epoch, the moment of class, which we postmoderns may or may not be on the other side of.[83] This is a question, I suspect, about which Renaissance sonnet sequences have a lot to teach us.

3 "An Englishe box": Calvinism and commodities in Anne Lok's *A Meditation of a Penitent Sinner*

Lok and the sonnet sequence

The first sonnet sequence in English appeared in print in 1560 at the end of a translation of four sermons by Calvin. *Sermons of John Calvin, upon the Songe that Ezechias made . . .* was entered into the Stationer's Register on 15 January 1560.[1] The translator of the sermons is named "A. L." at the end of the dedicatory epistle and since at least the nineteenth century has been identified as Anne Lok, a Marian exile and prominent member of the London merchant community.[2] Appended to the end of the sermons is *A Meditation of a Penitent Sinner: Written in Maner of a Paraphrase upon the 51. Psalme of Dauid*, a collection of twenty-six sonnets (five prefatory and twenty-one "meditations") which are deeply Calvinist in tone and content but which employ the particular form of the sonnet devised by Surrey a few decades earlier. A preface to the sonnets by the translator claims this "meditation" "was deliuered me by my frend with whom I knew I might be so bolde to vse & publishe it as pleased me," but no friend has been positively identified. Patrick Collinson has suggested that this preface indicates that Lok did not write the poems which follow (his candidate is John Knox).[3] Yet as Roland Greene notes, this is a "routine disclaimer of authorship" by a female writer in this period in which "one recognizes this [preface] as a circumlocution that generates an understanding beyond what it actually says, an acknowledgment that 'I wrote this book.' "[4] Because the writer protests too much, the note strongly suggests that Lok is in fact the author of the sequence. Almost certainly, then, the first sonnet sequence in English, over twenty years before sequences by Watson and Sidney, was written by Anne Lok.

For a history of sonnet sequences concerned with convention, Lok's work must remain invisible, for it is not Petrarchan in any traditional sense. Indeed, the first thing anyone looking at it is likely to notice is that these poems can be very hard to read – occasionally bordering on inscrutable. If this problem is partially due to the undeniable fact that Lok is not always the smoothest of poets, the main reason Lok's sonnet sequence makes such difficult reading is that it confounds the critical contexts – conventional Petrarchism included – that we might deploy to try to make sense out of it. As Greene suggests, "Lock's poem belies much of what we think we know about the cross-cultural valences and eventual domestication of the sonnet sequence – and that such a poet is a Calvinist, and a woman, complicates received literary history all the more."[5] Lok's work has been critically recovered largely in the terms set out in the title of Collinson's formative 1965 biographical article: "The Role of Women in the English Reformation Illustrated by the Life and friendships of Anne Locke." Lok has become visible within the renewed attention to women's writing and, as a matter of course, religious writing, since religion was a frequent, less closely regulated, outlet for women's writing.[6] Such work has been crucial in recovering writing ignored for centuries, but we should not read Lok only as "illustrative" of the "role" of Protestant women.[7] To Greene's list of contexts we might also add Lok's social position, for her poem also "belies" the connections between sonnet sequences and social distinction I outlined in the previous chapter. *A Meditation of a Penitent Sinner* is neither a product of court nor a product of a middle-class professional writer. Sidney Lee mentions Lok once, but only in his *Dictionary of National Biography* entry for her son Henry. Because the sequence completely lacks the conventional language of Petrarchism, it is difficult to place within the Bourgeois Paradigm. Viewing the work as a sonnet sequence consequently challenges the nineteenth-century conceptions of a rising middle class of professional sonnet writers, but it also challenges new historicist emphasis on ties between sonnet sequences and the reinforcement of absolutism. Much of what is interesting about Lok and her work, then, is that neither Renaissance writers nor current criticism offer compelling terms to describe people like her – in part, of course, because there do not seem to have been very many women like her at all. Exactly because it is *not* conventionally Petrarchan, then, *A Meditation* helps us to escape from the ossified questions that have defined the study of sonnet sequences and their conventions for over a hundred years – questions such as the relative influence of other nations upon English writers, the distinction between secular and devotional love poetry, and (above all) the question of whether sonnet sequences should be aligned with the aristocracy or the middle class. For a literary history of sonnet sequences, *A Meditation* becomes important less because of its negligible influence on later writers than because it opens up largely unexplored critical territory.

What critical territory? Lok's life situates her in a nexus of Protestant merchants who, while never constituting a distinct party or class in 1560, nevertheless formed a powerful voice in early Elizabethan England through the logics of Calvinism and mercantilism. Though Lok was not a member of court, her prominence in these circles meant that she was hardly as marginal as her nearly complete absence from literary history might suggest. Lok's father was, among other things, a Mercer and president of the Merchant Adventurers, Henry VIII's representative at the important Antwerp trade, Crown representative in the attempt to bring Tyndale back to England, an object of Sir Thomas More's attacks on suspected Tyndalians, and securer of a Crown loan from Antwerp merchants for £272,000. Her step-mother was a relative of Henry Brinkelow, whose *The Complaynt of Roderyck Mors* (?1542) and *Lamentacion of a Christian against the Citie of London* (1542) followed other apologists in arguing for further church reform and particularly criticized the distribution of recently claimed church property among aristocrats rather than the poor. Her father-in-law Sir William Lok was also a Mercer who had endeared himself to Henry VIII when, while on business in Dunkirk in 1533, he pulled down the papal bull excommunicating Henry; the king responded by allowing him £100 a year and making William a gentleman of the privy chamber (the king even dined at William's house once). Anne's brother-in-law Michael Lok was a prominent, polylingual merchant who traveled extensively throughout the world, and in 1576 he put up much of the money for Martin Frobisher's first attempt to find a Northwest Passage, a voyage in which the Sidneys also heavily invested. Michael Lok went bankrupt, however, and in 1582 dedicated a map of the world he had made to Sidney which was included in Hakluyt's *Divers voyages*, possibly in the hopes that Sidney would give him money. After her first husband died, Lok married the high profile Protestant preacher and brilliant scholar Edward Dering, who once, with shocking explicitness, criticized Elizabeth's handling of religion to her face in a public sermon. Most famously, Lok maintained a life-long friendship with the Presbyterian instigator John Knox, who stayed with her in London, persuaded her to travel to Geneva in 1556 (conspicuously without her husband, though no sexual relationship has been proven), and wrote to her to garner support and money for the Scottish Presbyterians. When in 1583 John Field sought to publish some of Knox's works, he seems to have acquired them from Anne. Her son Henry Lok carried on his mother's literary interests; in 1591 he contributed a sonnet to James VI's *His Maiesties Poeticall Exercises at vacant houres*, and he published his own sonnet sequence, *Sundry Christian Passions contained in two hundred sonnets*, in 1593. The later contains commendatory verse by, among others, John

Lyly, as well as an appendix of sixty sonnets dedicated to such notable courtiers as John Whitgift, Lancelot Andrewes, Sir Walter Ralegh, Sir Edward Dyer, and Fulke Greville. Henry also seems to have managed to obtain a position in the 1590s working for the Cecils. Even Lok's last husband, Richard Prowse, a draper from Exeter, was an alderman, three times mayor, and Member of Parliament. Anne appears to have been important enough for the puritan Christopher Goodman to travel to Exeter to preach – a place Collinson suggests he normally would not go.[8]

Lok's social position and her translation of Calvin consequently situate her at the center of what Robert Weimann terms the fundamental alterations in the "conditions of discursive practice" and reconception of locations of authority which took place in England partially as a result of the Reformation. While much authority remained "external," located in traditional ecclesiastical and political institutions, the Reformation created a new "internal," self-directed authority. Weimann stresses that in England the Reformation was particularly vexed, since Tudor absolutism used Protestantism to create the idea of a Protestant nation even while this combination divided locations of authority. In England "secular power and religious reform became intertwined" to create "an alliance between representation and the 'redemption of the world' through interpretation." The Protestant state simultaneously imposed Weimann's "external" institutional authority – an authority which exists, *a priori*, as a condition of its discursive utterance – as well as fostering the "internal" authority of Protestant subjects – an authority which emerged "in the perception of meaning as *process*."[9]

Recognizing this dynamic relation among politics, religion, and social position in Elizabethan England helps to make sense of Lok's work because it begins to clarify one of its most distinctive formal features – the difficult and complex relation between the sonnets and the text of the psalm that appears in the margin. On one hand, the psalm facilitates a specifically religious lyric authority by providing both a model and a text for the speaker to contemplate. On the other hand, the psalm provides a historical narrative of the founding of the "New Jerusalem" within which the speaker's lyricism occurs – England's return to Protestantism under Queen Elizabeth. The relation between sonnet and psalm thus sets in motion two incommensurable modes of authorization: a religious lyric authority and a political narrative authority. This relation is particularly evident in the final two sonnets in the sequence, numbers 20 and 21:

Shew fa-	Shew mercie, Lord, not unto me alone:
vour, o lord	But stretch thy savor and thy pleased will,
in thy good	To sprede thy bountie and thy grace upon
will unto	Sion, for Sion is thy holly hyll:
Sion, that	That thy Hierusalem with mighty wall
th [sic]	May be enclosed under thy defense,
walles	And bylded so that it may never fall
of Hierusa	By myning fraude or mighty violence.
lem may be	Defend thy chirch, Lord, and advaunce it soe,
bylded.	So in despite of tyrannie to stand,
	That trembling at thy power the world may know
	It is upholden by thy mighty hand:
	That Sion and Hierusalem may be
	A safe abode for them that honor thee.

Then shalt	Then on thy hill, and in thy walled towne,
thou accept	Thou shalt receave the pleasing sacrifice,
the sacri-	The brute shall of thy praised name resoune
fice of righ	In thankfull mouthes, and then with gentle eyes
teousnesse,	Thou shalt behold upon thine alter lye
burnt of-	Many a yelden host of humbled hart,
fringes and	And round about then shall thy people crye:
oblations.	We praise thee, God our God: thou onely art
then shalt	The God of might, of mercie, and of grace.
they offre	That I then, Lorde, may also honor thee,
yonge bul-	Releve my sorow, and my sinnes deface:
lockes upon	Be, Lord of mercie, mercifull to me:
thine al-	Restore my feling of thy grace againe:
tare.	Assure my soule, I crave it not in vaine.

As lyrics, these sonnets derive their power partially by ventriloquizing and ritualistically reenacting the voice of David, usually thought to be the author of the psalms. As Greene remarks, the psalms "require the reading voice to assume the identity of their represented speaker; in a certain sense a psalm scarcely represents a speaker at all, but is the script for sacred ritual cast in lyric discourse." As a psalmic ritual, Lok's work is a "prolonged incantation" that recreates in its performance the authority of a collective identity – here, quite specifically, English Calvinists.[10] The individual sonnets eventually become, literally, the psalm itself, as the speaker's extension of David's voice through sonnets gradually unfolds and articulates the lines of the psalm. Lyric authority here acts much like de Man's sense of "allegory" I discussed in the previous chapter: its incantatory feeling is distinctly anti-mimetic. Out of these enactments of the psalm emerges the New Jerusalem, an entity consisting of the

"people" praising God much as the speaker himself does by reading and
interpreting the psalm. As Norman Jones notes, for the godly in the 1560s
"the True Church [was] not built of stone and lime. Rather it [was] a
congregation of the faithful, where the pure and sincere word of God
[was] preached and the sacraments [were] duly ministered."[11] The
speaker's voice emerges as God "[s]hew[s] mercie" to him by assuring
his soul that mercy has been attained and the New Jerusalem has been
created; the speaker knows mercy has been attained when God decides,
as sonnet 17 puts it, to "loose my speche, and make me call to thee" –
itself a paraphrase of the psalm's request that the Lord "open thou
my lippes, and my mouth shal shewe thy praise." God's mercy is enacted
as it "resource[s]" in "thankfull mouthes." The realization of God's
mercy through the articulation of sin creates the New Jerusalem, the
true church; authority emerges, in Weimann's terms, through "the
perception of meaning as process." The creation of the New Jerusalem is
thus in one sense roughly equivalent to the emergence of the speaker's
lyric authority, for both stage the process by which God's mercy is
realized.

As a version of David, the "I" of the poems is male, a new embodiment
of the psalm's distinctly male authority, even though the poems
themselves never indicate a specific gender. For this reason I gender
the speaker male throughout this chapter. As we will see when we return
to the question of Lok's preface to the poems, however, the absence of a
specific gender marker itself points to a dynamic and shifting conception
of authority throughout the work. What the obscurity of the speaker's
gender makes initially apparent, however, is that the ritualistic script
provided by the Psalm is never seamlessly enacted. The speaker does not
simply become a contemporary David and a male speaker. The lyric
authority of these poems also emerges out of a *reading* voice, not just a
lyric ritual: Lok's sonnet "meditations" are as much interpretations of
the psalm as they are reenactments of it.

As a reading of the psalm, the sequence also represents a specific
historical story within which this interpretation occurs. The psalm
provides what de Man terms a "representational" mode: a narrative of
the founding of a historical New Jerusalem, a sequence that follows the
"plot" of the psalm. Margaret Hannay notes that building the New
Jerusalem, line eighteen of Psalm 51, had effectively become code for
Protestant activism – a connection Lok herself makes quite clearly in the
dedication to her other published work, the 1590 translation of Jean
Taffin's *Of the markes of the children of God*.[12] More than a theological
abstraction, "church" refers to the social activities of the godly
attempting to create and reinforce Protestantism in England. Reciting

and interpreting the psalm generates the speaker's lyric authority, but that authority is also facilitated by a "safe abode" "enclosed" under Queen Elizabeth's defense against the "tyrannie" of the Inquisition and papal authority generally. As the standard legal tag on the title page of the work suggests, Lok's poems exist *"Cum Gratia and privilegio Regiæmajestatis."* Elizabeth's protection facilitates this "safe abode" as the queen becomes the "Lord" who spreads "bountie" and "grace" on "Sion" by defending the church against "tyrannie." For Lok's speaker, the end of the narrative is not merely allegorical; the return to Protestantism under Elizabeth promises that the New Jerusalem will materially exist.

The form of Lok's work consists of the relation between these two modes, lyric and narrative, allegorical and representational: the internal authority of the lyric speaker becomes possible as a result of Elizabeth's institutional authority. And it is here that the strain between lyric and narrative, sonnet and sequence, becomes evident, for the religious ritual which Elizabeth's Protestantism facilitates potentially resists Elizabeth's institutionalized monarchical power. The formal contradictions of the work consequently participate in what Jones wryly terms "The Unsettled Settlement of Religion," the complex question of the relative authority of political, ecclesiastical, and social discourses which remained a central issue throughout Elizabeth's reign.[13] Lok herself was centrally involved in these issues through her own work, through her relationship with John Knox, and through her marriage to her second husband Edward Dering, who may well have been a Presbyterian.[14] But the power available to women like Lok was not only dependent upon their connections to men. In 1565 during the controversy over clerical vestments (which the godly felt were merely papist robes), Jones reports that

[o]ne man, a Scot who had earlier provoked a riot with a sermon against the surplice, appeared wearing one early in June. Some of the women of the parish stoned him, then dragged him from his pulpit, ripping his surplice and scratching his face in what Bishop Grindal described as a 'womanish brabble.'[15]

While Lok's privileged connections and social standing distinguished her from any mere "brabble," these circumstances, what Lok herself, writing in 1590, called the *"Halcyon daies"* of the puritan movement, provided the discursive conditions of her existence: "I have according to my duetie, brought my poore basket of stones to the strengthning of the walles of that Iuresalem, whereof (by grace) wee are all both Citizens and members."[16] The tension of the sequence is a tension between different modes of authorization: between the "Citizen" and the "member," between narrative and lyric, and finally, in a sense, between metaphoric and real stones.

Calvinism and commodities

English Calvinists are a group which have notably resisted attempts to assign them to a particular class. The "culture of puritanism," as a recent collection of essays terms it, was a religious, not an economic, phenomenon that crossed over many and varied socio-economic groups.[17] However, if the godly were not the rising middle class that volumes of historiography have wished they were, Lok's religion does not occur in a vacuum either. The context into which she brings Calvin's thought participates in English traditions with distinct social implications. English Protestant poetry like Lok's emerged out of native traditions of verse that were generally non-aristocratic; early Reformers, and especially Edwardians, took over native, medieval traditions of plain, didactic verse and applied Protestant messages to them. While Protestant verse enjoyed prestige at the Edwardian court, much of its purpose was to educate and inculcate the lower social strata.[18] Lok's use of the sonnet formally to embody these traditions complicates things further by introducing a form with quite distinct social and economic affiliations: her choice of the sonnet in 1560 associates her with an urban, non-aristocratic readership.

In 1560 the sonnet as a form was, at best, loosely defined in English. It might mean a love poem, or even just a short poem. Lok quite specifically chooses, however, the scheme devised by Henry Howard, Earl of Surrey. Where precisely she encountered and copied Surrey's format is a question open to historical speculation. Michael R. G. Spiller usefully suggests that Lok probably found the form in Surrey's sonnet "The great Macedon that out of Perse chasyd / Darius," a preface to Wyatt's *Psalmes*, arguing that "[t]his is a eulogistic and pious sonnet, and Locke would not even have had to know what a sonnet was to realize that here was a stanza form she might herself use for prefatory or translating purposes." Spiller goes on to note that "this is actually one of the very few sonnets by Surrey to obliterate the octave break," the form of the Surrey sonnet Lok usually employs.[19] The choice of Surrey's sonnet as Lok's main model is further supported by Alexandra Halasz's persuasive situating of Wyatt's *Psalmes* in relation to Henry VIII's control of church and state. Halasz argues that "Wyatt creates a perspective in his poem from which 'the values of a system that has an absolute monarch as head of both church and state' can be judged, the power of the monarch notwithstanding." Wyatt effects this critique by distinguishing "between himself, the narrator, and David . . . [Wyatt] can call the king to account, but he cannot do so from a position of innocence or spiritual purity."[20] Indeed, Wyatt's historicizing of David bears considerable resemblance to the paradoxical position of Lok's speaker between lyric and narrative senses of Psalm 51. Yet the high praise Spiller gives Lok for her technical poetic skill seems at odds with his description of her as "a completely innocent poet" who was "not even aware that she was looking at a sonnet."[21] Given that Spiller persuasively demonstrates Lok's familiarity with Wyatt's *Psalmes*, it seems much more likely that, were she "innocent" of the sonnet, she would employ Wyatt's quatrains rather than using Surrey's prefatory poem.

Instead, Lok seems quite familiar not only with "The great Macedon" but with the sonnet generally which she probably found in the great source of the sonnet form in English, *Songes and Sonettes, written by the ryght honorable Lorde Henry Howard late Earle of Surrey, and others*, the landmark publication of 1557 usually known as Tottel's *Miscellany*. It is exceedingly likely, though probably not provable, that Lok was familiar with Tottel's. Even assuming, as Spiller does, that Lok could not have seen Tottel's while she was in exile on the continent (which does not necessarily seem a likely assumption, since she was in Frankfurt, a center of the book trade, by late March 1559), she was back in England in June 1559, giving her six months to read Tottel's before her work was published in January 1560.

The probability of Tottel's influence on Lok suggests, even more strongly than Wyatt's *Psalmes*, the social stakes of writing sonnets in 1560. As a source, Tottel's removes Lok from an anachronistic religious vacuum and places her and her book in English society broadly conceived. What Lok and other non-noble readers found in Tottel's was a representation of aristocratic England meant to reinforce specifically the values of an urban Protestant. Mary Thomas Crane suggests that Tottel's shows evidence of a "middle-class," "humanist" emphasis on "aphoristic matter that tended to confirm the superiority of the middle-class's own unambitious way of life and frugal values."[22] Crane reads Tottel's famous preface to his book ("It resteth now, [gentle reader], that thou thinke it not evill done, to publish, to the honor of the English tong, and for profit of the studious of English eloquence, those workes which the ungentle horders up of such treasure have heretofore envied thee")[23] as emphasizing not the superiority of such aristocratic "treasures" but the power of those acquiring them:

To a readership including members of the urban merchant class, the social credentials of the authors of such poems were important not just because those readers were interested in the life-styles of the rich and famous, but because the effect of the poems is to judge the rich and famous by middle-class standards and to find them wanting.

In opposition to "social status" and "private, courtly luxury," Tottel presents, according to Crane, "a gathering designed to share among common people a textual commodity that is rightfully theirs," rather than a "courtly luxury" hoarded up by the "ungentle."[24] Wendy Wall similarly notes that "[i]n labeling the 'horders' of such texts as 'ungentle,' Tottel reverses the class distinctions generated by coterie circulation, inscribing the act of publishing as the more noble, 'gentle' mode of exchange and the book reader as the truly 'gentle' kind of textual consumer."[25] Social position, nobility and "gentleness" itself, becomes defined by the circulation of printed commodities. As a commodity, the stylistic matter in Tottel's attains value and authority not only through what Marx calls its "use value" – the tropes and stylistic matter one copies, for instance – but through its "exchange value," the circulation, purchase, and ownership of such tropes.[26]

What Crane somewhat misleadingly calls "middle-class values" points not at a specific group or class (the rising bourgeoisie) but at a distinct *process* of creating social distinction. The social distinction of Tottel's commodified stylistic material rests not in the social institution of the aristocracy or "the middle class" but rather in the possession and circulation of a commodity through ownership. This argument inverts what has become a critical commonplace about sonnets in the last forty years: rather than descending from the aristocracy (or at least court), the sonnet appears post-Tottel as a commodified form employed by often non-aristocratic writers to erect representations of social order, and conceptions of social distinction, from a non-aristocratic perspective. Rather than centralizing the authority of court and celebrating Tudor absolutism, Tottel's demonstrates a *dislocation* of authority, as Weimann puts it, out of institutions and into process. In the circulation of the book market, for instance, Tottel's published sonnets become the active embodiment of an authority based upon the possession of a commodity; prestige itself becomes objectified in the rhetorical phrases Tottel sells to his readers. By adopting a form of the sonnet found in Tottel, Lok is thus participating in the relocation of authority out of social institutions and into commodity ownership; more generally, she helps to transform what constitutes social distinction itself.

Such objectification of aristocratic "luxury" suggests a distinctly moralistic ambition to impose the tastes of those who socially distinguish themselves through commodity circulation. This moral imperative becomes clear in Lok's dedicatory epistle to the Duchess of Suffolk. Borrowing heavily from Calvin's theology, Lok is concerned in the epistle with an inward sense of depravity in the face of God's law. But she is even more occupied with the need for a *public* display of this inwardness. On the one hand, Lok emphasizes that "the greues of the body and calamities of fortune do so farre onely extende, to afflict, or make a man miserable, as they approch to touch the mind, and assaile the soule" (A3^v). The only sickness which really matters is an inward sickness, and one who has a "defense of inward understandyng" is safe from all outward, physical harm: "some men beynge pressed with pouertie, tossed with worldlye aduersitye, tourmented with payne, sorenes, and sicknes of body . . . Yet hauing theyr myndes armed and fournished with prepared patience, and defense of inward understandyng, all these calamities can not so farre preuaile, as to make them fall" (A2^r). The cure for this sickness of the soul ultimately lies only with God, but the existence of that cure is marked by a sign, an external indication of a mind "armed."

It is this material and outward indication of God's cure, her book, which Lok presents in the dedication to the Duchess of Suffolk: "this receipte God the heauenly Physitian hath taught, his most excellent Apothecarie master Iohn Caluine hath compounded, and I your graces most bounden and humble haue put into an Englishe box, and do present vnto you" (A3^r). Lok describes her relation to Calvin and to the duchess as a transaction, the delivering of a textual commodity Lok has packaged – "put into an Englishe box." The book becomes the objective embodiment of Calvin's cure, a public enunciation and response to an intense sense of inward sin. To possess the book is to possess the cure. But the published book, Lok's "Englishe box," also models the public declaration of sin. It provides individuals with "prepared patience, and defense of inward understandyng" by providing an *outward* and public display of sickness. The title of the book stresses "the *Songe* that Ezechias made after he had bene sicke" (my italics). The interest of Calvin and Lok lies not simply in the inward sickness of sin but, as the order of the wording of the title implies, the public response and articulation of Hezekiah to his sickness – his song.

In the most general sense, then, what Max Weber famously termed the "Protestant ethic" becomes in Weimann's terms "part of a larger culture of early modern appropriation in which the possession of objects could reward the spirituality of subjects."[27] The epistle describes the spirituality available from such "appropriation." While dedicatory epistles customarily sought to honor the book with the prestige of the (would-be) patron, Lok's epistle reads more like a lecture than flattery – telling the (admittedly very willing) Duchess of Suffolk, known as the mother of English puritanism, what she ought to know.[28] Instead of seeking to authorize the book with the prestige of the duchess, Lok's epistle presents and embodies a mode of authorized interpretation itself – Calvin's interpretation of Hezekiah's interpretation of sin, placed in an English box. Lok's "Englishing" of Calvin, the process of presenting him to the duchess, becomes a transaction of commodified authority which undermines the noble status ordinarily reinforced in dedications. In her book's title, Lok likewise plays down Hezekiah's own nobility. The title of the French edition is "Sermons de Jehan Calvin sur le cantique que feit le bon roy Ezechias apres qu'il eut ete malade et afflige de la main de Dieu." In the English version, Lok cuts out "le bon roy," the good king, though it is a phrase which she translates frequently in Calvin's sermons. Rather than seeking simply to praise the duchess, Lok's dedication *presents* a form of social distinction to her.

But at the same time, Lok's presentation of her book is not simply a circulation of commodities. This transaction occurs within a strenuously hierarchical society ruled by the government of an absolute monarch: God first, royalty second, Calvin third, and finally Lok herself, "most bounden and humble." In this sense, Lok's "Englishe box" is presented to a duchess in a familiar act of patronage, and it seems likely that Lok hopes the Duchess of Suffolk will use her social standing to help to disseminate the work. Even as Lok presents an individualized, commodified authority and "cure" of inward sickness, that transaction takes place within the aristocratic institution of patronage in which authority is located as an external social condition, not as an act of interpretation. If Calvin's name on the title page ensures that the book will possess a distinctively individual, commodified, and Protestant authority, the dedication to the duchess (despite, rather than because of, her endorsement of Calvinism) simultaneously invokes an authority which is based in social institutions rather than a discrete act of interpretation. In Lok's "Englishe box," in short, two radically different modes of authorizing discourse coexist: an external authorization, the system of patronage that reinforces, ultimately, Elizabeth's absolute rule; and an internal mode, the commodified interpretations that the book embodies.

These contradictions are likewise apparent in Calvin's sermons on Hezekiah, King of Judah (2 Kings 18–21) which constitute the bulk of the book.[29] The title page of Lok's book provides no hint that besides Calvin's sermons the book contains a verse meditation, never mind *sonnets*; what is advertised and stressed – the biggest words on the page – is *John Calvin*. The book is primarily a religious work meant to reinforce and reintroduce Calvin's interpretive methods into a specifically English context. It was published by John Day, who was responsible for a wide variety of godly books, including John Foxe's *Actes and Monuments*

(1563) and the French and Dutch versions of *A Theatre for Worldlings* (1568). Lok's book itself is a tiny, pocket-sized octavo volume probably meant to facilitate daily, individual contemplation of the sort stressed in Calvin's sermons. These sermons set out the theological framework within which Lok constructs her sonnet sequence.

In his discussion of Hezekiah, Calvin is specifically interested not only in the significance of sin and suffering, but more importantly in the reasons for recording one's suffering and presenting that record to others. He is concerned, in other words, with the significance of and procedure for commodifying declarations of sin. He begins in the first sermon by asserting that while God is immortal, his "trueth" in the world is not assured and requires constant attention: "our care should extende it selfe to the time to come, to the end we may have in store some continuing seede of religion, in such sort as the trueth of God may never be abolished" (B1ʳ). The example of Hezekiah shows, Calvin argues, the importance of recording one's penitence as a sign to others:

Behold now wherefore Ezechias was not contented to make this protestation whiche we read here with his mouth, but wold also wryte it, that to the end of the worlde men might knowe how he had ben vexed in hys affliction, and that the same myght serve for doctrine to all the worlde: so as at this day we may take profyt thereof. (B1ᵛ)

By recording his affliction in writing, Hezekiah provides an example and a means to maintain God's presence. Hezekiah is thus a typological symbol by which Calvin himself understands contemporary sins – Calvin takes "profyt" from Hezekiah's example because it establishes "doctrine": "let us not thynke it straunge that god sendeth us afflictions whiche seme grevous and sharpe unto us, seeing we see that Ezechias hathe walked before us to shewe us the waye" (B7ᵛ). Such a recorded example is necessary because while God is apparent in Nature ("For all the world is as a liuely image, wherein God setteth fourth vnto vs his vertue and highnes" C1ᵛ), God's presence in the world is mediated like an image in a mirror:

So nowe the good kyng Ezechias sheweth us, that it were better for us all to have died before we had been borne, and that the earth should have gaped whan we came out of our mothers wombe, to swallow us, than to live here by lowe, if it were not for thys, that we do here alreadie see oure God: not that we have a perfecte sighte. But first he showeth himselfe unto us by his worde, which is the trew lokyng glass. (C1ᵛ)

While God may exist in nature, in "so manye signes of his presence," Calvin stresses, using the mirror conceit common in the period, that the primary locale is scripture, "his worde, which is the trew lokyng glass."

The written Bible is the truth, for Calvin, to which one looks to see oneself.

Yet one does not look at the world or the Bible "with a perfecte sighte." The way to gain understanding for Calvin is not to attempt to clear up the picture – not to attempt to contemplate God's perfection. Instead, Calvin emphasizes the imperfection of the self we see in the mirror, the gap – sin – between a self and God's presence in the world. Hezekiah "did not here set fourthe his owne vertues to be praised of the world, for he might have kept in silence that which he hath declared of his owne waywardnesse" (B2^r). Instead of hiding his sin, Hezekiah displays it: "we see a poore man tormented even to the extremitye, and so striken downe, that he wiste not what myghte become of hym. We se a man astonished with feare of the wrath of God, lokyng on nothyng but his own affliction" (B2^r). Calvin closes the first sermon, as he does all four of the sermons that Lok translates, not with an attempt to see unadorned Truth itself through Hezekiah, but rather to use Hezekiah as a means better to see sin:

Nowe let us throwe oure selves downe before the majestie of our good God, in the acknowledgeynge of oure synnes, besechynge hym, that more and more, he wyll make us to feele them, and that he wyll in suche sort cleanse us from all oure fylthynesse, that we beynge perfectly awaked from oure dull drowsinesse, may grone and sobbe. (C4^r)

The way to make God present in the world is always negative: not through a contemplation of truth, but through a contemplation of "our fylthynesse." Rather than asking God for forgiveness, Calvin anxiously asks to feel sin more.[30]

Because God's presence becomes manifest in man's contemplation of sin, expressing sin becomes a complicated matter, for it necessarily implies God's presence as well as the salvation of the person doing the articulating. Consequently, the sign of a man who truly feels his sins, insists Calvin, is that he can barely utter them:

But whan that [Hezekiah] woulde frame anye request unto God, he was as it were dombe, and that on the one syde the sicknesse troubled hym, and yet he coulde not plainelye expresse what he ayled: so that he was in two extremities. Th[ ]one that he was in such sort locked up within, that with great payne could he fetch out any complaint. The[ ]other that he was oppressed with so vehement passyons, that he wyste no wheare too begynne to make his Prayer. (C8^r)

What marks the truly penitent sinner, Calvin suggests, is a pain so intense that a person cannot speak, and yet does; and an anguish so intense, a person does not know why he keeps silent: "And to be short, they that knowe in deede what the wrathe of God is, wyll speake and crye, and yet they know not on whiche side to begin: and again when they holde their peace they wote note why they doe it: but they are always in anguish. And we se a notable example of al these things in the good king Ezechias" (D1^{r-v}). True knowledge of God's wrath means true knowledge of sin, but this knowledge makes speaking of it difficult. The importance of Hezekiah lies thus in his capacity as both a sign of God's mercy and a model by which the "penitent sinner" knows where to begin.

The declaration of weakness, an awareness of sin so keen that one does not know where to begin, becomes the source of *authority* – a sign of God's presence. It is the precondition for writing and speaking, for a public display. Recording one's sins discursively becomes a sign of fallenness itself. Conversely, sin becomes the necessary precondition of all *authorized* discursive practice: if one were not fallen, a sign – a written sermon or poem – would hardly be necessary. In this sense Calvin's sermon, with its constant harping on man's filth and utter dependence upon God's good will, becomes a commodity: a negative sign of God's presence that depends upon the continual representation and objectification of sin in discourse. It is the process of interpreting Hezekiah's sign, or of reading Calvin's sermon, or of reading Lok's sequence, which establishes, via its own negation, the authority embodied in the written sign. The commodity itself becomes the sign of authority in a post-lapsarian world: only through the negation of the true does truth emerge.[31]

The presuming eye

At the start of her sonnet sequence, Lok adds a note which explicitly connects her work to the logic of Calvin's sermons. At the same time, the note backs off from the claim of authorship and authority generally:

I have added this meditation folowyng unto the ende of this boke, not as parcell of maister Calvines worke, but for that it well agreeth with the same argument, and was delivered me by my frend with whom I knew I might be so bolde to use and publishe it as pleased me.

While, as we have already seen, the prefatory note might complicate the identification of the author, it more crucially points directly at questions of *authority*, at the discursive practices by which the work understands itself to be true, convincing, and socially distinct. For Greene, this preface resembles what Patricia Parker calls "a poetics of dilation and delay" characteristically gendered female. Like Parker's "literary fat ladies," Greene suggests that the gender of Lok's speaker "is implied by the symbolic association with a postmedieval context of feminine copiousness and dilation."[32] One effect of this sense of the speaker's gender is to reiterate the gap between the speaker and the appropriation of David's masculine voice. Not only does the speaker interpret David's text, but that interpretation is performed within a context ordinarily labeled female. The question "what is the gender of the speaker" rearticulates the more general question of the speaker's social distinction because it points to the space between the allegorized, religious authority of a male lyric speaker and the existence of such a speaker in Lok's feminized "English box." The very fact that the "I" of the sonnets has no gender marker in the work sets in motion a dynamic process of authorization, a movement between a feminine book and a masculine speaker that enacts the "negative truth" of Calvin's sermons. This distinction depends on commodity circulation; publishing feminine dilation becomes the means whereby the work acquires a public, male authority. As it circulates publicly the sequence propounds the "same argument" as "maister Calvines work" because its social distinction becomes realized as it is exchanged and owned. The customary deflection of authorship by women becomes less a sign of the *author's* gender (though it may remain that) than a general model for all authoritative discursive practice.

The authority at stake in this dynamic similarly plays out in the structure of the work. *A Meditation of a Penitent Sinner* is divided into two sections: "The preface, expressing the passioned minde of the penitent sinner," and "A Meditation of a penitent sinner, upon the 51. psalme." In the preface, the speaker is scared, passive, and tentative, and his lack of power is expressed in the preface's rambling and difficult syntax. In the "Meditation" itself, however, the lyric voice changes dramatically. This change is largely attributable to the inclusion of the text of Psalm 51 in the margin of the sequence. The preface expresses "the passioned minde of the penitent sinner," a condition in which the speaker gropes about searching for salvation; that authorization emerges quite forcefully in the meditation as the speaker interprets the fragments of scripture included in the margin. Interpretation of scripture – or rather, the declaration of sin that interpretation entails – becomes the basis for the authoritative voice of the sequence.

The drama of the preface's "passioned minde of the penitent sinner" is a desperate, almost hysterical, search for comfort and the assurance of salvation. But Lok's "penitent sinner" hardly knows where to begin to look and blurts out a series of syntactically awkward assertions that articulate a "passioned minde." The first two sonnets consist of one long sentence that expresses the speaker's inability to "find the way wherin to walke aright." Initially, the speaker tries to maintain a distinction between himself and his sin. As the opening sonnet puts it, "The hainous gylt of my forsaken ghost / So threates, alas, unto my febled sprite." But the distinction between his "hainous gylt" and his "febled sprite," between sin and self, collapses when, in the third sonnet, the speaker finally encounters "despair":

> But mercy while I sound with shreking crye
> For grant of grace and pardon while I pray,
> Even then despeir before my ruthefull eye
> Spredes forth my sinne and shame, and semes to saye
> In vaine thou brayest forth thy bootlesse noyse
> To him for mercy, O refused wight,
> That heares not the forsaken sinners voice.
> Thy reprobate and foreordeined sprite,
> For damned vessel of his heavie wrath,
> (As selfe witnes of they beknowying hart,
> And secrete gilt of thine owne conscience saith)
> Of his swete promises can claime no part:
> But thee, caytif, deserved curse doeth draw
> To hell, by justice, for offended law.

Despair tells him what his "beknowyng hart, / And secrete gilt of thine owne conscience saith": that his curse is "deserved," and he goes to hell "by justice, for offended law." His guilt, God's wrath, and his "febled sprite" are all his own fault: he is a "[f]or damned vessel of his heavie wrath."

This knowledge of his own complicity in his suffering, of the fact that it is his very existence which offends God, conversely provides the means by which he will "try for mercy to releve [his] woes." In sonnet four, though his "conscience wanteth to replye" that he is not at fault, his "remorse" enforces his "offence" and "doth argue vaine" his attempts at mercy:

> This horror when my trembling soule doth heare,
> When markes and tokens of the reprobate,
> My growing sinnes, of grace my senslesse cheare,
> Enforce the profe of everlasting hate,
> That I conceive the heavens king to beare
> Against my sinfull and forsaken ghost:
> As in the throte of hell, I quake for feare,
> And then in present perill to be lost
> (Although by conscience wanteth to replye,
> But with remorse enforcing myne offence,
> Doth argue vaine my not availing crye)
> With woefull sighes and bitter penitence
> To him from whom the endlesse mercy flowes
> I try for mercy to releve my woes.

The speaker's despairing recognition of the "markes and tokens of the reprobate" becomes, implicitly, a mark that he is *not* one of the reprobate. As Calvin insists, Hezekiah's ability both to articulate his sin and to recognize it *as* sin becomes a sign of God's grace. Likewise, the speaker's ability to recognize the signs of the reprobate simultaneously becomes a sign of his elect status. In line three, "[m]y growing sinnes" are transformed into "of grace my senslesse cheare," a "senslesse" expression of grace. As his awareness of his sins grows, so, implicitly, does his "senslesse cheare" of grace. The speaker's emerging authority is constituted by his recognition of his sin – of his lack of authority – because he begins to identify and express himself as deservedly forsaken from the start.

But he cannot explicitly articulate this nascent sense of his election, for his "conscience" argues that his "not availing crye" is "vaine." Instead, his "cheare," his expression, must always be "senslesse." To consider himself elect would necessarily force him to stop recognizing his own sin because it would mean not emphasizing that the violation of God's law is the fundamental condition of his existence. He would be "vaine," one of the reprobate who doesn't feel his sins. Consequently, in the fifth and final prefatory sonnet, he determines to ask for grace by

> not darying with presumming eye
> Once to beholde the angry heavens face,
> From troubled sprite I send confused crye,
> To crave the crummes of all sufficing grace.

In 1560, "presume" pointed in many different, often contradictory directions. The speaker does not "presume" to look at God in the sense that he does not, as the *OED* puts it, "act or proceed on the assumption of right or permission." The speaker's position is one of abject humbleness, for he asserts that the grace he seeks is not his right, and that he does not have permission, as it were, to look upon God's angry face. To say that he does *not* dare "with presumming eye" underscores, however, his recognition that, though he does not dare look upon God and ask for mercy, he can conceive of doing so. Such protestation leads us to another, and quite contradictory, sense of "presume": "To take possession of without right; to usurp, seize." In claiming *not* to dare look upon God with a "presumming eye," the speaker simultaneously *stresses* his presuming eye. He has "taken possession of without right" in the sense that he *is* beholding here "the angry heavens face" even as he articulates the idea of a God he has offended, of a law he has violated. If the speaker "presumes" without right, he also presumes without authority. A third, equally current definition of "presume" is "[t]o take upon oneself, undertake without adequate authority or permission." Indeed, in his articulation of his lack of authority (the recognition that God's wrath is completely justified) the speaker *acquires* authority. This fact of the speaker's condition leads us to yet another definition of "presume": "To assume or take for granted; to presuppose." The speaker's "presumming eye" must always be *presumed*, presupposed, for the speaker to be capable of articulating his lack of presumption at all. As in Calvin, sin becomes the necessary precondition of discursive practice – here, of presuming.

This presumptuously active contemplation in pursuit of a largely passive relation to God recalls Calvin's declaration that not knowing where to begin itself marks a truly penitent sinner. Calvin himself points to Psalm 51 as a means out of the sinner's dilemma: "when God sheweth hym selfe mercyfull towarde us, and uttereth some signe of hys favor toward us, he openeth oure mouthes, as it is sayde in the li. Psalme" (F6ʳ). Not accidentally, then, it is precisely to Psalm 51 that the speaker (and Lok herself) turns to open his mouth and express his moan. As the headnote to the Geneva Bible argues, "[w]hen David was rebuked by the Prophet Nathan for his great offences, he did not only acknowledge the same to God with protestation of his natural corruption and iniquitie, but also *left a memorial thereof* to his posteritie" (my emphasis).[33] Lok's sequence, in one sense, is a reading of the psalm much like the marginal notes of the Geneva Bible – a "memorial" to "posteritie." Lok literally places the complete text of the psalm in the margin next to her sonnets, and by and large each sonnet is a meditation upon a verse of the psalm. But unlike the biblical glosses, the sequence is also an enactment of the authority of the psalm itself as the speaker becomes a contemporary David. The sequence emphasizes the truth of the psalm and redeploys that truth to become a sign of God's mercy. Lok's speaker and the sonnets themselves stand as both a ritualistic enactment of scriptural truth as well as an active example of the textual performance of that authority.

While in the preface the speaker sends "confused crye" and is "tost with panges and passions of despeir," in the first sonnet of the meditation the tone is authoritative and optimistic. The authority of the speaker derives from his ability to recognize and articulate his sin by interpreting scripture. In sonnet 1, for instance, the biblical text asks for mercy "after thy great merci," but the sonnet additionally stresses the speaker's own desire to "sound againe":

Have mer-	Have mercy, God, for they great mercies sake,
cie upon	O God: my God, unto my shame I say,
me (o God)	Beynge fled from thee, so as I dred to take
after thy	Thy name in wretched mouth, and feare to pray
great merci	Or aske the mercy that I have abusde.
	But, God of mercy, let me come to thee:
	Not for justice, that justly am accusde:
	Which selfe word Justice so amaseth me,
	That scarce I dare thy mercy sound againe.
	But mercie, Lord, yet suffer me to crave.
	Mercie is thine: Let me not crye in vaine,
	Thy great mercie for my great fault to have.
	Have mercie, God, pitie my penitence
	With greater mercie than my great offence.

What the speaker says, "unto [his] shame," is that he dreads to utter God's name "in wretched mouth." His voice is enabled by his ability to ask for mercy "that I have abusde" – that is, by his ability to ask to come to God even though he recognizes himself as "justly" accused. The imperative "Have mercy" which opens the sonnet repeats the opening of the psalm. The authority needed to use such a tense, to be able to ask for mercy derives, quite literally in this instance, from the biblical text. While in the preface the speaker can only "crave mercy," in the first sonnet of the meditation he is able to say "mercy" *ten times* in fourteen lines. Likewise, in sonnet 2 he declares that "My many sinnes in number are encreast," and in sonnet 3 he assures us that

> So foule with sinne I see my selfe to be,
> That till from sinne I may be washed white,
> So foule I dare not, lord, approche to thee.

> (2–4)

Like his "presumming eye," the speaker here claims he does not dare approach God, even as he does just that by announcing his foulness. By sonnet 4 the speaker insists that "I fele my sinne," and in sonnet 5 he puts it more emphatically:

> My cruell conscience with sharpned knife
> Doth splat my ripped hert, and layes abrode
> The lothesome secretes of my filthy life,
> And spredes them forth before the face of God.

Like both David and Hezekiah, Lok's speaker is not content merely to declare his sins; he also wants to publicly announce them, to anatomize them "before the face of God."

It is not just before God that these "lothesome secretes" are spread, of course. In sonnet 6 the speaker makes explicit the claim implicit in the published existence of Lok's work itself. In expressing his sin, he wants to become a sign and example for others, a textual embodiment and declaration of sin:

That thou   But mercy Lord, O Lord some pitie take,
mightest be   Withdraw my soule from the deserved hell,
founded just   O Lord of glory, for thy glories sake:
in thy say-   That I may saved of thy mercy tell,
inges, and   And shew how thou, which mercy hast behight
maiest over   To sighyng sinners, that have broke thy lawes,
come when   Performest mercy: so as in the light
thou art   Of them that judge the justice of thy cause
judged.   Thou onely just be demed, and no moe,
                     The worldes unjustice wholy to confound:
                     That damning me to depth of during woe
                     Just in thy judgement shouldest thou be found:
                     And from deserved flames relevying me
                     Just in thy mercy mayst thou also be.

The text of the psalm stresses that God's "sayinges" will be found just, but in the sonnet it is the speaker who desires to "tell" of God's mercy. God will be found "[j]ust in thy judgement" and "[just] in thy mercy," but that mercy is manifested in the voice of the speaker. He himself wishes to effectively *become* God's "sayings,"

> That I may saved of thy mercy tell,
> And shew how thou, which mercy hast behight
> To sighyng sinners, that have broke thy lawes
> Performest mercy[.]

As the speaker becomes increasingly concerned with his status as a sign, he moves gradually away from introspection toward public outbursts of optimism quite unlike anything we see in Calvin's sermons, which characteristically end by emphasizing the strictly negative articulation of God's mercy ("our fylthynesse"). At the close of sermon one, for instance, Calvin envisions a time when he and his followers will be "perfectly awaked from oure dull drowsinesse," but rather than imagining this as a joyful time, he hopes that then they will be able to "grone and sobbe." In other words, in the sermons Lok chooses to translate, Calvin adamantly refuses to impose a redemptive narrative onto his description of suffering: redemption remains abstract, and suffering remains immediate.

In Lok's work, conversely, the ability to "tell" of God's mercy produces a pervasive, if implicit, optimism derived from the narrative provided by

Psalm 51. The continual emphasis by the speaker on sin and filth gives rise to a glimpse, if not an actual manifestation, of cheer and joy. In sonnet 10, for instance, an initial emphasis on sin gives way to a vision of hope:

> *Thou shale*   Long have I heard, and yet I heare the soundes
> *make me*   Of dredfull threates and thonders of the law,
> *heare ioye*   Wich Eccho of my gylty minde resoundes,
> *and glad-*   And with redoubled horror doth so draw
> *nesse, a[n]d*   My listening soule from mercies gentle voice,
> *the bones*   That louder, Lorde, I am constraynde to call:
> *which thou*   Lorde, pearce myne eares, and make me to rejoyse,
> *hast broken*   When I shall heare, and when thy mercy shall
> *shal rejoyse*   Sounde in my hart the gospell of thy grace.
>   Then shalt thou geve my hearing joy againe,
>   The joy that onely may releve my case.

The speaker uses the possibility of joy in the psalm ("Thou shale make me heare ioye and gladnesse, a[n]d the bones which thou hast broken shal rejoyse") to construct an entire history. "Long have I heard, and yet I heare" situates him amidst a narrative of God's "dredfull threates." But this history of guilty echoes resounding in his mind seems at an imminent end. In line seven the speaker uses the present imperative to rejoice *now*: "Lorde, pearce myne eares, and make me to rejoyse." Only with the enjambed line "[w]hen I shall heare" is the present put off to the future. The language of the poem strongly suggests, in other words, that the future is now:

> And then my broosed bones, that thou with paine
> Hast made to weake my febled corps to beare,
> Shall leape for joy, to shew myne inward chere.

"And then" refers to a time when relief is realized, when mercy is actualized, and when the speaker "Shall leape for joy, to shewe myne inward chere." But of course the sonnet itself is a demonstration of that "inward chere," a realization of his interior countenance, and a manifestation of God's mercy as the speaker's mouth is opened, "constraynde to call" *louder*. We see in this sonnet not a syntactically confused, anxiety-ridden voice but rather a confident manifestation of God's mercy, of *authority*, in the speaker's ability to demonstrate his "inward chere." Likewise, in sonnet 16 the speaker actively imagines an act of praise that is not negative, is not simply a reiteration of sin:

> So, Lorde, my joying tong shall talke thy praise,
> Thy name my mouth shall utter in delight,
> My voice shall sounde thy justice, and thy waies,
> Thy waies to justifie thy sinfull wight.

God of my health, from bloud I saved so
Shall spred thy prayse for all the world to know.

(9–14)

Though he is careful to place everything in the future tense, the energy of the syntax ("thy waies, / Thy waies" begins to sound like fervent sermonizing) embodies a sense that salvation is at hand. In line thirteen he declares "I saved so" but catches himself at the start of line fourteen and places his salvation in the future ("Shall spred thy prayse") even as he imagines publicly spreading praise. Though sonnet 17 begins with the return of despair ("Lo straining crampe of colde despeir againe / In feble brest doth pinche my pinying hart") it ends with zealous optimism:

Lord loose my lippes, I may expresse my mone,
And findyng grace with open mouth I may
Thy mercies praise, and holy name display.

(12–14)

In displaying God's "holy name," the speaker also displays his own lyric authority, an authority made materially manifest by the declarations of sin the book makes possible.

The New Jerusalem

The optimism of *A Meditation* emerges, in contrast to Calvin's perennial anxiety, as a result of Lok's inhabiting a specifically English context, an "Englishe box," within which Protestantism rules. Only with England's return to Protestantism, after all, could a work like Lok's be published at all. Under Elizabeth, the time when God "releves" sorrow seems like it might be at hand. As a term, New Jerusalem means both a process of interpretation and the material activities of the godly. It sets in motion two different languages of social distinction in Lok's work: an allegorical, lyric authority, and a representational, narrative authority. Elizabeth's reinstatement of Protestantism promises that these two modes of authorization can be synthesized. Theoretically, at least, Elizabethan England and the New Jerusalem become synonymous terms. Absolute monarchy, like God, both embodies and enables the realization of commodified, Calvinist desires; the queen's authoritative social position resolves the dilemmas faced by people like Anne Lok. Much like Lok's presentation of her "Englishe box" to the Duchess of Suffolk, the representational authority of the monarchy acts to protect the "most bounden and humble." And like Lok's appropriation of the sonnet from Tottel's *Miscellany*, the speaker of the sequence utilizes the position of the monarchy to foster and articulate a distinct social authority – a true church where commodity circulation is both facilitated and, paradoxically, made unnecessary.

While the lyric authority of Lok's speaker emerges in what Greene describes as a "dilated" space, waiting for God's judgment, the optimism of the final two sonnets suggests that such judgment has, at least partially, arrived. The speaker begins to imagine himself as a character in a narrative, a participant, rather than an isolated subject groping about for grace. In sonnet 20, the speaker asks "Shew mercie, Lord, not unto me alone" and hopes that God's "favor" will be stretched to "Sion," "thy Hierusalem," and "thy chirch." Likewise, the first nine lines of sonnet 21 imagine "thankfull mouthes," "a yelden host of humbled hart," and the cry of "thy people." As the speaker imagines the realization of his desire, he effectively ceases to be a lyric speaker and is transformed into a character in a narrative. The "I" of the poems becomes just one of a "yelden host of humbled hart." Within this narrative vision, the New Jerusalem appears as a paradise where the realization of the speaker's desires simultaneously means the end of commodity circulation. When all the "people crye: / We praise thee," a textual sign of God's mercy – a sermon, a book, a poem – is no longer necessary. Situated amidst communal praise, "God" becomes the figure who embodies and makes possible the realization of desire, a figure of "might," "mercy," and "grace" in which sins are "defaced." As the shift away from a lyric "I" suggests, the realization of the speaker's desire in the New Jerusalem means the elimination of the very structures – commodity circulation – which provide the speaker with authority in the first place. It means, in other words, the elimination of the speaker himself. No longer an "I," the speaker disappears into a new mode of authorization: the "people."

Rather than celebrating his imminent erasure, however, this speaker ends up *resisting* the narrative realization of his desires. The sequence ends not with narrative closure, an allegorical vision of the undifferentiated people praising God, but with a contradictory reaffirmation of the lyric "I":

> That I then, Lorde, may also honor thee,
> Releve my sorow, and my sinnes deface:
> Be, Lord of mercie, mercifull to me:
> Restore my feling of thy grace againe:
> Assure my soule, I crave it not in vaine.

The speaker's desire to "honor" his "Lord" reaffirms his desire for lyric authority, for a material, commodified sign so that he "may also honor" God, but this desire rearticulates the very fallenness and sin which

separate him from relief. He must always "crave it . . . in vaine." The
rhyme "againe / in vaine" embodies both the hope and the fear of the
penitent Calvinist: any hope is always again "vaine" and "in vaine."
Reasserting the lyric "I" at the end of the sequence captures the
contradiction between the "I" and the narrative of the foundation of the
New Jerusalem. The speaker resists that narrative because it undermines,
even as it makes possible, his ability to speak at all.

This lyric resistance underscores that there remains an unbridgeable
gap between the New Jerusalem as a Protestant apocalypse – the
theoretical end of historical time – and the New Jerusalem as the
historical England which Lok seeks to transform and describe with her
work. From the speaker's point of view, Elizabethan England and the
New Jerusalem should be synonyms, but they aren't. As a result, the close
of the sequence moves from a tentative "presumming eye" to something
approaching open hostility. "Againe / in vaine," coupled with the
imperatives "Restore" and "Assure," sounds less like resignation than
anger. The speaker *tells* God – or Elizabeth – what to do, much as Lok
herself told the Duchess of Suffolk where to find mercy in the dedicatory
epistle. While the narrative of the foundation of the New Jerusalem
initially provokes the speaker's desire for mercy, his lyric authority comes
to oppose that very narrative when it paradoxically ends up endorsing a
monarchical power which threatens the speaker – a "tyrannie" of
"myning fraude" and "mighty violence." "Lord" suggests both the God
from whom the speaker wants mercy as well as the hoarder-up of
aristocratic treasure that the speaker's commodified, procedural authority critiques. The fact that these Calvinist exclamations take the form of
sonnets post-Tottel makes them socially critical from the beginning.
Equating Elizabeth with God, or even making her head of the church,
was, after all, largely what the godly resisted so insistently throughout her
reign. Were she not to support the more radical forms of Protestantism in
England (as indeed she largely did not), Elizabeth performs, within the
logic of A Meditation, the very "tyrannie" against which she is supposed
to protect Calvinists like Lok. Lok's speaker was hardly alone in such an
ambivalent portrait of Elizabeth's handling of religious matters. As early
as November 1559, John Jewel, also a Marian exile who eventually
became a bishop, complained to the Reformation figure Peter Martyr
back in Geneva, "[t]hat little silver cross, of ill-omened origin, still
maintains its place in the queen's chapel. Wretched me! This thing will
soon be drawen into a precedent."[34] The "ill-omened origin" of
Elizabeth's dimly Catholic cross acts much like the "myning fraude"
declaimed in A Meditation: both threaten to turn from protector to
persecutor. The paradox of the speaker's social distinction occurs as he

himself must assert his "presuming eye" and stand "in despite of tyrannie" against Elizabeth – against, in other words, the very historical narrative, the promise of the material founding of the New Jerusalem, that facilitates his utterance in the first place. In the absence of the apocalypse, he must finally act as his own "lord" and occupy the position – of God and the monarch – which promises to foster the circulation of commodities that is the basis of his social distinction.

It is surely no accident, then, that the speaker here comes to resist and to *resemble* the very monarch whose rule facilitates the meditation. In the movement between impassioned introspection and public show, between feminine and male authority, this speaker resembles nothing so much as the dynamic authority Elizabeth herself playfully employed. As Jennifer Summit suggests, Elizabeth routinely seized upon and made the object of performance the very limitations which her gender was supposed to put on her. "As an orator herself, Elizabeth tacitly acknowledges oratory's cultural status as a masculine art in ways that also allow her to appropriate it for her own uses: thus in her speeches she eloquently disclaims eloquence, and she violates the humanist injunction to female silence in the very act of articulating it."[35] Lok's speaker goes further, making feminine silence, the process of introspection, itself a necessary feature of any public, male authority. The implications of this dynamic for the social position of Lok are far-reaching: rather than reinforcing monarchical power, as do Elizabeth's manipulations of gender, Lok's work recasts the basis of social distinction from the institution of monarchy toward the movement between private and public that is entailed in the circulation of commodified declarations of sin. The dynamic movement that the sequence sets in motion – between genders, among commodities – begins to concretize a new social position.

In the resistance of the lyric "I" to the very narrative which provokes it, then, we see not only a powerful expression of a typically Calvinist speaker, or an example of the authority which might accrue to a woman in 1560; we witness the articulation of an emergent sense of social distinction both enabled by and resistant to monarchical authority. *A Meditation of a Penitent Sinner* is the formal embodiment of early-Elizabethan England as it is understood by a Calvinist, wealthy, mercantile woman. Lok's book not only exists "in" the "Englishe box" of Elizabeth's protection; it *is* the box – a textual construction of England circa 1560. The social contradictions that structure Lok's world also structure her sonnet sequence; indeed, those broader social contradictions are made visible through the formal paradoxes of the work itself. Early Elizabethan England from this perspective looks much like Lok's sonnet sequence – a world where authority is spread among both those who maintain Calvinist convictions and those who can enact those convictions in the form of textual commodities; but also a world where this procedural authority is enabled by and resistant to institutionalized conceptions of authority, particularly absolute monarchy.

In terms of literary history, Lok opens up an entirely new way of thinking about sonnet sequences. If writers like Lok depict the monarchy in the service of non-noble interests, conversely, to what degree was this possible because monarchical authority itself was in part modeled on the authority of interpretive process? When King James styles himself a "prentice" sonnet writer, when Astrophil checks himself in "Reason's audite," when Daniel claims that his sighs and sonnets are an account book, when Spenser's speaker claims the *Amoretti* emerge from "trade," when Shakespeare's speaker complains that his beloved is a "profitless usurer," and, finally, when Drayton describes these tensions as "the *English* strain" in sharp opposition to the king he despised – all these moments point to the need to reconceptualize social relations in Renaissance England and to the ways those relations are manifest in sonnet sequences. Only when we begin to address these questions will Lok find a secure location in the literary-historical landscape. To situate Lok in literary history means not only rethinking the relations between secular and religious poetry or imaging the effects of women's writing: it means conceptualizing the social distinction bound up in English sonnet sequences.

4   "Nobler desires" and Sidney's *Astrophil and Stella*

Anne Lok's impact on subsequent writers of sonnets probably ranged from minimal to non-existent. Though there is some evidence that the Countess of Pembroke, if not Philip Sidney, encountered her and perhaps her work, Lok's importance lies not in any explicit influence but rather in the capacity of her work to make apparent other forces that have been largely neglected in the study of sonnets.[1] These possibilities are especially apparent in the most influential sonnet sequence of the era, Sidney's *Astrophil and Stella*. As I argued in chapter two, Sidney was understood throughout much of the nineteenth century as either a dull conventional sonneteer or a passionate noble lover. Through the twentieth century Sidney became known as the great inheritor of Wyatt and Surrey, the writer of the first "authentically Petrarchan Petrarchism"[2] in England, and a proponent of the poetic taste that dominated continental courts. Since the 1960s, critics have stressed these courtly connections by arguing that the sonnet was a dominant form at court, employed by political insiders like Wyatt and Surrey, and written under Queen Elizabeth by Gascoigne, Watson, and above all, Sidney. Out of this narrative, Sidney emerges as the paradigmatic "courtier poet"; his use of Petrarchan conventions in *Astrophil and Stella* documents the dynamics of Elizabethan court life, and, for new historicist readings in particular, the frustrations and limitations of the ambitious Elizabethan courtier.[3]

Holding on to a vision of *Astrophil and Stella* as a conventional product of a courtly ethos, however, rearticulates the construction of the social space of the Renaissance inaugurated in the nineteenth century: it replays the dialectic between conventionality and originality, bourgeois and aristocratic, that has been proceeding for nearly two hundred years. In contrast, more recent descriptions of Sidney have begun to emphasize less his location in the Elizabethan court than his participation in a wide range of contemporary circumstances – an interest in the Americas, slavery, new forms of trade. Gradually, Sidney the "courtier poet" is being replaced with "the imperial Sidney." Alan Stewart has argued that

Sidney maintained an even higher international profile than had been previously suggested, and Roger Kuin has demonstrated Sidney's intimate involvement in the socio-economic issues surrounding the Americas.[4] *Astrophil and Stella* is in this revisionary sense a product not simply of Elizabethan court culture but also a participant in global shifts in nationalism, slavery, Protestantism, imperialism, and mercantilism. Such a shift of focus means that the move from *A Meditation* to *Astrophil and Stella*, from Lok's Calvinism and mercantilism to Sidney's international stature, seems less abrupt than it might in traditional narratives of sonnets in England. Rather than a homogeneous line of literary development, sonnet sequences are, as Roland Greene stresses, deeply generational and preoccupied with thinking through contemporary problems.[5] In this light, Sidney (b. 1554) has as much in common with Lok, probably about twenty years older than him, as with his traditional literary forebears Wyatt and Surrey, born a half-century earlier. Like Lok, Sidney's life located him at the intersection of a number of different discourses and in the midst of substantive changes in conceptions of social distinction. As the occasional heir to Leicester, Sidney was intensely aware of his quasi-aristocratic status, and he was, as Mary Thomas Crane argues, "more than any other writer of the period . . . located at the juncture of humanist and aristocratic systems."[6] William Kennedy similarly describes Sidney as "frustrated . . . by being stranded in the lesser nobility without earned title."[7] Sidney was, for example, the most celebrated pupil at Shrewsbury grammar school, owing largely to his father's virtually absolute rule over Wales, but he dined daily at the house of George Leigh, a leading figure in the local wool trade and a member of the Drapers' Company.[8] Sidney's meals at grammar school exemplify the issues he faced his entire life: though powerful family and political connections placed him in a position of the utmost social privilege, his daily existence led him to a continual interest in and interaction with forms of social distinction outside court politics and into, for instance, the mercantile world of drapers inhabited by people like Lok and her family – a connection facilitated by the Calvinist sentiment both generally shared. In light of these critical shifts, Sidney's decision to write a sonnet sequence can no longer be viewed as simply the product of a courtly environment. *Astrophil and Stella* participates in broader alterations in the production of social distinction at the end of the sixteenth century, and court is only part of these changes. What is crucially at stake in the sequence, then, is the question of social classification itself – how should we read Astrophil's social position and the social space of the sequence?

Astrophil and Stella presents another issue for any history of the sonnet sequence in England. Composed in the early 1580s, its massive influence apparently does not begin until nearly a decade later, when it is published in 1591 in a possibly pirated edition.[9] If the concerns of Sidney are distinct from those of Wyatt and Surrey, the same holds true for writers in the 1590s, a decade quite different from the 1580s.[10] A historical rendering of *Astrophil and Stella*, then, needs to examine two distinct issues: first, the conditions in the early 1580s within which the sequence was written; and second, the conditions of the 1590s, when *Astrophil and Stella* takes on a new life.

To address these issues, this chapter is divided into two parts. The first, longer section examines the construction of social distinction in *Astrophil and Stella*. It argues that Astrophil should be viewed as habitus paradoxically produced by two competing modes of social distinction: "status," where one's social legitimacy is determined by one's association with social institutions, particularly family; and "class," where one's social legitimacy depends (like Lok's speaker) upon the control of circulating goods. These contradictory fields provoke in Astrophil a desire for an imaginary social position that reconciles the strain between status and class – a new vision of nobility, what Astrophil himself terms "Nobler desires." The second section introduces the concerns of the rest of the book by examining the appropriation of Astrophil's "Nobler desires" by writers in the 1590s. "Our English Petrarke," as Sidney becomes known, indicates not only a poetic influence, but also a concern with a new, idealized conception of nobility. Writers following Sidney, however, were rarely noble themselves. Their appropriation of Astrophil's noble ideal tends to articulate more fully their own (non-noble) social position even as it seeks to reinforce a new definition of nobility. The contradictions so prevalent in *Astrophil and Stella* – both formal and social – consequently establish the terms by which a broader poetic and social process works itself out.

Nobler Desires

In sonnet 18, Astrophil articulates himself as a contradiction. After describing his squandering of the "birthright" and the "goods" which heaven has lent him, the idle spending of his wealth, the waste of his youth, and the mere toys that his knowledge brings forth, Astrophil adds in the couplet that he really wishes he could lose more:

> With what sharpe checkes I in my selfe am shent,
> When into Reason's audite I do go:
> And by just counts my selfe a banckrout know
> Of all those goods, which heav'n to me hath lent:
> Unable quite to pay even Nature's rent,

Which unto it by birthright I do ow:
And which is worse, no good excuse can show,
But that my wealth I have most idly spent.
My youth doth waste, my knowledge brings forth toyes,
My wit doth strive those passions to defend,
Which for reward spoile it with vaine annoyes.
I see my course to lose my selfe doth bend:
I see and yet no greater sorow take
Than that I lose no more for *Stella's* sake.[11]

Astrophil here consists of two things. On the one hand, he is a "birthright," that "which heav'n . . . hath lent," "Nature's rent." This self is immutable, God-given, and natural. On the other hand, he consists of "goods" and "wealth" which exist to signify his "birthright" but which he no longer possesses. The puzzle of the sonnet – and it is a puzzle for Astrophil as much as a reader – lies in the strain between these two selves and their relation to a desire for Stella. In the couplet, Astrophil suggests that his desire for Stella *expresses* his birthright. In spending or losing his goods and wealth for her, his birthright is tacitly, though forcefully, emphasized. As Maureen Quilligan suggests, "[h]e desires not only Stella but also all the riches, fame, and achievement he would happily throw away for her."[12] But that expression is contradictory, because the manifestation of his birthright in his desire for Stella simultaneously means the *loss* of his goods and wealth – that which also exists to signify his birthright. Astrophil's desire for Stella discloses a tension between two ways of distinguishing, of categorizing, himself. If his devotion to Stella expresses his birthright, it also expresses – even entails – his lack of wealth.

This internal contradiction is figured in the strain in the sonnet's form. As a character in a narrative "course," Astrophil is a largely passive creation of "goods" "lent" by heaven, a "rent" he owes "Nature" by virtue of his "birthright," a "wealth," "youth," "knowledge," and "wit" wasted on poetic toys. Astrophil's story "bends" "to lose" this "selfe" because he emerges as a character always already in debt; he is defined by his imminent erasure by the very processes producing him. While Astrophil understands himself in largely passive terms in the first ten lines ("I am . . . shent," "I do owe"), in the final three lines he becomes an active subject ("I see," "I see"). In opposition to this passive character, there is always also a lyric "I" who actively goes into "Reason's audit." By retelling in a lyric the "course" that the audit takes, this "I" implicitly resists that audit. If Astrophil is produced as a passive character, a subjective effect of a "course," he is *also* produced as a lyric subject – as an "I" who goes, sees, and represents himself in sonnets. Astrophil's self exists as both the passive product of a series of financial and social obligations (the "goods" heaven lends him, the "rent" he owes "Nature"), and as a subject who resists and seeks to lose the very forces which initially produce him.

"And yet" places us at the juncture between these two conceptions of Astrophil; the phrase marks that moment when Astrophil both most forcefully expresses his desire for Stella and understands the threat of his own dissolution – what David Kalstone describes as "the continued pointing of the poems toward the *discovery* of conflict, the frequent emphasis on disruption itself."[13] Astrophil is defined by his "birthright," "and yet" he also consists of goods and wealth. He is a passive character produced by a narrative "course," "and yet" he is also a lyric "I" who actively resists that narrative. But "and yet" also marks the relationship between these two contradictory versions of Astrophil's self and his desire for Stella. The ambiguous and elusive tone of "and yet" (smirking, resigned, witty, and puzzled all at the same time) expresses the strain of the entire sequence. Why does Astrophil's desire for Stella both reinforce a particular version of himself (his "birthright" and lyricism) and, at the very same time, undermine that self by exposing his lack of "goods" and his existence as a largely passive character in a socioeconomic "Audit"? Sidney uses the word "yet" sixty-seven times in *Astrophil and Stella* in forty-two different poems, and it tends to enact, as in sonnet 18, a moment of de Manian critical blindness, where Astrophil comments upon his own existence without successfully resolving the contradictions which produce his desire.

Astrophil's imagination of Stella does not resolve this paradox – it *expresses* it. To overcome his paradoxical existence, Astrophil tries to imagine a new object, a different character, who succeeds in wooing Stella and reconciles his contradictory existence. In other words, the overwhelming object of Astrophil's desire is less Stella than an idealized "Astrophil." As Jonathan Crewe suggests, this peculiar sense of Astrophil imagining an ideal narrative space, an "Arcadian story," is also a general feature of Sidney's work:

[t]he Arcadian story is definitively that of Philip Sidney, and the putatively ideal space of those poems, both songs and sonnets, is one that Sidney might hope to appropriate from Petrarch and others in such a way as to make it his own. But if he can put his distinctive mark on that space, he evidently cannot make it . . . into an Arcadia; indeed, there is a sense in which the speaker is never *in* Arcadia but inhabits the position of the privileged witness or prurient spectator *to* it.[14]

Astrophil is never "in" Arcadia and does not exist in a narrative in which he successfully wins Stella, but he often tries to imagine himself as if he were. *Astrophil and Stella* often depicts Astrophil as a speaker wishing he were in a different sort of story. Most famously, in sonnet 1 Astrophil seeks to "paint the blackest face of woe" in order to win Stella's "grace":

> Loving in truth, and faine in verse my love to show,
> That the deare She might take some pleasure of my paine:
> Pleasure might cause her reade, reading might make her know,
> Knowledge might pitie winne, and pitie grace obtaine,
> I sought fit words to paint the blackest face of woe
>
> (lines 1–5)

Astrophil is "faine," desiring, to show his love in verse because that representation of his "woe" will set off a narrative in which he obtains grace. What makes this sequence so complex, and the levels of personae so compelling and bewildering, is that Astrophil tries to imagine himself as a *new* idealized object ("the blackest face of woe") which will in turn set in motion a new narrative of success ("Pleasure might cause her reade, reading might make her know," and so on). But Astrophil is also already in a narrative of loss and desire for Stella ("Loving in truth"), and this desire *provokes* him to imagine a new narrative self. While "faine" means "desiring" and thereby implies a relatively stable subject who desires, "faine" also means (according to the *OED*) "obliged," suggesting a speaker who is interpellated, compelled "in verse [his] love to show." Astrophil the lyric speaker is "obliged" by his simultaneous existence as a character in a narrative of loss to create another persona – and another narrative – in the hope of success. This new persona would, moreover, effectively eliminate the desiring speaker by relieving the desire that defines him.[15]

This effort by Astrophil as lyric speaker to imagine himself as an idealized narrative character is especially clear in sonnet 45:

> *Stella* oft sees the verie face of wo
> Painted in my beclowded stormie face:
> But cannot skill to pitie my disgrace,
> Not though thereof the cause her selfe she know:
> Yet hearing late a fable, which did show
> Of Lovers never knowne, a grievous case,
> Pitie thereof gate in her breast such place
> That, from that sea deriv'd, teares' spring did flow.
> Alas, if Fancy drawne by imag'd things,
> Though false, yet with free scope more grace doth breed
> Then servant's wracke, where new doubts honor brings;
> Then thinke my deare, that you in me do reed
> Of Lover's ruine some sad Tragedie:
> I am not I, pitie the tale of me.

Astrophil's general lament here is that while Stella is moved to "pitie" by a "fable," she "cannot skill" to pity Astrophil himself. He complains, in an Aristotelian sense, that art moves Stella more than reality.[16] But of course, the "reality" of Astrophil's woe is itself "Painted" in his "beclowded stormie face." Astrophil's protest, then, is less that art is more powerful than life, than that a "fable," a different rhetorical mode, moves Stella more powerfully than his own lyric representation and "painting" of his "wo." In the competition for Stella's pity between Astrophil's lyric face and a "fable," narrative wins. The sonnet ends with the erasure of lyric in favor of narrative: "I am not I, pitie the *tale* of me." In place of his lyric complaint, Astrophil imagines himself as a character in a narrative. When he asks Stella to "thinke, my deare, that you in me do reed / Of Lover's ruine some sad Tragedie," Astrophil the sonneteer is replaced by Astrophil the tragic hero. He laments the inability of his lyric utterance to relieve his desire for Stella's grace, but he imagines that representing himself as a narrative character will do just that. The paradox of the sonnet is that such a representation is always a "*tale* of *me*," a lyric desire for narrative and for Astrophil as a character. The poem becomes contradictory because the imagination of this character depends upon the erasure of the speaker doing the imagining ("I am not I"). Conversely, the idealization itself is made unrealizable because it is articulated by the lyric speaker whose desire is defined by his existence in a narrative of loss. The very fact that Astrophil the lyric speaker imagines a character who wins Stella only rearticulates, as in sonnet 18, the condition of Astrophil's lyricism in the first place – his situation within a narrative of "woe" which paints his lyric "stormy face." The result is a contradictory lyric subject whose very power undermines the success he desires.

The contradictions internal to *Astrophil and Stella* are not unprecedented. Astrophil's lyric efforts continue the tradition of "autoreflexivity" that John Freccero influentially argues is the basis of much Petrarchan verse, a "totally autonomous portrait of the artist" where the Petrarchan laurel is an antitype to Augustine's fig tree. The laurel has no "moral dimension of meaning. It stands for a poetry whose real subject matter is its own act and whose creation is its own author," rather than grounding meaning in God or the logos, as Augustine insists all writing must.[17] *Astrophil and Stella* differs from other Petrarchan work, however, in the degree to which it stages the failure of Astrophil's autoreflexivity and the degree to which it views such autoreflexivity as itself conditioned by a broader social field. Astrophil's lyricism acts as habitus, not only an autoreflexivity, because the strain between lyric and narrative *stages*

Astrophil's idolatry as largely a response to his contradictory construction as "birthright" and "goods." While Freccero imagines autoreflexivity as a sort of subject freed from its object, reading Astrophil as habitus emphasizes that the very formal fact of Astrophil's desire expresses a specific position in social space. The desire for autoreflexivity itself, in other words, is a socially distinct position.

Emphasizing the relationship between Astrophil's autoreflexivity and the field within which that lyricism occurs rearticulates, in a historically more precise way, Kalstone's sense of Sidney's tendency to point continually to conflict in the sequence – those moments of disruption which Astrophil himself endlessly puzzles over and to which he has no easy answer. More than indicating a formal effect or a poetics, "Birthright" and "goods" correspond to different modes of social authorization, *status* and *class*.[18] Status and class should be read here as two components of a dialectical construction of Astrophil's self that draw on both existent (status) and emergent (class) organizations of social space. On the one hand, status sets in motion those political, familial, and legal institutions imagined as unchanging and constant. Astrophil seeks to "fulfill" and "repay" his birthright lent to him by heaven. In this sense, status is a static and largely legal term which identifies a conceptual category into which Astrophil fits and which, conversely, creates Astrophil in its own image. On the other hand, "class" sets in motion a dynamic process, Astrophil's identity as a production or bringing forth of those material goods which fulfill the parameters established by status and which, more importantly, signify the existence of status; in the sequence, class depends on riches, not on a birthright. These social contradictions are expressed formally in the paradox between lyric and narrative. Astrophil's formal urge to imagine a new narrative character, "Astrophil," should be seen as an attempt to imagine a new social position, a new idea of nobility, that reconciles the strain between status and class. The idealized conception of nobility acts something like a Lacanian imaginary that the speaker seeks to impose throughout the sequence, a conspicuously male figure who resolves the strain between birthright and goods. Astrophil's desire for a masculine noble ideal consequently represents in a concrete way the beginning of a breakdown of what Michael McKeon terms "aristocratic ideology." For McKeon, external and internal conceptions of aristocratic authority revolve centrally around the term "honor." Honor is an external quality expressed in wealth and political power. But it is also "an essential and inward property . . . that which the conditional or extrinsic signifiers of honor exist to signify."[19] Astrophil's problem is that the symbiosis between outward and inward honor so integral to aristocratic ideology keeps breaking down. Rather than reinforcing his honorific birthright, his goods (or lack of goods) tend to undermine any internal honor. The habitus of the poem consists of this structural contradiction, the social position that emerges in the increasing distance between birthright and goods, between inward and outward manifestations of honor.

In sonnet 21, Astrophil gives a name to this process. His birth, he tells his friend, produces in him "Nobler desires":

> Your words my friend (right healthful caustiks) blame
> My young mind marde, whom *Love* doth windlas so,
> That mine owne writings like bad servants show
> My wits, quicke in vaine thoughts, in vertue lame:
> That *Plato* I read for nought, but if he tame
> Such coltish gyres, that to my birth I owe
> Nobler desires, least else that friendly foe,
> Great expectation, weare a traine of shame.
> For since mad March great promise made of me,
> If now the May of my yeares much decline,
> What can be hoped my harvest time will be?
> Sure you say well, your wisdome's golden mine,
> Dig deepe with learning's spade, now tell me this,
> Hath this world ought so faire as *Stella* is?

Structurally, this sonnet acts very much like sonnet 18. After detailing a series of contradictions between his "Love" and his "Great expectation," between his "wit" and his "vertue lame," between his "coltish gyres" and the "wisdomes golden mine" of his friend, Astrophil asserts an "and yet" moment: "now tell me this, / Hath this world ought so faire as *Stella* is?" We are initially faced with effectively the same questions as in sonnet 18. What is the relation between his desire for Stella and the contradictions of the first thirteen lines? Is Astrophil admitting his shortcomings or making fun of the friend? Does his desire for Stella express his "young mind marde," or does it (somehow) transcend such criticisms? The strain here is figured explicitly in social terms: his writings are like "bad servants" that expose the contradictions of his "wits." But sonnet 21 holds out (as sonnet 18 only does implicitly) the possibility of resolution. In admiring the fairness of Stella, Astrophil is also expressing his "Nobler desires," his will to live up to "Great expectation" and produce a suitable "harvest." His desire is quite specifically a *social* desire for a different conception of nobility, a wish to be more noble – a "Nobler" desire. As an imaginary, this ideal nobility does not theoretically correspond to either Astrophil's existence as "birthright" or "goods." Nobility itself becomes an object of desire, a social position that imaginatively reconciles the contradiction between status and class.

As an imaginary, however, Astrophil's "nobler desires" disclose the specifics of the conditions which provoked that desire, rather than relieving it. In other words, throughout the sequence, the articulation of ideals ends up reiterating the specificity of a social position, not the realization of an aristocratic imaginary. As Žižek remarks about Lacan's term "the Real," it is "an entity which must be constructed afterwards so that we can account for the distortions of the symbolic structure." Likewise, the habitus of the sequence is the absent *cause* of the contradictory desires Astrophil articulates. Social position becomes apparent when we read backwards, as it were, from the desire it creates. "The 'class struggle,'" argues Žižek, "is present only in its effects, in the fact that every attempt to totalize the social field, to assign to social phenomena a definite place in the social structure, is always doomed to failure."[20] In sonnet 41, for instance, Astrophil attempts to present himself as just such a noble ideal:

> Having this day my horse, my hand, my launce
> Guided so well, that I obtain'd the prize,
> Both by the judgement of the English eyes,
> And of some sent from that sweet enemie *Fraunce*;
> Horsemen my skill in horsemanship advaunce;
> Towne-folkes my strength; a daintier judge applies
> His praise to sleight, which from good use doth rise;
> Some luckie wits impute it but to chaunce;
> Others, because of both sides I do take
> My bloud from them, who did excell in this,
> Thinke Nature me a man of armes did make.
> How farre they shoote awrie! the true cause is,
> *Stella* lookt on, and from her heavenly face
> Sent forth the beames, which made so faire my race.

"The true cause" of Astrophil's ability to "obtain the prize" is the fact that "Stella looked on, and from her heavenly face / Sent forth the beams, which made so fair my race." Astrophil's "race," both his tilting and his family lineage, is made "faire" by Stella's gaze: his tilting "race" expresses his family "race." Stella's gaze, and Astrophil's witnessing of it, demonstrates the inward honor that Astrophil demonstrates outwardly in his tilting performance. She reconciles his inward and outward shows by making both his "races" "faire" and enables him to "obtain the prize" of a nobler self. But this sonnet is crucially a recollection; he has already obtained the prize. Astrophil's triumphs are, especially within the sequence's narrative of loss, a retrospective fiction – notice, for instance, how the sonnet shifts back and forth between present and past tenses. If Stella facilitates Astrophil's story, she herself is not the object of his desire: the "Astrophil" who won the tilting match is. His representation of himself as a victorious feudal knight becomes the object of his lyric desire for an idealized nobility. Sonnet 41 imagines a narrative fiction in which Astrophil's desire finally gets realized, the story of how he "obtain'd the prize."

Reading this sonnet as *itself* an object of lyric desire helps to situate it historically by providing a formal frame for making sense of its many topical allusions. What is historical here is less the allusions themselves than the form they take – the sonnet's habitus, the construction of social space it seeks to enforce. The "Arcadian story" is, after all, at least partly the story of Sidney himself: as many have noted, Sidney goes out of his way in *Astrophil and Stella* to invite biographical readings. Aside from the allusions to Penelope Rich and her husband, the sequence is full of puns on Sidney's name and invocations of contemporary political events.[21] Sonnet 41 imports real historical events and real historical persons, but these events appear only in the recollection of the lyric speaker who presents a scene in which a character solves many of England's, and Sidney's, social and political problems. The retrospective "Astrophil" exists as an idealized object of the present "I's" desire, not a transparent depiction of Sidney himself. Any historical rendering of this sonnet must begin with this formal construction, its structuring structures. Though no specific tournament is (or should be) identified, the sonnet clearly invokes a variety of circumstances – Sidney's role in the *Triumph of the Four Foster Children of Desire*, the French Duke Anjou's negotiations of marriage with Elizabeth, Sidney's frequent participation in Accession Day tilts, the familial lines of his father and grandfather as well as his maternal uncles Leicester and Warwick, and so on. In presenting the details which construct Astrophil as an idealized feudal knight (his horsemanship, his military skill, his noble blood, his romance-like performance in front of others' gazes) the poem simultaneously presents the political battles Sidney participated in – most centrally, his relationship with Leicester that placed him in the Protestant faction vehemently opposing the possibility of Elizabeth's marrying the Catholic Anjou. But in the poem there is little factionalism or political conflict, but only wonder: how *does* he do it? The Astrophil imagined here becomes the historical realization of a figure who lives up to his blood and resolves international political crises all by performing the role of an idealized knight. He has "obtain'd the prize" not only in the sense of winning the tournament but also in reconciling the fierce factional fighting surrounding Elizabeth's courtship by Anjou; France is no longer the Leicester faction's most dangerous competition but instead becomes "that sweete enemie." These events, however, are crucially the object of desire of a particular lyric speaker rather than a representation of historical events.

There can be no question, consequently, of miraculously resolving either the formal contradictions of *Astrophil and Stella* or the broader social contradictions the sequence embodies. It is exactly these formal and social contradictions, the poem's habitus, which are historical in the work. In this light, sonnet 5 gives form to the forces which swirled throughout the controversy of the Anjou match. The iconoclastic imperatives of Protestantism (so apparent in Lok's work) meet up with an aristocrat's disgust with disorder, while at the same time the aristocrat bristles under the monarchy and the Protestant asserts the absolute rule of God over the monarch:

> It is most true, that eyes are form'd to serve
> The inward light: and that the heavenly part
> Ought to be king, from whose rules who do swerve,
> Rebels to Nature, strive for their owne smart.
> It is most true, what we call *Cupid's* dart,
> An image is, which for ourselves we carve;
> And, fooles, adore in temple of our hart,
> Till that good God make Church and Churchman starve.
> True, that true Beautie Vertue is indeed,
> Whereof this Beautie can be but a shade,
> Which elements with mortall mixture breed:
> True, that on earth we are but pilgrims made,
> And should in soule up to our countrey move:
> True, and yet true that I must *Stella* love.

The first thirteen lines of the sonnet consist of a passive assertion of what Kalstone calls "a series of moral axioms" "learned perhaps too well."[22] In the first quatrain, the "inward light," or "reason,"[23] is the "heavenly part," the divine, and ought to be served by the eye. This "inward" truth is expressed in an outward political hierarchy. Those who "swerve" from the king's rules are "Rebels to Nature." By resisting the king, they also rebel against God's rule and consequently only "strive for their own smart." But the image of a neat hierarchy of inward and divine order expressed in an outward political hierarchy is also disrupted by the inclusions of "Rebels" striving against it. The hierarchy threatens to disintegrate when we can no longer tell who is king and who is rebel. To claim that eyes should "serve / The inward light" and that the "heavenly part" "ought" to be king was certainly not, in the 1580s, a tired maxim. The phrase means, alternately, that the king-monarch is heavenly and ought to rule, but also that the heavenly part, a Protestant inward authority, ought to be king to which the monarch himself is subject – precisely the issue which obsessed Calvinists like Lok and her husband Dering. Indeed, Astrophil's use of "rules" rather than "rule" may suggest a covenant or a series of legal justifications rather than a reign of a single absolute monarch. The "rebels" might be those against the monarch or those supporting the monarch. If the monarch is "swerving" from the rules of the "heavenly part" ("whose" in this sense modifies "heavenly part") then the king and his party become rebels to nature. Indeed, the sonnet itself acts out these inversions: "Serve" becomes "swerve"; the "inward light" moves rapidly to the external "heavenly part"; "the heavenly part / Ought to be king" is enjambed, literally broken into two lines.

The speaker's relation to these contradictory "truths" is never clear. For instance, does Astrophil endorse monarchy as divine right, or does he support the Protestant rebels who insist on a distinction between monarchy and God? The relation of his desire for Stella and the other "truths" of the sonnet also remains untheorized. How should we read "and yet" in the final line? Does Astrophil's desire for Stella somehow trump these other truths? Is Astrophil aligned with the "fooles" who adore images carved for themselves (an idolatry with Catholic overtones impossible to ignore)? What is clear is that the lyric speaker of the sonnet emerges as a result of these truths and, at the same time, reacts against them. On the one hand, the voice of the first thirteen lines of the sonnet is largely passive, a conduit for truths articulated in clauses whose subject remains elusive and absent ("It is . . . ," "It is . . . "). In reaction to this passivity, the lyric "I" of the final line sounds almost defiant: "and yet" in this sense is an assertion of another truth – marked by the literal emergence of an "I" – apart from the mundane passivity of the first thirteen lines. At the same time, there seems to be a subject lurking somewhere behind the "moral axioms" in the first thirteen lines who makes fun of them. "It is *most* true" sounds like a verbal wink, and this irony sets up the assertion of the desiring "I" of the final line. Conversely, that final "I" is not just assertive; he is also a passive product who "*must* Stella love." The initial contradictory truths of the sonnet provoke and produce a speaker obliged to desire Stella. His desire for Stella becomes both an expression of his paradoxical existence and an attempt to articulate an object which will resolve those (extremely specific historical) contradictions. "And yet" once again suggests that Astrophil must love Stella as a result of these contradictions *and* that he must love her as a means of resolving these contradictions. It places us simultaneously at the moment in which Astrophil resists the social forces he has just detailed and at the moment when his desire for Stella is meant to reconcile those forces.

Beyond the intricacies of a particular political crisis, the social forces which motivate Astrophil, and within which the Anjou affair participates, are more general alterations in conceptions of social authority and the production and maintenance of social distinction. After all, the contradictions between the competing claims of status and class which I have been charting inform questions of the relation of Protestantism and monarchy generally. As Lok's *Meditation* suggests, in England the complications of Protestantism lie in the extent to which Calvinist discourse draws upon juridical discursive authority reinforcing the monarchy to facilitate a mode of producing social distinction based on the possession of commodities. This Protestantized commodity circulation, in turn, challenges the authority of status itself. In *Astrophil and Stella*, this logic also produces a desire for a new, idealized nobility: the monarch that protects godly people like Lok; the knight who solves the troubles involved in the Anjou affair. The difficulty that Astrophil faces, and one apparent in England generally, is that Stella is literally possessed by "Rich." Possession of "riches," rather than possession of inward honor, seems to define nobility in general, and it signals an emergent conception of social distinction at once modeled on the monarch and resistant to monarchy.

Far from resolving contemporary crises, *Astrophil and Stella* powerfully articulates them. The effort at objectification produces only more subjects, more historical specificity, and more social contradiction. As a result, Astrophil's social position becomes distinguished with ever greater nuance. When he seeks to distinguish himself in terms of social rank from the "Rich foole" who holds Stella, he ends up looking like a fool himself; when he tries to construct a conspicuously masculine social position in relation to Stella, he ends up looking more and more like her conspicuously feminine position. Consider first his efforts at distancing himself from Lord Rich. In sonnet 24, Astrophil tries to describe again a nobility that stands above mere control of goods and "riches":

> Rich fooles there be, whose base and filthy hart
> Lies hatching still the goods wherein they flow:
> And damning their owne selves to *Tantal's* smart,
> Wealth breeding want, more blist, more wretched grow.
> Yet to those fooles heav'n such wit doth impart,
> As what their hands do hold, their heads do know,
> And knowing, love, and loving, lay apart
> As sacred things, far from all daunger's show.
> But that rich foole, who by blind Fortune's lot
> The richest gemme of Love and life enjoyes,
> And can with foule abuse such beauties blot;

Let him, deprived of sweet but unfelt joyes,
(Exil'd for ay from those high treasures, which
He knowes not) grow in only follie rich.

What irks Astrophil here is that many "Rich fooles," and in particular one rich fool, Lord Rich, possess the trappings of a noble position, "the goods where in they flow." The thrust of the poem tries to distinguish Astrophil from "that rich foole." Astrophil would treasure Stella as a sacred thing, while that rich fool does not. In this light, Astrophil would be one of the fools of the octet who, despite their participation in the circulation necessary to produce wealth, also have "wit" imparted to them by heaven to recognize the true value of the good they possess. This wit acts as a sort of "birthright," a static social status set apart from the mutabilities of exchange. It is made apparent by devotion to a lady – specifically, a "rich" lady. The lady becomes a sign of an essential honor expressed through the admiration of her as a sacred thing. Astrophil's devotion to Stella should, he imagines, both express his wealth – his possession of goods and, literally, something "rich" – and also express his essential inward honor, the "wit" that sets him apart from "Rich fooles."

The octet initially sounds like a presentation of truths, much in the vein of the openings of sonnets 18 and 21 (we're all fools, and dependent upon heaven to tell us what has value). In the sestet, these abstract truths become historically focused with "But that rich foole." The specificity of "that" makes clear (if there were any doubt) that the sonnet refers, at some level, to Lord Rich – Penelope's husband, the person Astrophil must be distinguished from. Astrophil appears as an assertive speaker aggressively attacking Lord Rich, not a transparent vehicle for wisdom. Such aggression, however, merely underscores the similarity between Astrophil and "that rich foole." Rather than distinct from Lord Rich, Astrophil is *like* him, even inferior to him. They are both fools subject to the tantalizing logic of commodity circulation, "Wealth breeding want." Instead of "Lord" Rich, the sonnet only presents "rich"; Astrophil and Lord Rich are distinguished by the goods they possess (or lack) – by their "riches," rather than their titles (no doubt in part because, of course, Sidney did not have a title). The social position that Astrophil imagines overcomes this "breeding" – the "wit" imparted by heaven that should "breed" familial blood lines – is an *ideal* position that Astrophil, to his own annoyance, does not maintain. To be "rich" is to possess rich things, and Astrophil doesn't.

This tacit dismantling of Astrophil's social claims has significant implications for his gender claims as well. Instead of a sacred thing, Stella ends up looking pretty much like Astrophil – or rather, Astrophil ends up looking like Stella, a feminized, increasingly powerless speaker subject to the vicissitudes of wealth. Astrophil routinely seeks to imagine Stella as an abstract feminine gaze which reinforces his idealized masculine nobility. But just as that ideal is never realized, so Stella turns from an abstract "honor" that reinforces Astrophil's "honor" into a woman who is ruled by 'Tyran honour'" (Eighth song, l. 95). Stella's name implies that she will be a largely "absent presence" (sonnet 106), a stable "star" and transcendental signifier whose constancy enforces the speaker's "inward" nobility and honor. But throughout the sequence that abstraction is undermined by Sidney's constant association of Stella with another name and a real woman – Penelope Rich – and through the intimately related appearance of Stella as a speaking character and an active participant, a subject, in a seduction narrative.[24] Stella becomes subjected in ways similar to Astrophil himself – an identification, a similarity between characters, that the traditional title of the sequence, *Astrophil and Stella*, implicitly suggests.

In sonnet 52, the disjuncture between Stella's inward virtue and her "faire outside" replicates Astrophil's own contradiction between his inward honor and nobility. The sonnet details a split between a sense of nobility or "title" as a series of external "goods" ("Her eyes, her lips, her all") and inward honor (the "sure heire of heav'nly blisse"). This contradiction is played out in a "strife" between "Vertue" and "Love":

> A strife is growne between *Vertue* and *Love*,
> While each pretends that *Stella* must be his:
> Her eyes, her lips, her all, saith *Love*, do this,
> Since they do weare his badge, most firmely prove.
> But *Vertue* thus that title doth disprove,
> That *Stella* (ô deare name) that *Stella* is
> That vertuous soule, sure heire of heav'nly blisse:
> Not this faire outside, which our hearts doth move.
> And therefore, though her beautie and her grace
> Be *Love's* indeed, in *Stella's* selfe he may
> By no pretence claime any maner place.
> Well *Love*, since this demurre our sute doth stay,
> Let *Vertue* have that *Stella's* selfe; yet thus,
> That *Vertue* but that body graunt to us.

The surprise of the sonnet occurs in the last three lines when Astrophil enters on the side of Love. It is a surprise because up until that point the "strife" between Vertue and Love might reasonably be thought of as an internal dialogue, a sort of psychomachia. Whatever "strife" exists promises to be contained in the autoreflexivity of the sonnet itself, because it occurs inside Astrophil's head: Stella's scattered parts reinforce Astrophil's lyric prowess. Instead of such lyricism, Astrophil enters as a character in line thirteen, as a speaker in the narrative *Astrophil and Stella*. Freed from the gaze of Astrophil as lyric speaker – that is, emerging within a different mode of categorization – Stella appears in line twelve as a subject rather than merely the object of Astrophil's desire. Unlike an absent presence, Stella-as-subject can "demurre." In line twelve ("Well, *Love*, since this demurre our sute doth stay"), "this demurre" refers most immediately to Vertue's technical objection that stops the legal suit of Astrophil and Love. But "demurre" is also a pun. "Stay" means both to "stop" a legal proceeding and to "support" something like a crutch (as it does in sonnet 1, "wanting Inventions stay"). The "demurre" supports Astrophil and Love when we read "demurre" as "calm, settled, still." This meaning was applied to the bearing of people as "sober" and "serious; reserved or composed in demeanor," but the word also applied to its opposite – to an affected seriousness in those too young or unwise to bear it.[25] "[T]his demurre," then, invokes momentarily an act *by Stella*, her "demurring," her affected seriousness that encourages Astrophil and Love. Stella too makes fun of Vertue here. Rather than an objection halting the suit of Astrophil and Love, Stella's "demurre" supports their suit and aligns her with them against Vertue. Stella becomes a subject antithetical to an abstract singular honor and an active participant in the argument over possession of "Stella" the abstract ideal.

Similarly, we might think of the Eighth song as another attempt to realize an idealized position that resolves the contradictory habitus of the sequence. While the beginning of the song presents Astrophil and Stella as characters in a third person narrative, the poem ends, famously, by changing to the first person after Stella has rejected Astrophil's advances. In the attempt to tell the story, all the contradictory forces which provoke such an ideal rear up again. The song initially presents the couple as highly idealized characters in a highly idealized pastoral setting:

> In a grove most rich of shade,
> Where birds wanton musicke made,
> May then yong his pide weedes showing,
> New perfumed with flowers fresh growing,
> *Astrophil* with *Stella* sweete,
> Did for mutuall comfort meete,
> Both within themselves oppressed,
> But each in the other blessed.
> Him great harmes had taught much care,
> Her faire necke a foule yoke bare,
> But her sight his cares did banish,
> In his sight her yoke did vanish.

(lines 1–12)

Astrophil is here something like the figure of sonnet 41, a worthy male knight devoted to his lady whose gaze back at him reinforces the "cares" that he has learned. Problems immediately pop up, however, in the specifics of their encounter. The first disruption of the idealized setting occurs in the opening line. "[R]ich of shade" obviously invokes Penelope Rich and her husband. The allusion breaks the fiction of pastoral, the idealism of the poem, and marks it as an idealized (though witty) object: here is the masculine knight that Astrophil cannot be. Setting Astrophil within a "rich" grove immediately reproduces the contradictions of his social position: the "grove" is rich, but Astrophil is not; Lord Rich is rich, but Astrophil is not; Stella is rich, but Astrophil can't possess her. What initially promises to be a stylized realization of the desire of the sequence – finally, the lovers will get together – turns out to reiterate all the contradictions lurking throughout.

Likewise, though Astrophil initially tries to represent Stella as an idealized object (a "starre of heavenly fier," a "lodestar of desire" lines 31, 32), in making clear his desire to have sex with her, he admits that Stella is not an abstract object but a historical woman with a body. Stella becomes a subject, one who, as song four famously demonstrates, can say "no." This admission is partially forestalled by Astrophil's refusal actually to articulate his desire. "Graunt" he keeps asking,

> Graunt, ô graunt, but speech alas,
> Failes me fearing on to passe,
> Graunt, ô me, what am I saying?

(lines 45–47)

but never specifies what exactly he wants granted until he tries to grope her ("There his hands in their speech, faine / Would have made tongue's language plaine" lines 65–66). Stella's rejection reiterates what Astrophil's grope made "plaine" – the strain between his idealism and the social conditions which make him desire in the first place. Indeed, she goes so far as to argue that *Astrophil* is an ideal object for *her*: "All my blisse in thee I lay" (line 90). Her rejection replays the contradiction of the sequence, for it is "Tyran honour" which "doth thus use" Astrophil as well. Honor subdues Astrophil again because he is not rich, a contradiction embodied in the startling formal shift at the end of the poem:

> Therewithall away she went,
> Leaving him so passion rent,
> With what she had done and spoken,

> That therewith my song is broken.
>
> (lines 101–104)

The move from third person to first person "breaks" the song in the sense that the narrative mode is disrupted. It also breaks-*forth* a lyric mode, a desire that is provoked by the inherent contradiction in Astrophil's social position. Astrophil's idealized narrative collapses back into a conspicuously feminine lyric. He is "rent" by his lack of rent, by his lack of riches, and by the fact that honor uses him, rather than he using honor. Astrophil is, after all, like Stella – a feminized subject whose social position provokes a desire for a masculine imaginary that relieves that desire.

Throughout *Astrophil and Stella*, sonnets that seek on some level to establish truths – truths of social position, truths of gender – end up radically calling truth into question because they fundamentally interrogate the means by which truth might be legitimated. What social authority Astrophil has – and he obviously has quite a lot – emerges less and less from a "birthright" he can squander or a "wit" imparted by heaven than it does from his ability to manipulate goods: that is, from his similarity to the rich fools he despises. While the sequence cannot, of course, supply a resolution to these conflicts, the final sonnets register and lament a subtle, but apparent, move toward defining nobility through control of riches. Nobility itself, in other words, begins to be defined as class rather than status, a shift apparent in the sour note that many have seen emerging toward the end of the work.[26] While in sonnet 52 Astrophil lays claim to "this faire outside," in sonnet 108 he laments the uselessness of an inward sense of honor without an external demonstration of riches:

> When sorrow (using mine owne fier's might)
> Melts downe his lead into my boyling brest,
> Through that darke fornace to my hart opprest,
> There shines a joy from thee my only light;
> But soone as thought of thee breeds my delight,
> And my yong soule flutters to thee his nest,
> Most rude dispaire my daily unbidden guest,
> Clips streight my wings, streight wraps me in his night,
> And makes me then bow downe my head, and say,
> Ah what doth *Phoebus'* gold that wretch availe,
> Whom iron doores do keepe from use of day?
> So strangely (alas) thy works in me prevaile,
> That in my woes for thee thou art my joy,
> And in my joyes for thee my only annoy.

Though Astrophil possesses "Phoebus' gold," he is a "wretch" because he is barred from "use of day." His control of "Phoebus' gold" does not "availe" him because he cannot put it to "use" – that is, express that inward quality in the light of day as an external show. This external show becomes synonymous with "use," the process of turning an abstract "Phoebus' gold" into wealth through the production of monetary interest – the "*Tantal's* smart" of sonnet 24. Without interest, "Phoebus' gold" is literally useless – an argument that Shakespeare's *Sonnets* will develop at considerable length. This argument is formally embodied as the lyric speaker of the first nine lines of the poem has his wings clipped by Despair and is turned into a character after line nine: "And makes me then bow downe my head, and say." If we read this moment of characterization as lasting only through line eleven (as does, for instance, Katherine Duncan-Jones, who reasonably inserts quotation marks around lines ten and eleven),[27] then with line twelve the lyric voice reenters with an "and yet" moment: "So strangely (alas) thy works in me prevaile." The relation between the speaker's desire for Stella and his social existence remains strange, puzzling, and resistant to his understanding. In this sense, sonnet 108 is really not much different from the rest of the sequence. It reiterates the complex relation between desire and social existence, the moment of "and yet," which troubles the speaker throughout.[28]

Such a reading, however, does not account for the increasing emphasis on despair and powerlessness in the final poems that many readers have felt. "So strangely (alas)" lacks the subjective, lyrical force of "and yet," the assertive resistance to the narrative contradictions that provoke and disintegrate the speaker. This thematic emphasis on despair is, in part, the result of a formal shift apparent in the final sonnet. The three published editions of the 1590s include no quotation marks at all in the sonnet to distinguish the speaker from the character, with the result that it is just as plausible to read the final five lines as spoken by the character bidden by "dispaire." In this sense, the sequence ends with an inversion of the Eighth song. In the song, the failure of narrative produces the lyric speaker, breaking forth a lyric of brokenness; Astrophil's failure to gain Stella is the ground upon which his lyric complaint rests. In sonnet 108, conversely, the lyric speaker is effectively erased by a story of his inability to "use" what gold he has. Rather than ending, in other words, with a reiteration of the lyric desire with which the sequence begins, it ends, at least in part, with Astrophil turned into a character who cannot finally realize any nobility because he lacks "use." Status – the urge to express birthright through the squandering of wealth – is replaced with class – a social position defined in part by gold, by economic capital. Though he remains wrapped in despair's night, his desire for "use," for an economy of exchange, marks him precisely as one of the "Rich fooles" of sonnet 24 who are damned to "*Tantal's* smart, / Wealth breeding want, more blist, more wretched grow." Indeed, the final lines of sonnet 108 forcefully recall this logic:

> So strangely (alas) thy works in me prevaile,
> That in my woes for thee thou art my joy,
> And in my joyes for thee my only annoy.

The formal elimination of the lyric "I" here places the speaker within the dialectic of exchange which provides wealth only to recreate "want." The "thee" of the final lines is, in this sense, not so much Stella, or some idealized lyric object which reconciles "want" by providing what sonnet 24 terms "wit" imparted by heaven. Instead, "thee" is "use" itself whose "works . . . prevaile." Noble status becomes an effect of "use," of a new form of social distinction; status starts to be an object with no existence outside the vicissitudes of exchange.

While there is no doubt that Sidney's work emerges partially out of courtly traditions of love poetry that create and recreate noble subjects, the close of *Astrophil and Stella* suggests that that tradition itself becomes subsumed into the social forces we witnessed in Lok's sequence. The crucial point here, then, is that noble identity, and the social and epistemological stability associated with it, becomes an object produced out of exchange – out of "use." And yet it is precisely the location of a noble status within the dynamics of class which makes Astrophil, and the English sonneteers who follow him, desire that noble status all the more intensely.

Our English Petrarke

In looking for a tragic story to move Stella, and one somehow superior to his own contradictory lyricism, Astrophil could have done worse than turn to the story of "Sir Philip Sidney," Protestant humanist and noble knight. Named after the most powerful king in Europe, this Sir Philip traveled widely in the best court circles, charmed everyone he met, championed Protestant causes, married the daughter of an important courtier, and died a heroic death in a worthy cause. He was mourned at a gigantic and hideously expensive funeral, was lamented in a series of poetic miscellanies, and was emulated by one aristocrat who failed to overthrow a queen and by one king who failed to get the locals to like him very much. What's more, he invented English poetry, wrote the best defense of it then and possibly since, and brought superior continental learning to bear on backwards English thought. If any "fable" could convince Stella to give Astrophil what he wanted, the story of "Sir Philip Sidney" ("[t]he argument cruell chastitie, the Prologue hope, the Epilogue dispaire")[29] might do.

Unfortunately for the Astrophil of *Astrophil and Stella*, he is not "Sir Philip Sidney," and he remains perpetually frustrated by his inability to fashion a self-representation half as compelling. Astrophil very much resembles, however, a less inspiring figure named Philip Sidney who was, as Dominic Baker-Smith suggests, "haunted" by the "great expectation" of sonnet 21.[30] This Sidney was often hot tempered and brooding, accomplished little as a diplomat, got in squabbles with the queen, possibly flirted with Catholicism, quested perpetually after money, and died, in Horace Walpole's opinion, "with the rashness of a volunteer."[31] In short, this Sidney never came close to living up to what people in England and on the continent, including himself, thought the nephew of the Earl of Leicester ought to be like – a leader of an international Protestant movement, an alternative "Philip" to the Catholic King of Spain.[32] Like Astrophil's desire to recreate himself in narrative, Sidney "tried to realise himself through roles which he selected, and others proposed roles to him; in life others read him in terms of roles which may not have been his own, while after death the poets conspired to embody in him an ideal type."[33] Astrophil's desire for a noble ideal is finally realized in the figure of "Sir Philip Sidney."

As recent criticism has exhaustively demonstrated, the legendary "Sir Philip Sidney," tragic-hero and shepherd knight, was largely invented after his death in 1586. The funeral was paid for by his father-in-law Walsingham, and the two poetic miscellanies mourning Sidney's death published by Cambridge and Oxford were dedicated to Leicester. Both the funeral and the miscellanies probably reflected the interests of the Protestant faction at court seeking to increase England's intervention in the Netherlands where Sidney lost his life.[34]

But praise of Sidney was always also implicated in literary concerns. As Richard Helgerson notes, "when contemporaries praised [Sidney's] works, they did so in terms that could have been inspired by his own definition of what poetry should be and do." Thus for Matthew Roydon, Sidney reconciles the contradiction between "love" and "honor":

> Above all others, this is he
> Which erst approved in his song,
> That love and honor might agree,
> And that pure love will do no wrong.

Roydon imagines Sidney overcoming the difficulties of the prodigal, making him "an unquestionable hero who was also a gentleman, a poet, and a defender of poetry."[35] Such praise of Sidney was, Raphael Falco concludes, integral to the formation of an English poetic tradition. He points out that the line between praise of Sidney and a literary tradition is opaque: the famous accounts of Sidney's death (giving his water to another soldier; his thigh wound), whatever their historical validity, also depend on literary, romantic accounts of Alexander and Adonis.[36] Such praise, and the literary tradition it facilitated, was, moreover, not exclusively the terrain of ambitious courtly insiders. As John Huntington has recently argued, Roydon was a member of a "group of disadvantaged men," including Lodge, Marlowe, and Chapman, who were in the process of "discovering how by asserting a higher standard of literacy they [could] challenge courtly privileges and the styles that signify them."[37]

It is with these social and literary constructions of Sidney in mind that we should approach the production of Sidney as what Sir Walter Ralegh termed "our English Petrarke," his emergence as a model sonneteer. Both Ralegh and John Harington quite explicitly link Sidney's sequence with a reconciliation of love and honor, of erotic devotion and military service. In the notes to Book Sixteen of his translation of *Orlando Furioso*, Harington reiterates Ralegh's description in terms of Sidney's "worthiness":

Petrarke in his infinite sonets, in the midst of all his lamentation, still had this comfort, that his love was placed on a worthie Ladie: and our English *Petrarke*, *Sir Philip Sidney*, or (as *Sir Walter Raulegh* in his Epitaph worthely calleth him) the *Scipio* and the *Petrarke* of our time, often comforteth him selfe in his sonets of *Stella*, though dispairing to attaine his desire, and (though that tyrant honor still refused) yet the nobilitie, the beautie, the worth, the graciousnesse, and those her other perfections, as made him both count her, and call her inestimably rich, makes him in the midst of those his mones, rejoyce even in his owne greatest losses, as in his eighteenth sonet which many I am sure have read.[38]

The reconciliation between "the *Scipio* and the *Petrarke* of our time" is here expressed through desire for Stella, whose "nobilitie," "beautie," "worth", "graciousnesse," and "other perfections" effectively mirror those qualities which Harington seeks to praise in Sidney himself. Harington goes on to quote in full sonnet 18, but with a number of textual variants from the three versions published in the 1590s which temper the contradiction between love and honor:

> With what sharpe checks I in my selfe am shent,
> When into reasons recknings I do goe,
> And by such counts, my selfe a bankrout know,
> Of all those goods which heau'n to me hath lent,
> Vnable quite to pay eu'n natures rent,
> Which vnto it, by birthright I did ow,
> And which is worse, no good excuse can show,
> But that my wealth I haue most idly spent:
> My youth doth wast, my knowledge brings foorth toyes,

My wit doth striue those passions to defend,
With my reward (spoyled with vaine annoyes)
I find my course to loose it selfe doth bend:
I see, yet do no greater sorow take,
Then that I leese no more for *Stellas* sake.

Viewed from the largely postmodern perspective I have been pursuing, where the social implications of the formal contradictions of the sonnet are especially conspicuous, the sonnet articulates Astrophil's paradoxical existence. But for Harington writing in 1591 the poem demonstrates Sidney's worthiness; it reconciles contradictions. Among the variants in Harington's version, two subtle but important textual differences facilitate this reading. First, the tense changes in line six. In the published versions in the 1590s, Astrophil continues to owe rent to nature. In Harington's version, the use of the past tense suggests that the rent has been paid. And similarly, in line twelve of the three versions published in the 1590s, Astrophil loses himself ("I see my course to lose my selfe doth bend"). In Harington's version, however, the self remains intact and finds instead that the "course" is lost: "I find my course to loose it selfe doth bend." The separation of self from course, like the use of the past tense, helps to stabilize the identity of Astrophil and the "worthiness" which Harington sees the sonnet express.

"Our English Petrarke" consequently becomes for Harington short hand for "the *Scipio* and *Petrarke* of our time," for a realization of the political and military ideals expressed through devotion to an idealized female. In other words, "our English Petrarke" comes to stand not only for a particular conception of poetry, but for an ideal of nobility which was continually desired by Astrophil, and Sidney, himself. In the 1590s, Sidney and Astrophil are made into the figures that I have been arguing are the objects of Astrophil's lyric desire: an idealized masculine figure that reconciles the gap between nobility as a status and nobility as a class, between the inward nobility expressed by devotion to Stella and the outward show of nobility expressed by riches. It is a truism of sonnet criticism that the publication of *Astrophil and Stella* in 1591 sets off the vogue for sonnet sequences in the 1590s, and that Sidney's work largely establishes the terms and concerns within which later writers work. One crucial aspect of this influence is the lingering desire for an idealized nobility which reconciles the competing categories of class and status. For if Sidney's nobility is only secured as a textual ideal by writers like Harington, writing sonnet sequences in Sidney's wake meant always at the same time trying to recreate an idealized nobility which Sidney himself could never actually live.

After Sidney, and in the midst of the reinvention of him as a noble imaginary, the challenge for subsequent sonneteers is to reimagine and represent this ideal. In one of the few considerations of sonnets outside the poems themselves, Giles Fletcher the Elder argues quite explicitly in the dedicatory epistle to his sequence *Licia* that sonnet writing is a socially distinguishing act:

And for the matter of love, where everie man takes upon him to court exactlie, I could justlie grace (if it be a grace to be excellent in that kinde) the Innes of Court, and some Gentlemen like students in both Universities, whose learning and bringing up together, with their fine natures makes so sweet a harmonie, as without partialitie, the most injurious will preferre them before all others: and therefore they onelie are fittest to write of Love. For others for the moste parte are men of meane reach, whose imbased mindes praie uppon everie badde dish: men unfitte to knowe what love meanes; deluded fondlie with their owne conceit, misdeking so divine a fancie, taking it to bee the contentment of themselves, the shame of others: the wrong of vertue: and the refiner of the tongue; boasting of some fewe favours. These and such like errours (errours hate-full to an upright minde) commonlie by learnlesse heades are reputed for loves kingdome. But vaine men naturallie led, deluded themselves, deceive others.[39]

By insisting that "some Gentlemen" "are onlie fittest to write of Love," Fletcher raises more questions than he solves. His emphasis on "learning" and its association with the universities and Inns of Court rearticulates ideals of "gentleness" in terms associated less with blood aristocrats maintaining an essential inward honor than with the social ambiguities associated with humanism and the merchants who funded schools and contributed sons to these institutions. "[U]pright minde[s]" are conspicuously contrasted to "learnlesse heades . . . reputed for loves kingdome"; the "kingdom" of love poetry for Fletcher belongs to the learned mind, not to the "heades" of the body politic. Despite their close association in criticism of the last thirty years with court, sonnet sequences after Sidney were rarely written by actual courtiers.[40] Fletcher himself was an important political figure, but he was not noble. Aside from *Astrophil and Stella*, really only Fulke Greville's *Caelica*, Sir Robert Sidney's sonnets, and Lady Mary Wroth's *Pamphilia to Amphilanthus* can reasonably be considered significant sonnet sequences that are products of "court." Instead, sonnet sequences in the 1590s and after tended to be written by men from socially ambiguous backgrounds, often in service of social, economic, and poetic, though not necessarily political, ambition.

Nevertheless, as Fletcher's dedication suggests, sonneteers in this period are intensely concerned with what constitutes social distinction, but they enact this concern, as does Fletcher, from an uncertain social position and conspicuously in the emerging public sphere of print. The writers of most sonnet sequences, and in particular the most

influential ones, created idealized conceptions of nobility from a
distinctly non-aristocratic, and non-courtier, perspective. Like Anne
Lok, writers such as Daniel, Spenser, Shakespeare, and Drayton (not to
mention Barnabe Barnes, Thomas Lodge, Henry Lok, Henry Constable,
William Percy, Bartholomew Griffin, Richard Linche, William Smith,
Richard Barnfield, and Robert Tofte) generally inhabit a murky social
position and tend to be dependent on print – either directly for money
or as a means of securing a financially advantageous patron. Unlike
Sidney, the sonneteers who follow him (more often than not) lack not
only the riches but also the birthright to demonstrate and produce the
noble ideal which becomes so central a feature of imitating the "English
Petrarke." These writers are forced (and enabled) by their social position
to take "use" even more seriously than does Astrophil. For them, the
authority and value produced through exchange rather than through
"*Phoebus'* gold" simultaneously produces and undermines the desire for a
nobility set somehow apart from it. Writing sonnet sequences meant
increasingly taking into "account" that narrative of economic exchange,
the "Audit" that shames Astrophil, and the "use" whose logic finally
determines him.

The remainder of this book examines sequences by Spenser,
Shakespeare, and Drayton within the forces of "use" and market
exchange to understand the ways their representations of nobility, and
their desires for a masculine, noble status, paradoxically illuminate
instead their positions within new social relations. In desiring to honor
and imitate the "English Petrarke," and sometimes in trying to become
such a figure themselves, these writers articulate in increasingly precise
ways the contours of an emergent discourse of class. As a way of
introducing the next chapters, I want very briefly to turn to Samuel
Daniel's *Delia*, the first sonnet sequence published after *Astrophil and
Stella*. Some of Daniel's sonnets were initially published with the
"pirated" edition of *Astrophil and Stella* in 1591, and in the dedication to
Sidney's sister the Countess of Pembroke of his 1592 version of *Delia*
Daniel responds publicly to this purported injustice. He sets "Astrophel"
into an idealized space of nobility while placing himself firmly within the
vicissitudes of publication and an exchange economy:

Right honorable, although I rather desired to keep in the private passions of my
youth, from the multitude, as things utterd to my selfe, and consecrated to silence:
yet seeing I was betraide by the indiscretion of a greedie Printer, and had some of
my secrets bewraide to the world, uncorrected: doubting the like of the rest, I am
forced to publish that which I never ment. But this wrong was not onely doone to
mee, but to him whose unmatchable lines have indured the like misfortune;

Ignorance sparing not to commit sacriledge upon so holy Reliques. Yet *Astrophel*, flying with the wings of his own fame, a higher pitch then the gross-sighted can discerne, hath registred his owne name in the Annals of eternitie, and cannot be disgraced, howsoever disguised. And for my selfe, seeing I am thrust out into the worlde, and that my unboldned Muse, is forced to appeare so rawely in publique; I desire onely to bee graced by the countenance of your protection: whome the fortune of our time hath made the happie and iudidiall Patronesse of the Muses, (a glory hereditary to your house) to preserve them from those hidious Beastes, Oblivion, and Barbarisme. Whereby you doe not onely possesse the honour of the present, but also do bind posterity to an ever gratefull memorie of your vertues, wherein you must survive your selfe. And if my lines heereafter better laboured, shall purchase grace in the world, they must remaine the monuments of your honourable favour, and record the zealous duetie of mee, who am vowed to your honour in all observancy for ever[.][41]

Though the works of both Daniel and Sidney have been "betraide by the indiscretion of a greedie Printer," "Astrophel" flies to "a higher pitch then the gross-sighted can discerne" and becomes timeless. Like Harington's reading of sonnet 18, Daniel sees Sidney's work as embodying a status above the social level of the "gross-sighted." More specifically, this status is distinguished from a "greedy Printer" and the public world of a print market in which Daniel's work, conversely, must "*purchase* grace." Daniel likewise sets the Countess herself outside of this process of public exchange, since she not only possesses "the honour of the present, but also . . . [binds] posterity to an euer gratefull memorie" of her "vertues." The Countess' "honor," like Astrophil's "wings of his own fame," marks an internal nobility. But at the same time, Daniel deploys this nobility in the service of his own work and in his own interests. The dedication to the Countess assists his work in its efforts to "purchase grace." Both Sidney's poetry and the Countess' "honor" become instrumental components in Daniel's own socio-economic endeavor. Sidney is finally transformed into his published persona "Astrophel," his very name finally determined by a greedy printer, a purchasing poet, and the market in which they participate. Indeed, Henry Woudhuysen has recently speculated (with, he emphasizes, only circumstantial evidence) that Daniel may have been partially responsible for the purportedly pirated 1591 edition of *Astrophil and Stella* which he used to work his way into the circle of the Countess of Pembroke.[42]

The opening sonnet of *Delia* similarly records its debt to Sidney. Yet while Astrophil found himself "shent" in "Reasons audit," Daniel's speaker, and the sequence which follows, exists entirely as a more literal audit, the financial "booke" of his "charg'd soule" where he has "cast th'accounts of all my care":

Vnto the boundles ocean of thy beautie
Runs this poore riuer, charg'd with streames of zeale:
Returning thee the tribute of my dutie,
Which heere my loue, my youth, my playnts reueale.
Heere I vnclaspe the booke of my charg'd soule,
Where I haue cast th'accounts of all my care:
Heere haue I summ'd my sighes, heere I enroule
Howe they were spent for thee; Looke what they are.
Looke on the deere expences of my youth,
And see how iust I reckon with thyne eyes:
Examine well thy beautie with my trueth,
And crosse my cares ere greater summes arise.
Reade it sweet maide, though it be doone but slightly;
Who can shewe all his loue, doth loue but lightly.

Astrophil in sonnet 18 spends his birthright in his devotion to Stella, but Daniel's speaker consists entirely of a *"poore* riuer" perpetually flowing into "the boundles ocean" of Delia. And though he momentarily conceptualizes this flow as a "tribute" which returns to its source, by the end of the sonnet the speaker exhorts her to "Examine well thy beautie with *my* trueth." The "beauty" of Delia, like the "honour" of the Countess or the "wings" of Astrophil, is measured by the truth of the ever flowing market in which the speaker exists – the truth of the account book where he "sums" his "sighs."

The next three chapters examine in more detail the strain between an ideal nobility and a group of writers who associate themselves and their distinct social position with market exchange. While Lok's work suggests the ways authority and value will be produced in these sequences, Sidney's work establishes the concerns within which that production will occur. In Spenser's *Amoretti and Epithalamion*, the speaker attempts to use his poetic capital to possess an ideal nobility, but the very forces which permit him to imagine such an upwardly mobile move undermine the status that possession (of his lady, of a landed estate) entails. Shakespeare's speaker similarly attempts to draw upon the distinction he derives from the market to construct an ideal nobility in the figure of the young man. He tries to distance this noble imaginary from the market by gendering it male and the market female. Finally, I argue that by continually revising *Idea* over twenty-five years, Drayton and his speaker gradually create a distinct social position which turns away from Sidney as a model to King James' well-documented status as a Poet-King. But rather than using this absolutist model to reinforce monarchical authority, Drayton uses his position sharply to criticize Jacobean policies and champion his own "Libertine" authority. Drayton's speaker gradually becomes, in formal terms, a subject whose story lies within his own lyricism. By explicitly celebrating his own social power against his monarch-model, Drayton names this new social distinction: "the *English* straine."

5 "So plenty makes me poore": Ireland, capitalism, and class in Spenser's *Amoretti and Epithalamion*

Spenser in Ireland

Nowhere are Astrophil's "Nobler desires" played out with more ferocity than in the sprawling poetry of Spenser. Spenser himself contributed quite explicitly to the myth of Sidney with the pastoral panegyric *Astrophel*, and throughout his work Spenser rearticulates Astrophil's desire and tries to create a new kind of nobility. This desire by Spenser becomes activated in two interrelated arenas – his literary activity and his participation in English colonialism in Ireland. In the past decade scholars have persuasively argued that Ireland was far more than a backdrop for the work of the "Poet's poet," and that his poetry is fundamentally implicated in an English colonial project. They have also shown, however, that Spenser was not merely an apologist for Elizabethan imperialism; his outlook concerning Ireland was as often equivocal as it was resolute. As David Baker argues, "[w]hatever Spenser was at the end of his life, he was no longer (if he ever had been) purely 'English.' Spenser, rather, was the product of a life lived on – and 'between' – two islands, and the inheritor of the complexly imbricated histories of both."[1] What, then, might these revisions tell us about the conceptions of social distinction emerging out of such "complexly imbricated" utterances? For if Spenser existed between islands, he also existed between modes of social distinction. I want to address these questions through a reading of *Amoretti and Epithalamion* in part to build on the long association of the work with Spenser's personal experience in Ireland. Spenser's sonnet sequence is often thought to express his turn from the world of court to a more private, even bourgeois, identity – the final turn to modernity in his cursus virgiliem. But I also want to consider what exactly a "personal experience" might mean. Given its long association with Spenser's "private" concerns, *Amoretti and Epithalamion* is a particularly compelling test case for the influence of post-romantic conceptions of poetry, the tendency to read lyric as expressing in a formal rhetoric an opposition between the aristocracy and the bourgeoisie. Like

Spenser in Ireland, the speaker of *Amoretti and Epithalamion* tries to distinguish himself socially by mimicking a noble imaginary – in part Astrophil, but more especially the idea of nobles in Ireland. Through this desire for and imagination of noble, and especially royal, privilege, however, the poem embodies a new mode of creating social distinction. As habitus, *Amoretti and Epithalamion* expresses the contradictory social longing of an existence that has no name for social authority outside of "nobility."

In a partial revision of his influential earlier view of a Spenser inextricably tied to court power, Louis Montrose suggests that Spenser's position in Ireland offers an "alternative center" which implicitly challenges the centrality of the English court. In "generically marginal texts" like *Colin Clouts Come Home Againe* and *Amoretti and Epithalamion*, "Spenser calls attention to his position on the social and geo-political margins of Elizabethan courtly and aristocratic culture; and the Poet's persona – variously shepherd, lover, and bridegroom – reinvents this margin as an emergent and alternative center."[2] Montrose's attention to Spenser's position in Ireland complicates ties between his work and court because the colonial project participates in a reimagination of the locations of power. No longer seen as a reflection of Elizabethan absolutism, texts such as *Amoretti and Epithalamion* create an "alternative center," a new social force at the end of the Elizabethan era. On the one hand, how can we describe this "alternative center" without implying that it remains a reflection of the *real* authority centralized in Elizabeth's court? And on the other hand, how can we describe it without aligning this "alternative" with the interiorized privacy of a teleologically rising middle class confronting its arch historical antagonist, the nobility? What is at stake in reading the *Amoretti and Epithalamion* within the discontinuous arena of English colonialism in Ireland, in short, is reading the struggle by which classificatory constructions of social space *emerge*, not the speaker's relation to systems of classification ("the court"; "the bourgeoisie"). *Amoretti and Epithalamion* not only reinforce or undermine existing social classifications; they participate in the production of new ways of conceptualizing social distinction itself. The alternative of seeing Spenser's work as either belonging to court or to a bourgeois private realm is a false choice, a product of post-romantic conceptions of lyric. In contrast, recent examinations of the Elizabethan colonial project in Ireland, with their emphasis on the production of "hybrid" subjects "between" discourses, offer a model for fundamentally reimagining these possible social positions.

The traditional critical problem of whether *Amoretti and Epithalamion* points to the court or a private love, however, makes one thing apparent.

It is never entirely clear throughout the work what "system" is dominant, though the speaker clearly articulates what sorts of persons and things he wishes were dominant and what sorts of persons and things he wants to dominate. Throughout the poems, Spenser's speaker tries to fashion himself, like the elusive object of *The Faerie Queene*, as a "gentleman or noble person."[3] Maureen Quilligan has shown how this "or" in the letter to Ralegh complicates gender identities in its attempt to accommodate Queen Elizabeth as a female reader.[4] The "or," however, similarly complicates questions of social standing. Like the voice of the letter to Ralegh, Spenser's speaker in *Amoretti and Epithalamion* encounters a great deal of difficulty trying to be both a "gentleman" and a "noble," for he is uncomfortably aware that whatever those terms might mean, they do not simply mean the same thing. The gap between "gentleman" and "noble person" tries to accommodate Queen Elizabeth as a conspicuously female reader, but it also tries to accommodate the socially ambiguous Spenser himself, who like the speaker of the *Epithalamion*, sings "unto [him]selfe alone."[5] In *Amoretti and Epithalamion*, Spenser's speaker repeatedly tries to imagine himself as a kind of Astrophil, a noble lord controlling a virtually feudal estate, and the primary vehicle he uses for this fantasy is his attempt to control his female poetic object. That object proves, like the Irish and the Old English lords whose lands Spenser himself tried to possess, remarkably and complexly uncooperative. The lady of *Amoretti and Epithalamion* is not only an object of the speaker's desire; she is also a *subject* whose relations with the speaker make apparent the struggles for social classification in which he finds himself.

These struggles emerge, as Montrose argues, in conjunction with new conceptions of land tenure – in the construction of what he terms, following Paul Alpers, Spenser's "domestic domain" in its initial, most literal sense.[6] Spenser had been acquiring land in Ireland since at least 1581, and primarily two conditions made this possible: first, Spenser's government posts as a secretary and his position in a system of patronage; and second, the reconceptualization of Irish land under an "English" model of agricultural innovation and market rents. These two conditions are, however, intimately related. Spenser drew on his public offices and in particular his position as secretary to Lord Grey, leader of the English forces, to acquire rights to a variety of lands, which he then successively sold in pursuit of more prestigious estates – a process which culminated with his acquisition of Kilcolman.[7] In buying and selling land, Spenser thus participated in the reimagination of Ireland in nascent capitalist terms. As Julia Reinhard Lupton notes, the 1584 survey of Munster land was intended to reorganize conceptually the Irish landscape, to "compound," to "convert to English tenure . . . the lands not held by the Crown." The "act of 'composition' entailed conversion to a fundamentally different conception of land, based not on the brief leases and nomadic displacements of Brehon law, but on the fixed, transmittable 'plots' of what we now call private property."[8]

This reorganization of land occurred continuous with the terms of modernized agriculture. In place of Irish pastoralism, the New English planters desired to impose a system of modern tillage. As Sir John Davies wrote in 1612,

For the husbandman must first break the land before it be made capable of good seed; and when it is thoroughly broken and manured, if he do not forthwith cast good seed into it, it will grow wild again, and bear nothing but weeds. So a barbarous country must be first broken by a war before it will be capable of good government; and when it is fully subdued and conquered, if it be not well planted and governed after the conquest, it will eftsoons return to the former barbarism.[9]

Similarly, in Spenser's *A View of the Present State of Ireland*, Irenius insists upon tillage as synonymous with civilization: "And to say truth though Ireland is by nature counted a great soil of pasture, yet had I rather few cows kept and men better mannered than to have such huge increase of cattle and no increase of good conditions."[10] The principal historian of the Munster plantation likewise stresses that "[t]he equation hammered home by every English commentator was that pastoralism encouraged sloth, instability, and the Irish way of life. The settlers' job was to transplant the new England to Munster, and in agricultural terms this meant the promotion of arable farming."[11]

Describing the imposition of land tenure and agricultural reforms as a "civilizing" process invokes a framework of historical development. The New English planters depicted themselves as ushering in a new era of land relations and obedience to an absolute monarch and her law. Ireland thus became a space where the New English could imagine and enact nascent capitalism by representing the local Irish and the Old English, regardless of the conditions within which they actually existed, as anachronistic, uncivil remnants of a feudal past. Nicholas Canny notes that Sir Henry Sidney, Philip's father and the Lord Deputy Governor of Ireland, "was conscious that feudal society in Ireland . . . was still at a stage of development beyond which England had advanced."[12] Because the "feudal" authority of the Old English in the Counties Palatine seemed to threaten the authority of the monarch, the New English worked to eliminate them. Writing in 1607, Sir John Davies noted that "when England was full of tenants-at-will our barons were then like the mere Irish lords, and were able to raise armies against the crown; and as this man was O'Neal in Ulster, so the Earl of Warwick was O'Nevill in Yorkshire, and Bishopric and Mortimer was the

like in the Marches of Wales."[13] The Liberty of Tipperary, ruled by the Old
English Earl of Ormond, Black Thomas, was the only one left by 1596, and
it was viewed by men from Sir Henry Sidney to Sir John Davies as a place
immune from the Queen's rule. As Baker observes, "[w]ithin Ormond's
borders, as Davies realizes, the status of English authority was at its most
uncertain – at once present and excluded, authoritative and unfounded . . .
Like Davies, Sidney believed Black Thomas was more king than a subject;
in Tipperary, they had 'never herd of other prince than Ormond'."[14] By
representing Old English lords as anachronistically feudal and dangerous to
Elizabeth's monarchy, New English writers like Spenser endorsed, and
created, the progressiveness of their own social position. In becoming a land
owner, Spenser was consequently participating in a key transitory moment
between the social capital promised by ownership of a domain and,
simultaneously, the undermining of that capital by the very processes which
made it possible for a socially ambiguous person like Spenser to become a
"lord" at all.

   And yet at the same time, Spenser uses the new language of capitalist land
relations associated with the New English to desire a social distinction, and
a control of property, which is, on the one hand, strikingly similar to the
very Old English lords such language was deployed to eliminate; and which
is, on the other hand, partially a reconstruction of the Elizabethan
absolutism which this "alternative center" challenges.[15] Even as Ireland
was represented as a barbaric place requiring English civility and market-
based conceptions of land, Ireland was also a place where the New English
planters desired to live out an ideal of feudal land possession. In marking
himself as progressive, Spenser constructs a feudal ideal which emerges out
of his participation in the "civilizing" process. This idealized social
distinction is partially constructed by attributing to merchants (and thereby
concealing) the economic exchange essential to such land possession. The
Munster plantation was unusual in that it was run by the government, not a
private joint-stock company of merchants (as, for instance, the Virginia
colony was).[16] As Michael MacCarthy-Morrogh points out, the planters
for Munster originally were supposed to come from wealthy gentry.
Because merchants were excluded from the enterprise, the initial costs of a
seigniory – from £278–£500 just for the first year – ensured that only the
social, rather than the monetary, elite could participate. Yet it was the fact
that Munster was a government enterprise, and consequently susceptible to
those with political influence, which enabled Spenser to participate.
Prominent courtiers like Sir Walter Ralegh and Sir Christopher Hatton
received huge, plum estates. Current and former army men who had fought
in Ireland claimed land in lieu of back-pay. Lord Grey handed out land to
loyal followers like Edward Denny and Spenser. While largely excluding

merchants from the plantation gave the project more social capital, the inclusion of army men and government officials like Spenser tempered that social distinction. Sir William Herbert, for instance, "considered that he was disgraced by being associated with such companions."[17]

As we will see, the speaker of *Amoretti and Epithalamion* is similarly at pains to distinguish himself from the wealth of merchants; he claims social superiority by ascribing nascent capitalism entirely to them. However, the insistence upon "English" agriculture methods and market rents which was so integral a part of the plantation project tended to erode, in the long term, the economic basis of feudal estates upon which the social distinction of "lords" – in contrast to merchants – was in part based.[18] Spenser's realization of his own domain came, in other words, as a result of the emergence of capitalist land relations defined against the social distinction of the lord of the domain – and in particular Old English lords like Ormond and Roche. For men like Ralegh, Hatton, and Herbert, who enjoyed a wide range of high social markers, the decline of feudal land relations mattered little for their social standing. They became, in Richard Lachmann's trenchant phrase, "capitalists in spite of themselves."[19] And similarly, Old English lords like Ormond or Roche (with whom Spenser was engaged in a protracted legal haggle over land) repeatedly appealed directly to the crown to address the wrongs they felt were inflicted on them by the New English. But for Spenser, a man whose very education depended upon the emerging dominance of English merchants (he was educated at the Merchant Taylors' School), and who did not come from an important family, such markers were crucial.[20] Possession of an estate (and it should be noted that Spenser's was one of the smallest in the entire plantation) both marks Spenser's upward mobility and, at the same time, the limits placed on that mobility by its basis in emergent capitalist land relations. Gaining control of his own domain thus signals, as Montrose suggests, a reaction against Elizabethan absolutism by creating an alternative center constructed at the cultural margins; but it performs this resistance paradoxically by enacting the logic of Elizabethan absolutism in pursuit of an idealized feudalism, a desire for land ownership, that is produced and made possible by nascent capitalism.

Lyric and narrative in the *Amoretti*

Spenser's ability to control his own Irish domain becomes thematized as content in *Amoretti and Epithalamion* in the speaker's attempts to control his lady like a piece of Irish land. To read merely the thematization of "Ireland" in the works, however – for instance, through the invocation of

Irish places ("Mulla" in line 56 of the *Epithalamion*) or particular dates (the apparent dates of sonnets 22–68 placing the sequence in Lent 1594) – tends to adopt the effort of Spenser's speaker to conceptualize and classify Ireland, and the poems themselves, in a particular way (this is a holy sequence, beyond the vicissitudes of Elizabethan Irish policy). As a result, the struggles for classification within which Spenser and his speaker act, and the conditions which make his particular construction desirable, tend to remain invisible. These struggles become apparent when we look beyond Ireland as a theme in the poems and instead interrogate the speaker's classificatory struggle as also a struggle over *form*: as an effort to impose upon both Ireland and the poems themselves a definite shape. In the *Amoretti*, this formal effort becomes apparent in the strain in its formal rhetoric, the tension between a lyric and narrative mode of representation. This formal contradiction is especially apparent in the contradictory presentations of the lady of the poems. Read as lyrics or isolated sonnets, the *Amoretti* tends to present a speaker who controls both his lady and his landscape; read as a narrative sequence, it presents a speaker uncomfortably aware of his subordination to social mechanisms which he can never quite comprehend – mechanisms associated with the lady as subject. These formal oppositions form the contours of the work, the social struggle within and out of which desire emerges. The effort of the speaker to classify his lady and Ireland according to lyric criteria is, at the same time, an effort to create and impose a distinct classificatory system upon himself and social space generally. Read in relation to the narrative of the sequence, however, that lyric rhetoric is continually undermined, enabling us to see not only the speaker's lyric version of Ireland and his lady but also the conditions which provoke his desire for just such a mode of classification. The form of the poem consists of the social struggle embodied and expressed in these rhetorical contradictions; it is defined by the contradictions between its two primary schemes of classification.

Sonnet 75, for example, moves back and forth between lyric and narrative classificatory modes as the speaker and his lady argue about his poetry. Despite the repeated razing action of the "waves" that wash away his attempts to write her name, and despite the lady's dismissal of his "vaine assay," the speaker insists that his verse "shall eternize" her "vertues." Against both the flow of time's waves and the lady's protest, the speaker claims the superiority of his own representation of the lady as object against the lady as subject:

> One day I wrote her name upon the strand,
>   but came the waves and washed it a way:
> agayne I wrote it with a second hand,

but came the tyde, and made my paynes his pray.

Vayne man, sayd she, that doest in vaine assay,
a mortall thing so to immortalize.
for I my selve shall lyke to this decay,
and eek my name bee wyped out lykewize.

Not so, (quod I) let baser things devize
to dy in dust, but you shall live by fame:
my verse your vertues rare shall eternize,
and in the hevens wryte your glorious name,

Where whenas death shall al the world subdew,
our love shall live, and later life renew.

Depending upon which scheme of classification is highlighted, the lady looks quite different. Indeed, there are effectively two ladies here, two products of different rhetorics: a narrative interlocutor, who thinks the speaker's project is "vaine," and the "name" of the lady, her "vertues rare," a lyric object that he plans to write in the heavens. Not only does the interlocutor object to the project, but she becomes identified with the very processes of "decay" which her name (in his hands) is meant to overcome. The sonnet is a dialogue between the writer and the lady, but it is also a structural defense by the speaker as his sonnet wraps itself around and seeks to contain the lady's argument presented in the second quatrain. As the final couplet has it, "subdewing" her argument allows him to "renew" his claim to transcendence. Viewed as a lyric, the sonnet presents a masculine speaker bravely resisting what he depicts as the baseness and mutability of the world by controlling a female object. Viewed as a narrative, the sonnet presents a male writer attempting, with limited success, to defend his project against both Time and the lady; he is, as she suggests, a "Vayne man" whose authority is circumscribed by the very mutability she articulates. While the sonnet presents an exemplary instance of lyric power, it also dramatizes the process by which that power is constructed and the specific, historical ways the speaker's subjection occurs.

Attending to the rhetorical strain between sonnet and sequence helps to begin to account for the apparently inconsistent representation of the lady in the work – long a critical crux of the sequence – as an issue of form. J. W. Lever infamously found the "characterization of the heroine" so uneven that he opted to exclude eighteen sonnets from the sequence. Instead, he emphasized that "in general the sonnets are more concerned with the state of mind of the poet and his lady than with the circumstances of their love affair."[21] Louis Martz, conversely, suggested that Lever's sense of inconsistency "tend[s] to disappear within a dominant tone of assurance and poise and mutual understanding that controls the series." Martz describes sonnet 28 as striking "exactly the tone that an older man, of experience and wisdom (someone a bit like Emma's Mr. Knightley) might adopt toward a bright and beautiful and willful young lady for whom he feels, not awe, but deep admiration and affection."[22] Whereas Lever seems to think of the work primarily in lyric terms ("the sonnets are more concerned with the state of mind of the poet and his lady"), Martz's invocation of Austen's novel suggests that he tends to regard the speaker and his lady as characters in a narrative. We need to recognize, in short, both the speaker's idealized representations of the lady – what O. B. Hardison termed a *"donna angelicata"*[23] – as well as the representation of the lady apart from the speaker's desires: in other words, to recognize the lady as both the necessarily silent object of a lyric "I" and as a relatively independent character in the narrative of the sequence itself.[24] Thus, for instance, in sonnet 79 we see both a lady who is "fayre" and, to the speaker's mind, a bit vain about it, even as he lectures her that she ought to be more like "the trew fayre" that he seeks to praise. Similarly, in sonnet 28 the speaker interprets the lady's wearing of laurel as a sign of his own power ("the powre thereof, which ofte in me I find"), but in sonnet 29 the lady appears as a character who reinterprets the sign of the laurel to her own advantage; in sonnet 54, she willfully misinterprets the act the speaker puts on in "this worlds Theatre." And as we have seen already, in sonnet 75 the speaker's transcendent lyricism literally attempts to surround the pragmatic narrative voice of the lady, who dismisses his pretensions toward immortality as a "vaine assay."

These competing representations of the lady make clear the extent of and the limitations on the speaker's lyric authority. In sonnet 45, the speaker's exasperation with his position and his lady points directly at his ability to construct his own social distinction. Sonnet and sequence confront each other quite openly as she rejects his entire ideological program. There are, again, two ladies here: the lady the speaker addresses who "evermore" stares at herself in the mirror, and "the fayre Idea" that lies in his heart. The first lady acts largely as a character in the drama of the sonnet – refusing to look at the image the speaker has constructed by, presumably, refusing to read his sonnets. The second lady, the "fayre Idea," becomes more closely identified with the speaker himself:

> Leave lady in your glasse of christall clene,
>   Your goodly selfe for evermore to vew:
>   and in my selfe, my inward selfe I meane,
>   most lively lyke behold your semblant trew.

> Within my hart, though hardly it can shew
>   thing so divine to vew of earthly eye:
>   the fayre Idea of your celestiall hew,
>   and every part remaines immortally:
>
> And were it not that through your cruelty,
>   with sorrow dimmed and deformed it were:
>   the goodly ymage of your visnomy,
>   clearer then christall would therein appere.
>
> But if your selfe in me ye playne will see,
>   remove the cause by which your fayre beames darkned be.

His heart ("it" in line ten) has become "dimmed and deformed" because the narrative lady won't look at it. The reciprocity between lyric subject and object, between speaker and "Fayre Idea," is disrupted by the lack of cooperation from the narrative lady. On one hand, then, the dialectic of subject/object is set against the narrative lady's view of herself in the mirror. Were she to look, she would see her "semblant true," an essential self beyond the world of mere appearance represented by the "glasse of christall clene." On the other hand, the lyric itself and the speaker's authority, like his heart, becomes "dimmed and deformed" by her unwillingness to cooperate. In line three ("and in my selfe, my inward selfe I meane"), the speaker himself is effectively split in two, into a narrative "selfe" and a lyric "inward selfe." Caught up in a narrative dialogue with the lady, he attempts to extricate himself by insisting upon the priority of his lyric self. But the exasperation and irritation of the line ("my inward selfe *I meane*") betrays the dependence of that inward self upon the speaker's relation with a possibly vain and certainly uncooperative narrative subject. Rather than lyric idealism overcoming narrative mutability, the desire for such idealism and the authority it promises are situated as an effect of a narrative field.

Possession of the lady presents the (always elusive) possibility for the speaker to extricate himself from a narrative of dispossession, loss, and contingent value. When we turn, then, to those moments in the sequence where the speaker's will to control of her seems especially strong, what we find is a complex interplay of possession and dispossession, of social authority and subordination. The intensified urge to possess betrays a more historically specific sense of dispossession. In sonnet 15, for instance, Spenser employs the blazon, a form that many critics have seen as particularly embodying the speaker's urge to dominate and control:

> Ye tradefull Merchants, that with weary toyle
>   do seeke most pretious things to make your gaine:

and both the Indias of their treasures spoile,
what needeth you to seeke so farre in vaine?

For loe my love doth in her selfe containe
all this worlds riches that may farre be found:
if Saphyres, loe her eies be Saphyres plaine,
if Rubies, loe hir lips be Rubies sound:

If Pearles, hir teeth be pearles both pure and round;
if Yvorie, her forhead yvory weene;
if Gold, her locks are finest gold on ground;
if silver, her faire hands are silver sheene,

But that which fairest is, but few behold,
her mind adornd with vertues manifold.

Building on the influential arguments of Nancy Vickers and Patricia Parker, Kim Hall remarks that "Spenser's blazon [in sonnet 15] clearly demonstrates the dismemberment and control of the female and also the competitive rhetoric of display that reveals – even as the poet denies – his economic motives."[25] The speaker controls the lady by trying to turn her into a commodity – or rather, a series of commodities – and this control in turn enables him to articulate his social superiority to the "tradefull merchants." In contrast to the expansive movement of the merchants for mutable, material "things," his lady "doth in her selfe containe" value – there is no need for the speaker to leave home. The merchants and their jewels come to represent a transitory, changeable economy, a relentless and continuous search for value. The lady, conversely, represents an internal constancy ("in her selfe") that trumps the necessarily external movement of the merchants. This identification of the lady's constancy enables the speaker to distinguish himself from the merchants. But unlike the lady, the speaker claims no internal, immutable value for himself. Instead, he claims to possess such value ("*my* love"). His possession of the lady distinguishes him socially; she is a "fairest" thing which "few behold" and even fewer own. The speaker distinguishes himself from the merchants in terms of an economy he ascribes to them: he is superior because he presents a commodity so rare that it is invisible.

The dismemberment of the lady into commodities enables the speaker to define his relation to the merchants. The lady's body becomes, in Eve Sedgwick's influential phrase, a site for the construction of relations "between men."[26] But between what men? When we take class into account, these male bonds look tenuous and contradictory. The speaker certainly does not (at least initially) seek a homosocial bond with the merchants; as an object of the speaker's lyric desire, the commodified lady *distinguishes* him from the merchants and makes possible his domination of them, rather than sealing a bond between them. Instead, in his desire for a possession free from the endless ranging of the merchants, for a possession which is right in front of him, the speaker desires to be like nothing so much as New English representations of Old English land owners like the Earl of Ormond. These men possessed their estates – at least as far as the New English were concerned – free from the vicissitudes of exchange and from the new, "civilized" English mode of agricultural production. But in this sense, the homosocial relation secured through the female body is again a relation that the speaker in part does not desire; the Old English, and the mode of production they represent, is largely what the New English sought to eliminate. As the speaker becomes identified with the merchants, he loses the very possession which his relation to them is meant to facilitate. Thus the specter of an absolute possession, of a desire for a homosocial bond with the Old English or the merchants, only arises because the speaker also desires *not* to be like them.

The desire for control of and through the female body should be seen as habitus; the desire discloses the conditions which provoke it and the limits thereby set upon the desiring subject. Consequently, we should stop reading sonnet 15 and other similar moments as strictly a conventional lyric blazon apart from its contextual production. Reading the sonnet as a generic blazon identifies with and tacitly accepts the speaker's version of his lyric self; that is, it involves a critical investment with the speaker's desires, whether in the service of a feminist or anti-colonialist politics that seeks to identify him with patriarchal or imperial power or a more conservative desire to witness the *Amoretti*'s ability to overcome mutability.[27] Instead, attention to the strain between lyric and narrative highlights the lady's double existence. For while she is an object of the speaker's lyric desire, she is also a subject, a participant in the narrative interaction which *produces* the lyric. The lady's status as subject discloses the speaker's similarity to the merchants – a relation between men that he does not want. While his social distinction from the merchants depends upon his ability to construct a sonnet set against their mutability, his economic similarity to them, his mode of production, becomes apparent when the lady is no longer merely a commodified lyric object but a subject in a narrative of exchange. He too works with "weary toyle" to make his "gaine," but his search lies in his attempt to create the lady as something which we can retrospectively recognize as a commodity. Indeed, in his attempts to objectify her, the speaker tries to create something like the idea of a fetishized commodity, rather than simply turning her into one. "Commodity" as a capitalist category is here coming into existence; it is not a stable idea being imposed on the lady but an abstraction the speaker tries to produce. Likewise, it is worth remembering at this moment that the ostensible object of the poems, Spenser's second wife Elizabeth Boyle, was herself also a subject. Even Spenser's biographer, who largely embraces the speaker's account ("[m]uch that we know about Spenser's marriage to Elizabeth Boyle is found between the covers of a small octavo volume published in 1595"), notes that the three extant letters by Elizabeth suggest an educated woman "free from any hint of subservience."[28]

The speaker's attempt to identify exchange with the merchants is largely a red herring, for the paradigmatic capitalist here is the speaker himself. Sonnet 15 consequently places us at a very precise historical juncture, a moment when social distinction began to depend less on landed wealth and more on wealth from land, not on feudal domains but on capitalist landlord–tenant relations that produced the wealth to buy the merchants' "pretious things." "[T]radefull," for example, identifies these merchants quite specifically as members of the newly founded long distance companies like the East India, Muscovy, and Virginia who imported commodities into England. And yet this very capacity to produce wealth also creates the possibility of imagining goods *as* commodities, even as it produces the desire to secure a domain to establish a more permanent sense of social prestige apart from commodities.

This situating of male lyric desire and control within a female narrative is especially apparent in probably the most famous sonnet in the sequence. In sonnet 67, exhausted from his metaphoric chase of an elusive deer, the speaker sits down, only to discover that possession presents itself apart from his action:

> Lyke as a huntsman after weary chace,
>   Seeing the game from him escapt away:
>   sits downe to rest him in some shady place,
>   with panting hounds beguiled of their pray,
>
> So after long pursuit and vaine assay,
>   when I all weary had the chace forsooke,
>   the gentle deare returnd the selfe-same way,
>   thinking to quench her thirst at the next brooke.
>
> There she beholding me with mylder looke,
>   sought not to fly, but fearelesse still did bide:
>   till I in hand her yet halfe trembling tooke,
>   and with her owne goodwill hir fyrmely tyde.
>
> Strange thing me seemd to see a beast so wyld,
>   so goodly wonne with her owne will begyld.

The speaker's power through possession is here formally expressed as he is literally placed (and places himself) within a narrative that ends, equivocally, with his tying up the deer with "her owne will begyld." The securing of his masculine position ("lyke as a huntsman") only occurs within a chase, again (as in sonnet 75) a "vaine assay," dominated by an uncooperative female. The myth of Actaeon is effectively reversed: the lady, the deer, looks, rather than the male hunter. The speaker admits that he and his masculine huntsmanship had nothing to do with the capture: she is "beholding" (looking at, possessing) him even as she looks "with mylder looke" at his own "mylder looke" – he is apparently not playing the huntsman anymore. Despite the location of the modifier in line eleven, "till I in hand her yet halfe trembling tooke," the speaker, as much as the deer, seems to be trembling. The result of this approaches a comic inversion of the scene; the deer seems as, if not more, controlling – more masculine – than the speaker who ties her up.

The tenuous possession of the deer by the speaker is further mediated by his awkward invocation of social ambition; desire for possession of the deer is also a desire to be noble. The conceit of the hunter and deer is of course routine, beginning (at least in terms of sonnets) with Petrarch's *Rime* 190,[29] but Spenser's sense of social position here is anything but conventional. In the other well known English sonnet version of the myth (which Spenser may or may not have known), Wyatt's "Whoso List to Hunt," the speaker fails to possess the deer because, among other things, it belongs to "Caesar."[30] The desire of Wyatt's speaker bumps into social, and specifically royal, boundaries. The deer, like the hunt itself, belongs to the king, even as the speaker invites "Whoso list to hunt" to participate themselves (a potentially subversive invitation appealing, no doubt, to the largely aristocratic audience who first encountered Wyatt's poem in manuscripts like the Arundel Harrington and Egerton). In positioning himself as a hunter of deer, Spenser's speaker is implicitly trying to adopt an aristocratic stance, to become, like the Earl of Ormond, a virtual prince himself. But unlike Wyatt's speaker, the speaker of sonnet 67 succeeds; he possesses the deer. This was a position which Spenser himself had recently come to enjoy: his lease on Kilcolman, for example, allowed him to impark 150 acres for horses and deer. In adopting the stance of the hunter, Spenser's speaker, like Spenser himself, adopts the position of the idealized feudal lord who masters his possessions and land.

But this social position is substantially undermined when we view the deer as not merely his lyric object but as a representative character in a narrative chase, a "vaine assay." This speaker is only "lyke" a huntsman, and he is only partially successful at playing the part. First, he fails to catch the deer, and then he fails "lyke as a *huntsman*" to kill her. His possession consists only in tying up (albeit "firmly") a "beast so wyld." The speaker himself doesn't understand how this possession could occur, for it seems to follow a logic entirely outside his comprehension. His "goodly" possession (like a good) of the "beast" is the result not of his efforts but rather emerges from "her owne will." The dialectic of possession and dispossession, of the nascent capitalist relations which provoke, enable, and finally limit the speaker's social mobility, appears as this "strange thing" – a beast beguiled, deceived by its own "will," a systematic power whose logic he cannot understand. Even in her capture, the deer maintains an elusive power which the speaker does not have. But the deer also partially mirrors the position of the speaker – tied into a narrative chase, beguiling himself. After all, he is as much a part of the narrative as she is. His control of the lady/deer does not lead to a satisfying closure, a fixing of meaning, and the realization of social prestige and conquest; instead, as the continuance of the sequence makes clear, it leads to only a moment of possession in the dialectic into which the socially mobile hunter has (been) unwittingly entered. Possession is an expression of masculine dominance, but it occurs only momentarily in the otherwise continual flight of a feminine, narrative beast.

The contradiction of the sequence, finally, is the strain between the speaker's attempts to impose a lyric mode of classification upon the space of both the poem and Ireland, of his sometimes disturbing attempts at masculinist and colonialist control, and a capitalist dialectic that provokes his lyric voice and makes him long for a secure possession – like that of the Old English he seeks to eliminate or the queen he tacitly challenges with his "alternative center." As the speaker describes it in sonnet 35,

> My hungry eyes through greedy covetize
> still to behold the object of their paine:
> with no contentment can themselves suffize,
> but having pine and having not complaine.

Or, as he puts it a few lines later, "so plenty makes me poore." It's hard to imagine a more succinct description of the contradictory social distinction set in motion by nascent capitalism. His economic plenty marks him as socially poor because he requires plenty to construct a noble social position in the first place. Whatever possession and stability – both social and epistemological – the speaker achieves in these moments of lyric control is continually situated within and against the material and physical dispossession he suffers. The last five sonnets of the *Amoretti*, which have troubled critics looking for a satisfying conclusion to the possession enacted in sonnet 67, are rather an extension of the contradictions present throughout the sequence. Though the speaker's contemplation of *his* "purest part" in sonnet 88 allows him to behold "th'Idæa playne," the sonnet ends with him stressing his starving body and blind eyes. In sonnet 89, he tries to sing "Lyke as the Culver on the bared bough," but decides instead that "Dark is my day" as he finds his life "dead . . . that wants such lively blis." Whatever moments of lyric control he erects continually threaten to collapse back into the narrative of the sequence – a death less of the speaker in the abstract so much as his existence as a lyricist. As habitus, the speaker and the sonnets struggle to impose a "lyric" system of classification, and this struggle occurs as the speaker reacts back upon the narrative field that creates his desire.

Amoretti to *Epithalamion*

Many critics have remarked on the *Epithalamion*'s apparent capacity to "solve," at least partially, the critical problems of the *Amoretti*. In particular, Spenser's use of marriage is often thought to subject the sonnets' erotic tension to a "Protestant ideology" embedded, for instance, in the poem's numerology.[31] At the same time, this reconciling capacity of the *Epithalamion* also marks a crucial turning point in conceptions of Spenser's poetic career; the turn from *Amoretti* to *Epithalamion* enacts in miniature a more general pattern from concerns with the public politics of court to a more private realm. This career trajectory has recently come under severe scrutiny. As Richard Rambuss remarks,

[w]hether formulated in terms of his incipient 'modernism,' or his inauguration of a brand-new author function, or his final contemplative withdrawal to a private Acidale cordoned off from the historical world, the inevitable but deeply misguided next step for any critical or biographical account that abstracts Spenser and his poetry from other careerist pursuits – including those attendant upon his service as a colonial bureaucrat in Ireland – is the proffering of a transcendent Spenser.[32]

This "transcendent" Spenser is, of course, quite historical. In his capacity as private author whose power emerges from his Protestant interiority, he embodies the traits usually called bourgeois. What is "misguided" about such depictions of Spenser is their privileging of the categories of middle class or bourgeois subjectivity (inwardness, privacy) over the historical forces which in this period begin to produce such categories of analysis. The emergence of class as a means of making social distinctions becomes conflated with a particular class that clearly does not exist yet. Viewing Spenser as bourgeois may have a "genuinely explanatory theoretical function,"[33] because it makes possible a description of the sorts of authority at work in his earlier and later work. Using bourgeois as a category, however, risks obscuring the struggle to produce not only the bourgeoisie as a class but the idea of "class" itself as a historical issue by adopting as a primary critical lens the bourgeois category *par excellence* – class itself – as a historical given. Spenser's "alternative center" thus becomes a celebration of the private, the interior, and the bourgeois. An "abstracted" Spenser posits the real existence of a bourgeois class that only exists theoretically. Such a "Bourgeois Paradigm," as we saw in chapter two, has proven amenable to the liberal "profferings" that Rambuss rightly critiques. But it has also facilitated (more or less) Marxist accounts that look to career moves like Spenser's as a challenge to noble privilege instigating a crisis of the aristocracy as well as new historicist renderings of the containment of the Spenserian subject by Gloriana's gaze. However, an emphasis on and sense of new forms of authority themselves is not necessarily misguided: Spenser and *Amoretti and Epithalamion* do enact shifts in locations and conceptions of social distinction. Instead, what is at stake in rethinking the transition in authority from *Amoretti* to *Epithalamion*, and in Spenser's career generally, is renegotiating the gap between the real, emergent, social distinction that Spenser puts into play and the theoretical class (the rise of the bourgeoisie) customarily put in place to understand that emergent position.

Such issues are especially compelling in the *Epithalamion* in part because, as Montrose emphasizes, "Spenser draws attention to his appropriation for a personal and bourgeois occasion of a celebratory genre normally reserved for the politically and dynastically significant marriages of members of royalty and the aristocracy."[34] This appropriation is apparent in Spenser's most striking departure from convention – his conflation of the speaker with the bridegroom. As Thomas Greene points out, classical epithalamia (Sappho and Catullus) place the speaker as a master of ceremonies at an aristocratic occasion who directs the day's action – who enters when, who sings, which gifts are given by whom, and so on. And yet in classical and Renaissance models the speaker's function is social, not private: "The poet-speaker acts as an advocate for society . . . the typical epithalamion is a ritualistic *public* statement, unconcerned with the actual intimate experience undergone by individuals."[35] Because speaker and bridegroom are the same, the social experience of the *Epithalamion* is perpetually filtered through the lyric rhetoric of the speaker – invocations of gods and nymphs, and descriptions of the beauty of the bride take on a poignancy unavailable to a speaker who is only a master of ceremonies. The poem presents the events of the speaker's wedding day, but this narrative occurs, as the first stanza makes clear, as the speaker "unto my selfe alone will sing." The result is that the troubles the speaker runs into are converted from problems of social relations into abstractions (Time, Death) for which lyric is particularly suited. He comes to seem less a participant, a character, in a narrative drama (though he still is that), and more a lyric speaker who transforms his troubles into mythic and theological significance.[36]

While the apparent closure of the *Epithalamion* emerges as a result of a formal emphasis on lyric, as in the *Amoretti* this rhetoric, and the masculine subjectivity it makes possible, appears in relation to the narrative of the occasion. In this vein, Montrose brilliantly reads the moment in stanza 21 when Cynthia "peepes" through the window at the newly married couple: "here the private is not merely defined by its juxtaposition to the public; it becomes apprehensible precisely in the moment of its violation. In this instance, by evoking that aspect of Cynthia-Diana which connects her to childbirth, the poet-bridegroom rhetorically assimilates the militantly virginal Queen / goddess to his epithalamium; he seeks to put her into domestic service."[37] But something similar needs to be said about the speaker's construction of a social hierarchy in stanza 11 where "vertue raynes as Queene in royal throne, / And giveth lawes alone." The speaker is not only reacting against Elizabeth's court, and thereby celebrating his domestic domain; he is also reacting against the "merchant daughters" and desiring to be like either the Old English – an "English" lord over an Irish estate – or like Elizabeth herself, a mini-monarch:

> Tell me ye merchant daughters did ye see
> So fayre a creature in your towne before,
> So sweet, so lovely, and so mild as she,
> Adornd with beautyes grace and vertues store,
> Her goodly eyes lyke Saphyres shining bright,
> Her forehead yvory white,
> Her cheeckes lyke apples which the sun hath rudded,
> Her lips lyke cherryes charming men to byte,
> Her brest like to a bowle of creame uncrudded,
> Her paps lyke lyllies budded,
> Her snowie necke lyke to a marble towre,
> And al her body like a pallace fayre,
> Ascending uppe with many a stately stayre,
> To honors seat and chastities sweet bowre.
> Why stand ye still ye virgins in amaze,
> Upon her so to gaze,

> Whiles ye forget your former lay to sing,
> To which the woods did answer and your eccho ring.

While the "domestic domain" comes into existence as it is violated by Cynthia/Elizabeth's peeping, that domain, and the control it implies, also comes into existence as it is "violated" by the presence of the "merchant daughters" who provoke the speaker into the blazon which stanza 11 completes. The speaker's blazon is meant to dazzle the eyes of the "merchant daughters," while the bride's "inward beauty," which the daughters cannot see, reinforces the social superiority of speaker and bride – a distinction furthered since the bride is apparently not from the town ("did ye see/So fayre a creature in your towne before"). A social and political hierarchy, topped by the male lyric speaker, emerges from imagining a commodity so precious and rare that it cannot be seen (these are "unrevealed pleasures") as the lady becomes not only a commodity but also a "pallace fayre." As in sonnet 15, the blazon always threatens to expose the speaker's economic similarity to these merchants daughters; his control of queen and palace ultimately depends upon his control of a commodity and the violation of the idealized feudal position he desires to occupy. Fair palaces become commodities, and *vice versa*. This exposure occurs, paradoxically, as the lady herself ceases to be a commodity and becomes a subject that betrays the speaker's desire.

But unlike sonnet 15, the speaker here not only attempts to conceal his own participation in exchange by ascribing it to the merchants; he also specifically genders these merchants as female and makes them subordinate daughters. The implicit gendering of mercantile economics as female in the *Amoretti* – the dialectic of dispossession that animates sonnet 67 – is here made quite explicit. The speaker defines his masculinity and his social position against the changeableness of the "merchant daughters," who by association gender female the nascent capitalist exchanges which make possible the speaker's claims at all. If the speaker is not "bourgeois," if he is not socially identical with the merchants and their daughters, he is self-conscious about his economic similarity to them, and he uses gender markings to try to distance himself. Consequently, it is only a half truth (but not untrue) to suggest that in stanza 17 "there is a distinctly bourgeois pleasure in the 'silken courteins,' 'odourd sheets, and Arras coverlets' of the bridal bed"; but is certainly untrue to suggest that such "a pleasure . . . would be unseemly at an aristocratic occasion."[38] The distinction between "middle class" and "aristocracy" here is much murkier because the criteria used to make such a distinction are not entirely clear. Rather than embodying a bourgeois challenge to aristocratic authority, the speaker employs an economic mode of authority (control of capital) to create a new sense of social distinction. But he also seeks to hide his use of such capital by labeling as feminine that process of deployment. Far from unseemly, these are the items which the speaker uses to construct his social distinction from the merchant daughters; they are the sorts of goods that Spenser might deploy as a sign of the income he enjoys from the possession of land in Ireland. The masculine possession of feminized commodities, and their spectacular display, becomes in this period less a mark of a particular class – the "rising" bourgeoisie, the dominant aristocracy – and more a means of creating social distinction itself. Such display marked bourgeois aspirations, but it also distinguished the aristocracy and the landed gentry, whose economic dominance increasingly depended not on forcefully extracting purveyance from peasants but from market rents. Aristocrats used this new cash increasingly to buy goods imported by the newly founded merchant companies.[39] Yet such a means of distinction consequently made it increasingly difficult to maintain a socially distinct position. What is "mobile" here, finally, is not a particular class (the rising bourgeoisie, the aristocracy in crisis) but rather the very idea and means of producing "classes," distinct social groups.

The most prominent good the speaker displays, of course, is the poem. As Jacqueline Miller suggests, the ending of the *Epithalamion* "clearly reflects its author's sense of the poem as a poem – as a fiction ultimately defenseless against the external world of destructive elements."[40] The sense of possession in the *Epithalamion* first arises out of the speaker's ability to control social relations by abstracting those relations into myth or supernatural forces within his masculine lyric voice. But while the *Epithalamion* partially solves the problem of the *Amoretti* by internalizing and abstracting narrative intrusion as masculine control of feminine goods, the fact of the lyric utterance itself betrays the speaker's complicity in a contingent economy. This dialectic is most conspicuous in the tornata, which represents the poem itself as a mediator between transcendence and time in largely economic terms:

> Song made in lieu of many ornaments,
> With which my love should duly have bene dect,
> Which cutting off through hasty accidents,
> Ye would not stay your dew time to expect,
> But promist both to recompens,
> Be unto her a goodly ornament,
> And for short time an endlesse moniment.

The song itself becomes a commodity by taking the place of the "many ornaments" – like the "silken courteins" and "odourd sheetes" – which the economically strapped speaker apparently cannot afford.[41] It also creates the spectacle that marks the speaker's social superiority, for it "promist both to recompens" – both to pay the debt the speaker owes to the lady (as an ornament) and to himself as his own patron (as an unfinished song). Like the commodities of sonnet 15 and stanzas 10–11, the song displays the superiority of the lady (it is an "ornament") while also displaying the superiority of the speaker who possesses both the lady *and* the song (he is, after all, his own patron). However, while his social status permits him an epithalamion on his wedding day, his socioeconomic position and his masculinity are insecure enough that he must do the job himself.

The song thus stands in as a commodity, an ornament, that both marks the speaker's lack of commodities and his dependence upon commodities to distinguish himself socially. His possession of the song, the day, the lady – like Spenser's possession of Kilcolman Castle – are not enough, since the desire to possess betrays his participation in an endless promise of "recompens." The poem itself becomes the feminine object the speaker tries to control, but his dominance is again tempered as the poem becomes figured as capital "recompens." As he puts it earlier, in stanza seven, "let this day this one day be myne."[42] The repetition here displays a speaker who is both creepily controlling and pathetically powerless; his compulsive desire for possession betrays the fact that he does not possess very much. Such poetic self-awareness nevertheless signals Spenser's astonishing poetic capacity, for it is difficult to maintain a sense of sympathy for this speaker without, at the same time, accepting his categorization of social space. His struggles seem like our struggles as we try to read him (let this one stanza be mine), but this process reenacts the dialectic of possession the speaker finds himself in from the start of the *Amoretti*:

> Happy ye leaves, when as those lilly hands
>   which hold my life in their dead doing might
>   shall handle you and hold in loves soft bands
>   like captives trembling at the victors sight.

The anxiety of this speaker is, among other things, that of a writer – the dread of turning over one's "leaves" to another's hands, of becoming subject, or object, to the "dead doing might" of a reader. The stability of circulating pages only among patient friends, or just in his own head, gives way to the anxiety of a published book, a commodity defined and valued by the whims of a fickle market that always holds him captive –

even though, and especially because, this speaker *likes* being a captive. There is a palpable erotic thrill in all the holding, handling, and trembling here, and this excitement likewise suggests how much the speaker likes the social position such authorial captivity affords him. He consequently reads his reader, attempting to seize an interpretive authority he nevertheless knows must be denied him for his commodity to become valuable. "Happy," then, is both wishful thinking, an effort to forestall an inevitable doom, as well as an expression of the exhilaration such subordination entails.

The *Epithalamion*, rather than resolving, powerfully rearticulates the historical contradictions of the *Amoretti*: a masculine, lyric speaker whose desire for possession and a socially distinct position is provoked, enabled, and undermined by the feminine narrative of exchange within which he speaks and to which he contributes. The relation between sonnet and sequence provides the model by which Spenser, and perhaps we as well, construct social space, the means to understand the relation between poetry and society and the precarious authority of a new social position. And in this sense, finally, *Amoretti and Epithalamion* is symptomatically Elizabethan not simply because it marks a moment of movement from one conceptual economy or class to another, or because it embodies a centripetal court culture, or even because it exists "between" English and Irish cultures. Rather, in the strain between lyric and narrative, *Amoretti and Epithalamion* embodies the paradoxical process of subjection that nascent capitalism produces, as well as the subjects in which nascent capitalism exists. Within and out of this very social contradiction, sonnet sequences and those who wrote and used them begin to express a distinct social disposition. To the extent that the subject's desires are realized and his mode of distinction is reinforced, to the extent that the *Epithalamion* fills the role of "many ornaments," to the extent that a masculine speaker asserts control over a contingent feminine object, to the extent that Spenser does become a kind of lord in Ireland, and to the extent that lyric comes to internalize and partially control narrative – and it is at best a deeply equivocal realization – to this extent, finally, the contradictory struggle for classification in *Amoretti and Epithalamion* acquires a historical force for which we have no better term than class.

6 "Till my bad angel fire my good one out": engendering economic expertise in Shakespeare's *Sonnets*

"Two loves I have": classification struggle in the *Sonnets*

This chapter makes more explicit the intersection of social position, gender, and economic language in sonnet sequences by looking at Shakespeare's *Sonnets*. We have already seen that the recourse to financial metaphors is a central component of the imaginative construction of social space in sonnet sequences in this period. Biblical interpretation in Lok's work is aligned with commodity circulation. Astrophil's interaction with Stella takes the form of his succumbing to "Reason's audit," a procedure that makes clear his dependence upon Stella's feminine "riches." Daniel represents *Delia* as an account book, and Spenser's *Amoretti and Epithalamion* invokes new conceptions of capital and land possession in the speaker's desire for his lady. In each case, social distinctions are also partly set in motion by gender distinctions, and both are intimately related to a financial language – the "use," "accounts," and "audits" that compulsively appear in these works. Such economic language pervades Shakespeare's *Sonnets*, as a number of studies have detailed.[1] What has been less remarked on is the function of this language in producing, rather than reflecting, a social position; my interest in this chapter is less the economy, the market, or usury as autonomous discourses, than the social position that emerges from Shakespeare's appropriation of them.

The production of this social position is apparent when we focus on the form of the *Sonnets*. As generations of readers have noted, one remarkable thing about Shakespeare's work is its construction of two objects of desire – the young man and the dark lady. This divide literalizes through gendered categories the processes we see in other sequences; it is as if Spenser's lady has suddenly been split in two. Though much has been made of this literalization – that it is original, unconventional, and stands at the end of an exhausted poetic tradition – it is clear that Shakespeare is operating firmly within both generic and historical conditions.[2] Shakespeare's work participates in general, deep connections between gender and economic language in the period, and not only in poetry: economy itself appears in gendered terms. As Mary Poovey argues, seventeenth-century merchants helped to create the laws of "the economy" – specifically, the economic doctrine ordinarily known as mercantilism – by labeling feminine those aspects of markets which they could not control. In the process, they created for themselves a distinct social position tied to their expertise about, control over, and invention of "economic" discourse.[3] Like the merchants Poovey describes, Shakespeare's speaker creates much of his celebrated lyricism by using economic language to distinguish himself as a sort of economic expert.

Also like Poovey's merchants, such expertise emerges through the speaker's use of gender categories. Throughout the *Sonnets*, Shakespeare's speaker attempts to construct a masculine noble imaginary in the figure of the young man. The speaker tries to stabilize this object by associating with the dark lady, and thereby labeling feminine, those social forces which threaten to undermine the young man's social position. Fairness, masculinity, and lyricism become associated with nobility. Darkness, femininity, and narrative become associated with those who are not noble or who participate in the market (these are not necessarily exclusive categories). The speaker consequently uses gender categories to extricate the abstracted ideal of the young man from the economic mutability of the dark lady. Nevertheless, his desire for that lyric ideal emerges because he identifies – not in terms of gender but in terms of social position – with the dark lady and the mutable forces she both embodies and wields. His identification with the position of the dark lady consequently expresses the latent contradiction throughout the entire sequence: the speaker's desire for an imaginary nobility emerges out of an economic and class narrative which provides the vocabulary for him to create sonnets at all; but that very language continually undermines the noble imaginary he tries to construct. Like Spenser's speaker in *Amoretti and Epithalamion*, Shakespeare's speaker authorizes himself by resisting the economic forces that supply his desire and his language; in the process, such differentiations end up defining the speaker's habitus.

Sonnet 144 narrates what appears to be, at first glance, something very much like a transition from a feudal to a mercantilist economy, and it does so in part by distinguishing these attitudes in terms of gender. The sonnet begins with the speaker presenting a sort of allegorical psychomachia – a conceptual universe with himself placed at the center. In the first quatrain the speaker exists inside a world of absolutes, where comfort, goodness, and masculinity are lined up against despair, badness, and femininity:

Two loves I have, of comfort and despair,
Which like two spirits do suggest me still;
The better angel is a man right fair,
The worser spirit a woman coloured ill.
To win me soon to hell, my female evil
Tempteth my better angel from my side,
And would corrupt my saint to be a devil,
Wooing his purity with her foul pride.
And whether that my angel be turned fiend
Suspect I may, yet not directly tell;
But being both from me, both to each friend,
I guess one angel in another's hell.
　　Yet this shall I ne'er know, but live in doubt
　　Till my bad angel fire my good one out.[4]

We have no sense of time, no sense of change, no sense of mutability in the first quatrain – just a constant symbiotic opposition that "suggest[s]" the speaker. "Suggest" here means that the "spirits" not only "insinuate" or "prompt" the speaker;[5] these spirits also "suggest" the limits of his existence by reproducing allegorically aspects of him – the better and worser angels are, in this sense, extensions of the speaker himself. But in the second quatrain, this static structural opposition starts to break down as "my female evil" begins to act. While the speaker perceives her actions as specifically directed at him ("To win me soon to hell"), what is especially striking is that the "female evil" "[t]empteth" not the speaker but the "better angel." The effect is twofold. First, though the speaker insists that he remains the center of all action and mediates between the binaries established in the first quatrain ("To win *me*"; "*my* female evil"; "*my* better angel"; "*my* side"; "*my* saint"), the "female evil" and "better angel" suddenly no longer seem allegorical extensions of the speaker's universe. They seem instead independently operating agents not necessarily concerned with him – even though he continues to emphasize his own reactions. Second, by tempting the "better angel" and not the speaker himself, the "female evil" disrupts the entire moral and ontological spectrum constructed in the first quatrain. In tempting – and possibly succeeding at tempting – the "saint," the balanced structure of good versus evil, male versus female, comfort versus despair, is radically undermined. In place of the balanced binaries of the opening quatrain comes uncertainty and doubt ("Suspect I may, yet not directly tell"). The two angels, once virtual extensions of the speaker, are now "from me, both to each friend," and he can only "*guess* one angel in another's hell." Rather than the angels marking allegorical extensions of the speaker – marking, in other words, his stability – the action of the female angel disrupts his very status as a subject. As Eve Sedgwick suggests – in a reading that I am merely nuancing here – the "coolness with which the possibility of a 'heaven' for the poet (and, indeed, the question of the poet's destiny at all, even the centrality of the poet) is made to evaporate from the poem is rather breathtaking; surely that, more than particular suspicions about the two spirits, makes the poem so disconcerting and moving."[6]

But this evaporation also *creates* the speaker as a subject – what Joel Fineman calls "the resonant hollowness of a fractured verbal self" that the speaker experiences "*as* his difference from himself. His identity is an identity of ruptured identification, a broken identity that carves out in the poet's self a syncopated hollowness that accounts for the deep personal interiority of the sonnets' poetic persona."[7] Rather than just undermining a pre-existing integrity – the psychomachia with which sonnet 144 appears to begin – the movement of the "female evil" expresses a subject continually living in doubt but crucially able to *articulate* that doubt. In this sense, the psychomachia of the first quatrain is a component in the construction of the broken subjectivity of the speaker, the imaginary stability against which brokenness understands itself. Likewise, the movement of the worser angel, and the speaker's response to it, are expressions of the unstable, shifting categories which "suggest" or structure the speaker and which he, in turn, uses to distinguish himself. The two angels here become part of a classification struggle that constitutes the subjectivity of the speaker: these are the very categories that he deploys to distinguish himself.

This classification struggle plays out throughout Shakespeare's sequence, most notably in the traditional "division" of the sonnets between those generally concerned with the young man (1–126) and those generally with the dark lady (127–154). Originally made explicit (or made up) in Malone's 1780 edition, this division has been called into question of late as an unexamined remnant of Romantic understandings of the sequence. Indeed, the division is a particularly glaring instance of the sort of post-romantic assumptions about sonnet sequences I discussed in chapter two: it makes possible all the by-now tiresome arguments about Shakespeare's intentions, the correct order of the sequence, the true identity of the dark lady and young man, and so on. That the division facilitates these critical hobby-horses does not mean, however, that Malone's division is simply wrong. As Valerie Traub emphasizes, "[o]ne need not accept the 1609 Quarto as authoritative nor agree that the collection constructs a diachronic narrative based on coherent character-ization (biographical or fictional) to assert that specific gender positions nonetheless are inscribed."[8] The young man and dark lady are not real people, the "addressees" of the poems: they are gendered objects of desire. The bipartite division of the sequence is a function, as Fineman insists, of the speaker's desire, an urge to distinguish dialectically between male / noble / lyric and female / market-class / narrative. In this sense, the division expresses the classificatory struggle of the sequence, a conflict that effectively *is* the speaker: as in sonnet 144, the desire for the order of "two loves," the fear that it is impossible to tell them apart, the sense of a subjective wholeness coming apart, the urge definitively to articulate this instability in order to stabilize a subject.

Rejecting Malone's romantic emphasis on the story of the sonnets, moreover, does not mean we are magically extricated from the construction of Shakespeare in the eighteenth and nineteenth centuries: what remains, apart from the story, is the naturalized social position, the lyric "subjectivity," that the division helps to produce.[9] As in *Amoretti and Epithalamion*, the question of the relative "lyricism" of Shakespeare's speaker is always a social question, because such lyricism depends upon a social position which sonnet sequences in this period labor to create. The emergence of the narrative division in Malone's eighteenth-century hands should be understood as marking the concretization of a social position, its historical transformation into a clearly demarcated class – the bourgeoisie. What requires further investigation is how that social position begins to emerge in Shakespeare's sequence; this is the sort of historical contextualization that Sedgwick warns at the outset that she will not pursue in her largely formal reading or that gets rendered invisible by Fineman's dependence upon a "conventional" understanding of sonnet traditions.[10]

"Bad angels": the emergence of economic discourse

With the intrusion of narrative in the second quatrain of sonnet 144 comes a more historically specific sense of some of the forces "suggesting" the speaker. In the couplet, the once abstract "better" and "worser" angels are transformed into, among other things, money. Though these lines have generally been read as either invocations of the "fire" of venereal disease or a hunting metaphor (smoking out prey), at least two commentators – Stephen Booth and John Kerrigan – see "Till my bad angel fire my good one out" as recalling the economic saying known as Gresham's Law, "bad money drives out good," because "angel" was a highly conventional pun on coins stamped with the image of the angel Michael.[11] Coins were a particular concern of Thomas Gresham at the start of Elizabeth's reign; in the 1560s, he advised the Queen to remint all circulating coins to try to solve the seemingly intractable issue of currency devaluation and price inflation, a problem contested at least through the mercantile debates of the 1620s. If the first quatrain of sonnet 144 begins with an idealized, anachronistic, medieval psychomachia, it ends with a relatively contemporary sense of monetary crisis. The "narrative" within which sonnet 144 implicitly places itself is the constantly recurring action of bad angels firing out good, of bad money driving out good money. This process radically destabilizes the ontological position of the speaker, even as it both provokes the speaker's desire for increased stability *and* gives him a language in which to gain authority himself. Bad angels driving out good puts a name on a process of subjection and value production.

What we witness in the couplet of sonnet 144, then, is a moment when economic language begins to acquire an authority, a distinct power, to explain social change previously maintained largely by the axis between religion and the state – angels here are not only spiritual anymore. Let me be clear, however, that I emphasize the economic implications of this language not because I think it provides access to a more fundamental substructure, or because I think that the sonnets are, in the last analysis, "about" or "reflect" the well-documented economic changes in the period. Instead, the shift in the significance of angels registers a moment in a long process when the very idea that the economy constitutes a social "base" begins to be imagined. Rather than a mythical reality that irrupts into language, "economy" here is itself part of the classification struggle in the poem.[12] Shakespeare's language actively participates in the production of a new idea of a market and a newly conceptualized social position able to describe it. The categorical struggle of the sequence depicts (as characters, as "angels") the emergence of a name for the social and material instability, the "transformative power," which instigates the speaker's desire.[13] What is at stake in examining the speaker's deployment of economic language is not his position in the universal laws of economics but rather his participation in the production of an economic field and a social position authorized to describe it. Put another way, I see my analysis here not as an example of a new economic criticism but rather as a social critique of which economics, though important, is only a part.[14]

In this light, sonnet 144 cannot be said, strictly speaking, to echo Gresham and his famous law because the law was not actually coined by Gresham at all. As S. T. Bindoff explains, the saying was "let loose" in the nineteenth century by the British economist and former banker Henry Dunning Macleod in three books: *Elements of Political Economy* (1857), *The Theory and Practice of Banking* Volume I (1875), and *The History of Economics* (1896), where Macleod added "unrepentantly that it had been universally accepted."[15] Macleod's denomination of Gresham-as-lawgiver consequently participates in the Enlightenment project of imagining "economics" as a universal discourse, true in every period and in every place. What Macleod's focus on Gresham suggests is less that a universal law is discovered in the 1560s than that Gresham, courtesy of Macleod, participates in the broader production of a social position able to claim its social distinctions as economic universals – the classical political economy that Marx mocks in the *Economic and Philosophic Manuscripts of 1844* because "sie unterstellt, was sie entwickeln soll [it takes shelter in what it should explicate]".[16] For Macleod writing in the nineteenth century, this position seems inextricably connected to the Renaissance. Though he admits that "[t]he fact of the disappearance of good coin in the presence of bad, was noticed by Aristophanes," he insists on crediting Gresham with explaining this monetary puzzle.[17] The connection between Gresham the Renaissance man and economic laws stuck. As Bindoff notes, "[d]espite the swift refutation of the claim (which Macleod later accepted), a hungry public swallowed it whole, and by 1912 the *Dictionary of National Biography* had to concede that the term was 'universally adopted by writers on currency.' Today his Law remains the one thing that everybody knows about Gresham who knows anything about him at all."[18] What this entire episode suggests, then, is that the emergence of an economic field always also depends upon the simultaneous emergence of a social position which legitimates that discourse, a figure who can nominate economy and economists as the source of truth.[19]

Despite the fact that Shakespeare cannot be said to be alluding to "Gresham's Law," the financial implications of the couplet place the *Sonnets* amidst the very social processes which Elizabethans struggled to understand and which were, by the nineteenth century, labeled as "economic." The pun on "angel" is so common (Donne can never leave it alone) that it would be unusual were it *not* present here, and it seems to me to be the central issue for the speaker to try to determine what, exactly, these two angels *are*. Are they religious figures? Characters? Vehicles for venereal disease? Angels-as-coins promises a tacit metadiscourse able to tie together all these possibilities into a coherent meaning: economics emerges from a social position able to link religion, drama, and sex together into a seamless totality. Sonnet 144 places us directly in the middle of the epistemic shift Foucault describes from a sixteenth-century conception of exchange based in "resemblance" to the mercantilism of the Classical Period. During Shakespeare's lifetime, "economy" emerges as money itself becomes "the instrument of the representation and analysis of wealth."[20] But the sonnet crucially also suggests that epistemes always depend on social positions, on agents that can put them into effect.

As a number of historians have suggested, the responses of Shakespeare and his contemporaries to what we would call monetary crisis and inflation were multiple and contradictory. What was at stake in these crises was not only the origin of the value of money, but the question of who could explain the question of value itself. Often enough, the government and the monarch tended to react by trying to reinforce a traditional conception of their authority. Yet their attempts to control inflation exposed the limits of the power of the monarch over monetary value while presenting the monarch as a powerful participant in the market. Queen Elizabeth inherited, the economic historian D. M. Palliser suggests, "the belief that if the debased coins could be replaced with good ones the inflation would stop." While Elizabethans understood that scarcity – particularly bad harvests – drove up prices, they could not explain why "prices rose [when] the circulating medium increased while the supply of goods remained stable."[21] As Norman Jones notes, "[m]onetarists in their economic theory, most Tudor people thought of the economy as static and of inflation as the result of both greed and money whose face value did not match its bullion content."[22] By the time of Elizabeth's reign, coins in England had been massively devalued by Henry VIII's "Great Debasement" – the practice of removing metal from coins while assigning them the same nominal value (the loose modern equivalent is when governments print more money).[23] One principal result of this debasement was an increase in inflation (what contemporaries intriguingly termed "dearth"),[24] and it was precisely to address inflation – which had nearly tripled the price of food in thirty years, while wages showed only modest increases – that Gresham advised Elizabeth to remint all circulating coin so that its value would be restored.[25] But the recall didn't work: in the early 1560s prices remained the same even though the coins contained more bullion. As a result, the crown began considering a new debasement to borrow more money in Antwerp, apparently planning to pay off the loans with bad money (as Henry VIII had done). Rumors of the possible debasement set off a panic and caused a rush on the real estate market. Robert Jones, one of Cecil's servants, claimed that people were willing to pay thirty-six times the value of annual rents for land, perhaps because land seemed to represent value partially exempt from such fluctuations.[26]

The Queen set up a commission to address these monetary troubles in 1563, and its report, presented in 1564, recommended the establishment of an international bank and the use of French and Imperial coins in England. It also blamed bankers, who were thought "able to rule the exchange rather than being controlled themselves by market conditions."[27] In the end, Elizabeth neither debased the coinage nor allowed foreign currency as legal tender, but her government did apply "the other popular economic theory" of the time: "The government moved to punish greedy people by legislating against the importation of foreign goods, fixing wages and prices, enforcing the statutes regulating apparel, and applying a regulatory solution when the markets failed to respond to the currency cure." Currency devaluation appears here as a political and religious problem that called for a political and religious solution. Unfortunately, one effect of these measures was to contribute to a "trade war"[28] between England and the Duke of Alva, the Spanish Governor of the Netherlands. As G. D. Ramsay has shown, "the dependence of the English kingdom and the English economy upon the international emporium at Antwerp in the mid-sixteenth century" – as an outlet for English cloth, as a source for imports, and as a source of royal financial loans – "was, if not total, dangerously tight."[29] The massive political and financial repercussions from Elizabeth's monetary policy may suggest that the centralization of power in the monarchy expressed by the attempt to punish "greedy people" was itself as much a reaction to the contingent value of currency exchange as a reassertion of some quasi-traditional absolute authority. Indeed, the two are hardly separable. One aim of the embargo, according to Sir Walter Mildmay addressing the Privy Council in 1570, was to demonstrate "how this realm might fynde sufficient traffique without [the Netherlands], and had not so much neede of them as by their continuall injuryes they seemed to thinke, and thereby to bring them to more reasonable condicions."[30] Elizabeth's reactions to the currency fluctuations were not only an attempt to impose her institutionalized authority; they were also a paradigmatic instance of a powerful market participant.

This paradoxical position of the monarch – the embodiment of both traditional and market authority – was reinforced sixty years later in the other great financial crisis of this period: the stagnation of the wool trade in the 1620s. The depression in the cornerstone of the English economy had massive financial and social effects, causing unrest among the working poor all over England.[31] Its monetary effects were hotly argued in a series of pamphlets, which began in 1603 but reached their height in the 1620s in the writings of Gerald de Malynes, Edward Misselden, and Thomas Mun. As Joyce Oldham Appleby argues in her seminal study, Malynes, assay master of the English mint and a royal appointee, insisted that the financial crisis should be addressed primarily in terms reinforcing social order. The financial crisis arose, for Malynes, "because merchants, ill-informed and selfishly motivated, overvalued foreign coins and had the audacity to give up more English coins in exchange, thus causing an unnecessary loss." Malynes' solution was "a revitalization of the Royal

Exchange in London, to enforce published official rates of exchange between English and foreign coins."[32] The value of coin should be determined by the monarch, acting as God's representative. As Poovey remarks, such value

both reflected and reflected upon the authority of the king . . . The power to make the extrinsic value of gold and silver correspond to their intrinsic value . . . was a sign of the monarch's authority, and the king's willingness to honor this value (that is, not debase or enhance the currency) was considered [by Malynes] an 'essential Mark' of the monarch's embodiment of justice.[33]

Malynes, in other words, attempted to assert James' monarchical power much as Elizabeth did in her move to punish "greedy people." The value of the currency pointed for him to the "values" inherent in political order.

But whereas under Elizabeth, for example, the Mercers had promised to lower their prices if everyone else did, by the 1620s conditions had changed. Merchants, with their newly imagined expertise over the "market," "were able," Poovey argues, "to enhance the status of their own profession . . . by representing the conventions that prevailed among merchants as providing the necessary *theoretical* support for modern government."[34] Edward Misselden, a Hackney merchant, argued in *The Circle of Commerce . . .* (1623) sharply against Malynes by emphasizing the necessity of profit in trade. Misselden rejected both Malynes' solution and his conception of the problem by pointing out that profit by merchants *drove* exchange, rather than inhibited it: "Exchange transactions enabled merchants to operate on credit, which enabled more people to enter trade. Take the profit out of exchange, and you have inhibited rather than enhanced trade." What this meant was that "traffique" maintained an authority "beyond the power of the prince to control."[35] Opposed to Malynes' conception of "eternal values grounded in the nature of things" and ultimately subject to the power of the prince, Misselden conceived of a world lacking any fixed point of reference outside of "traffique," the endless circle of international mercantile commerce itself.

The other participant in the debates of the 1620s, Thomas Mun, located the authority to articulate, understand, and control this new economic sphere in the figure of the merchant and his control over the new language of economics, particularly the double entry account book that permitted merchants to articulate the balance of trade. This new economic field required "specific knowledge . . . to understand its workings," and this knowledge was constructed in part by excluding those parts of the market which could not be controlled (but which were simultaneously necessary for profit) – for instance, the risk involved in bills of exchange. This assertion of authority through exclusion was effected in part, Poovey suggests, by gendering the risky aspects feminine; the authority of merchants emerges by excluding women "from the ranks of those considered eligible to produce knowledge" about market transactions. Indeed, this "exclusion was necessary because the unlawfulness associated with women could be made to stand for other kinds of unlawfulness essential to the idea of a law-abiding market."[36] As a result, "economics" emerges as a discourse dominated by the new "objective" language of accounting; a discourse which implicitly challenged the authority of the crown with the authority of the merchant who has mastered double-entry bookkeeping; and a discourse which is gendered as exclusively male in order to separate those facets of the market which are fundamentally and necessarily uncontrollable. And yet all of these factors also depend upon the emergence of a social position able to put them into motion. For Poovey,

[t]he tendency of mercantile accommodation to create a positional status system instead of referring status to birth was the implicit issue in the debate between Misselden and Malynes: Malynes wanted to preserve a social order in which value was an expression of identity, whereas Misselden insisted that value was a function of various relationships within the system of commerce as a whole.[37]

Within the emergence of mercantilism, and within bad angels firing good ones out, is a fundamental shift in the mode of producing social distinction itself. The power of the merchant, and the power of Shakespeare's speaker, emerges as a "positional" system, one based upon the mastery of economic discourse rather than based upon noble status.

Published in 1609 and probably written and revised over a period of more than ten years,[38] Shakespeare's *Sonnets* emerges between the currency crisis at the start of Elizabeth's reign and the mercantile debates of the 1620s. The work responds in ways reminiscent of other reactions to the gradual growth of the market I have just briefly outlined. In the young man sonnets, the speaker reacts much like Elizabeth and Malynes by attempting to ground value in the identity of a dominant noble status. This attempt is, however, internally contradictory, since it is in part the emergent market which erodes noble hegemony but which provides the speaker the authority and the desire to (re)produce this noble imaginary. In the dark lady sonnets, the speaker reacts much like Mun. Though the speaker does not pretend to control an "objective" language, he does seek to naturalize the language of exchange by labeling as female those portions of the market from which he seeks to extricate both himself and the nobility. And he does both of these by trying to represent the young man as a lyric object.

Use and a man right fair

As generations of commentators have discovered, it is simply impossible to identify conclusively who the young man is.[39] The mystery is not simply a matter of a lack of biographical details. "Who is the youth" is also a question the speaker himself asks. For it is the perceived lack in the youth – his lack of "increase," the speaker's dissatisfaction with him – which provokes the speaker to attempt to represent him as an idealized object. What is clear about the youth's elusive and unstable identity, however, is that it is centered on his social standing and his gender. As Margreta de Grazia suggests, the real "scandal" of Shakespeare's sequence is its obsession with class. She argues that the young man is linked to the "dominant class" by the speaker's concern to reproduce "fairest creatures" in the first line of sonnet 1:

there can be no pretence of fair being either an abstract value like the Platonic Good or a disinterested one like the Kantian Beautiful. *Fair* is the distinguishing attribute of the dominant class, not unlike Bourdieu's *taste* that serves both to distinguish the dominant class and, by distinguishing it, to keep it dominant. The first seventeen sonnets urging the fair youth to marry and beget a son have an open and explicit social function: to reproduce, like an Althusserian state apparatus, the *status quo* by reproducing a fair young man[.][40]

What the speaker himself desires, in other words, is something like the "status quo" that maintains social order. And yet the very ambiguity of the term "fair" (and, as we will see, of the similarly vague "free") implies that this status quo is not nearly as dominant as the speaker would like. After all, if his desire is to reproduce just such a ruling nobility, the cumulative effect of the sequence is that such reproduction does not take place. As Thomas M. Greene suggests, the "worth of the friend may reside after all in the poet's own fancy."[41] De Grazia's invocation of a status-quo social hierarchy (facilitated by the tacit equation of Bourdieu and Althusser) erases the process of distinguishing here, positing an ideological state apparatus that the speaker labors to *imagine* by making "status quo" and "Platonic Good" appear to be synonyms.[42] The young man is not an addressee; he is the object of the speaker's desire. Even though de Grazia recognizes the biographical identity of the young man as largely a product of Malone and his post-romantic readers, she nevertheless posits a real group of people here: "[t]he 'private friends' among whom according to Francis Meres these sonnets circulated as well as the patron to whom the collection is ostensibly dedicated can be assumed to have recognized this rhetoric as a blueprint for reproducing the fair values of the dominant class."[43] Yet this sonnet is not a wink to a preexisting class but an on-going effort at making social distinctions;

whereas de Grazia views the opposition between the young man and the dark lady as alternatives between "hierarchy and anarchy,"[44] social positions in the sequence are not clearly bifurcated. The sonnets never definitively articulate the youth's social standing because how such standing might be construed constitutes one central preoccupation of the work.

The desire for a status quo should be understood as the speaker's lyric desire; the imagined stability of a dominant class reveals the position of the speaker in a mutable narrative, not the actually existing conditions of early modern England. Such a relation informs the attempt in the opening sonnet to reconcile a metaphor of natural "increase" with the financial implications of increase – interest on a loan:

> From fairest creatures we desire increase,
> That thereby beauty's rose might never die,
> But as the riper should by time decease,
> His tender heir might bear his memory;
> But thou, contracted to thine own bright eyes,
> Feed'st thy light's flame with self-substantial fuel,
> Making a famine where abundance lies,
> Thyself thy foe, to thy sweet self too cruel.
> Thou that art now the world's fresh ornament
> And only herald to the gaudy spring
> Within thine own bud buriest thy content,
> And, tender churl, mak'st waste in niggarding.
>   Pity the world, or else this glutton be,
>   To eat the world's due, by the grave and thee.

On the one hand, "increase" here means quite specifically a child, a "tender heir." Procreation is figured as a natural phenomenon: "rose," "riper," "spring," and even "famine" are all words conveying a sense of a circular, agricultural cycle tied to the seasons, so that "increase" also means something like "harvest" (a sense used in sonnet 97, "The teeming autumn, big with rich increase"). The "tender heir" will eventually also grow "riper" like his father, with the result that familial reproduction is closely tied to agricultural production and *vice versa*. "Increase" in this sense is an effectively static term: nature is continually produced and reproduced. In procreating, the young man is (according to the speaker) simply participating in the natural order. Like an Althusserian Ideological State Apparatus, change in this cyclical sense is understood as the re-production of stability and social order, what Althusser famously terms the "reproduction of the conditions of production."[45] Heirs take over their father's estates, thereby maintaining both the agricultural production seen as a basis of this "natural" view and the social order that is itself recognized as a circular reinforcement of similarity.

But "increase" also means financial interest or "profit."[46] It suggests the production of an "heir" who "tenders," pays off in money his debt, a sense picked up elsewhere in the sonnet: "heir," "abundance," "niggarding." But more importantly, "increase" as a financial concept fills the void left as the social, agricultural, and putatively natural order breaks down. "Increase" as interest becomes a new, alternative means of achieving this same stability, set inside "natural" metaphors invoking agricultural reproduction and the changing of the seasons. This metaphoric combination is expressed in the final line, where "this glutton" eats "the world's due" – "due" here meaning both the natural expectation of the world as well as the interest which the young man owes to the world.

Tying the re-production of a ruling class to "increase" points to the radical social implications, also examined in the last chapter, of the gradual shift from defining nobles through land to defining them through control of capital. Whereas expressing the reproduction of a ruling class in agricultural metaphors attempts to tie the authority and value of that status to the imagined circularity of harvests, reproducing nobility through interest – that is, through usury – locates authority and value in a contingent series of exchanges, in capital.[47] Rather than a "tender heir," the youth becomes a "tender churl." "Tender churl" is certainly, as Kerrigan comments in his notes to the poem, "a bundle of paradoxes" suggesting "sensitive boor," "loving begrudger," and "young old skinflint," but its social implications directly undermine the speaker's attempts to reproduce "fairest creatures." According to the *OED*, while the first meaning of "churl" is simply "a man, *esp.* 'man' as correlative to 'wife,'" its second and third meanings are tied directly to social position. "Churl" means a man "without rank; a member of the third or lowest rank," "the antithesis of *king, noble, gentle*." It also means a "tenant in pure villeinage; a serf," and it is through these social implications that it acquires the sense of a "rustic" or "boor." Rather than a circular reproduction of natural order, increase as interest reconceptualizes the "tender heir" as a participant in an endless, contingent narrative of "increase" which *undermines* his nobility – the very social distinctions the sonnet attempts to draw.

The sonnet tries to naturalize such usury by attributing greed to the youth when he does *not* produce "increase," rather than when he does. But the "greed" attributed to the young man is no less paradoxical than Elizabeth's attempt to punish "greedy" people. The youth eats "the world's *due*," rather than, as sonnet 2 suggests, producing a child that will "sum [his] count." Natural balance occurs as a result of financial order, not the other way around. This alteration becomes explicit in sonnet 4 in the idea of a "loan." The sonnet begins by figuring the youth's procreation once again in largely natural and static terms: his beauty is his "legacy," "Nature's bequest." The youth is expected to pay his debt to nature, and the payment itself constitutes a sort of natural balance – what he has been loaned he gives back. Yet the sequence becomes more and more complicated as, in sonnet 4, the terms of that loan and the position of the debtor become less and less clear:

> Unthrifty loveliness, why dost thou spend
> Upon thyself thy beauty's legacy ?
> Nature's bequest gives nothing, but doth lend,
> And being frank she lends to those are free.
> Then, beauteous niggard, why dost thou abuse
> The bounteous largess given thee to give ?
> Profitless usurer, why dost thou use
> So great a sum of sums yet canst not live ?
> For having traffic with thyself alone
> Thou of thyself thy sweet self dost deceive;
> Then how when nature calls thee to be gone,
> What acceptable audit canst thou leave ?
>   Thy unused beauty must be tombed with thee,
>   Which, usèd, lives th'executor to be.

"[F]ree," the last word of the first quatrain, is of course a pun meaning, as Booth points out, both "generous" and "licentious." The youth would be more generous to the world were he more sexually active – if he would produce an heir. But Booth also notes that "free" here suggests "noble," and Kerrigan proposes that "Shakespeare playfully glances at the stock phrase 'frank and free,' meaning 'not a serf,' 'nobly open in temperament,' and 'without let or hindrance.'" Through the word "free," the cliché of paying a debt to nature through death (a pun Shakespeare is particularly fond of in, for instance, *1 Henry IV*) is quickly mediated through a complex and contradictory conception of social status and land ownership: what constitutes a "free" loan? The social stability implied in "legacy" and "bequest" gives way, by the end of the quatrain, to unstable and uncertain social positions. Is the youth "noble" or merely "not a serf"? In what sense is his status tied to land ownership? In the space between the two senses of "free" – both "of noble temperament" and "not a serf" – lies a vast social terrain, as we saw in Spenser's own awkward social identities in the previous chapter, or in the uncomfortable proximity of merchants and nobles that Richard Helgerson charts.[48]

The ambiguity of social standing arises, moreover, specifically in relation to usury. The trouble with the status quo, as line seven puts it, is that it is a "Profitless usurer." The young man represents the worst of two concepts – he fails to produce profit even though he loans at interest to himself. The poem seeks to create the inverse of this – a "profitable non-usurer," so to speak, one who generates gain while maintaining social distinctions. As sonnet 6 usefully puts it, "That use is not forbidden usury, / Which happies those that pay the willing loan" (5–6). The speaker wants to produce a class which can generate profit while simultaneously concealing that generation. The result would be a sort of "balance," an "acceptable audit" that recalls the cyclical natural imagery of sonnet 1.[49] Sonnet 4 works toward such a justification by identifying Nature herself as just such an entity. She loans at interest, but the repayment of her loan produces a balance, a circular closure. That the youth's "unus'd beauty" lies with him when he dies implies that he has a finite store of beauty. But it also implies a beauty not put to "use," a beauty not employed in the service of generating interest. Much like Malynes, the speaker tries to ground exchange within a metaphoric "nature." Yet he does so because the identity of the youth – his nobility – seems to depend entirely on "use" and interest: "Thy unused beauty must be tombed with thee." Thus if the dependence of the youth's identity on exchange and use is partially obscured inside the speaker's "natural" metaphors, natural order itself also becomes conceived of in terms of exchange.

While the terms of exchange complicate the youth's social standing, they more specifically identify the *speaker's* social position within the market narrative from which he seeks to distance the youth. In sonnet 1, when the speaker claims "From fairest creatures *we* desire increase," that "we" is no less a social marker than "fairest." It distinguishes the speaker *from* the "fairest creatures" – he is neither noble nor "fair" – while also, by articulating our "desire," identifying him with that vaguely defined position of open participants in monetary exchange. The very fact that he utilizes financial language to articulate his desire for "fairest creatures" places the speaker inside the narrative of exchange.

The often remarked on compulsion of the speaker to distinguish himself from the youth thus should be read in part as a social anxiety. As Sedgwick notes, "[i]n the sonnets addressed to the fair youth, there is plenty of dissonance, doubleness, and self-division, but it is all described as located outside the youth himself, and whenever possible, within the speaker."[50] This insistent separation of the youth from the speaker occurs perhaps most famously in sonnet 73, where the speaker imagines the young man's own perceptions of him ("That time of year thou mayst in me behold") in order to reinforce the stability of the observer ("This thou perceiv'st, which makes thy love more strong"). The familiar enabling fiction of sonnet writing – that the absence of the object produces the presence of the writing – is consequently given a specific social dynamic. The youth must be absent so that he does not become contaminated by the market narrative and, more specifically, by the social position identified with that narrative – namely, the speaker himself. Poetry becomes a function and product of the youth's distance, not of his presence. In sonnet 30, solitary lyric thinking on the youth restores "All loses" of the "sad *account*," the "summon[s]" (*sum*-on, totaling) of "remembrance of things past." The lyric remembrance thereby provides the "acceptable audit" (4.12), a financial balance, the speaker seeks to construct.

Most explicitly, in the obsequious sonnet 26, the final desire of the speaker is not to join with the love but to stay away. The exaggerated, anachronistic, feudal language of the poem itself enacts the socially stabilizing relationship in lyric which the socially discontinuous narrative provokes; in other words, here is a lyric *desire*, not a transparent record of actual experience:

> Lord of my love, to whom in vassalage
> Thy merit hath my duty strongly knit,
> To thee I send this written ambassage,
> To witness duty, not to show my wit –
> Duty so great, which wit so poor as mine
> May make seem bare, in wanting words to show it,
> But that I hope some good conceit of thine
> In thy soul's thought, all naked, will bestow it;
> Till whatsoever star that guides my moving
> Points on me graciously with fair aspect,
> And puts apparel on my tattered loving
> To show me worthy of thy sweet respect.
>   Then may I dare to boast how I do love thee,
>   Till then, not show my head where thou mayst prove me.

The symbiotic relation between lord and vassal is mutually reinforcing only in the speaker's continued absence.[51] Were the lord able to "prove" the speaker, and, conversely, were the speaker able to "prove" the lord, the relationship would evaporate. Thus to read this sonnet as evidence of an existing patron-client relationship misses the point of the poem: that such a relationship only exists ideally, in the speaker's lyric. The language of patronage here is less an extension of a traditional social organization than a delicate balancing act between latent social mobility and the idealized feudalism to which it gives rise. Whatever the relation of Shakespeare and the *Sonnets* to the mysterious "W. H." of the dedication, the sonnet strongly argues that such a patron-client relationship is an ideal produced and provoked by the position from which the speaker speaks.[52] The search for the identity of "W. H.," like the search for the identity of the young man generally, replicates at the level of criticism the speaker's lyric desire for the production of "fairest creatures." He wants to imagine himself as a vassal rather than as a writer produced by the vicissitudes of market exchanges.

Such subtle lyricism threatens to collapse in those sonnets where narrative becomes most explicit. What most obviously ties together the poems which invoke a love triangle or complaint about the rival poet is the presence of other characters which intrude upon, undermine, and provoke the speaker's lyricism. The effect of highlighting such narratives is not so much to remind us of a story, or a history taking place outside the sonnets – though it does do that – so much as blatantly to emphasize the speaker's own position in a relational field. Rather than a disembodied or internalized voice, the speaker becomes clearly subject to the forces he describes. In the sections of the sequence most explicitly concerned with the rival poet or the dark lady, the speaker appears not, as in sonnet 30, summoning and controlling remembrances of things past to produce an acceptable audit; he instead appears as an uncomfortable participant, a sort of character himself. Whatever one's attitude toward the speaker in the rival poet sonnets (he is wronged, or jealous, or petty), judgment of him is always made in relation to the implied narrative within which he is situated. The effect is similar to the shifts in our understanding of Hamlet's "To be or not to be" soliloquy by the ways his speech is situated in the scene. The extent that Hamlet is aware of being watched by Polonius and Claudius (which must always be a directorial decision) dramatically alters the "lyricism" of his meditation. The framing of the speech by the scene calls into question the degree to which that meditation is an instrumental act within the narrative of the play: to what extent is Hamlet "acting" his soliloquy? Similarly in the *Sonnets*. The more explicitly embedded a particular sonnet is within a narrative field, the more limited its lyric scope. And yet just as Hamlet's meditation on un-being is in part provoked by the actions of Claudius and Polonius, so the lyric idealizations of the speaker of the sonnets emerge as a reaction to the narrative which lurks in each lyric.[53] Hamlet's authority – and much of the power of the "To be or not to be" soliloquy – emerges less from some secret interior power than his ability to manipulate the narrative which creates him.

The idealization of the youth, the desire to depict him as a sort of ideological apparatus, is consequently an expression of the speaker's own decidedly un-idealized position. In Fineman's terms, his identity is fractured, but it coheres in its articulation of that very brokenness through its imaginary idealization. The speaker's disposition emerges less from his ability to exit time or overcome mutability than from his ability to keep both the young man and his readers concentrating on the lyric imaginary. It is a mark of the historical triumph of this social position that readers since Malone have focused so obsessively on the lyric idealization, rather than on the construction of the desire that makes such an imaginary. Indeed, to even mention the forces which provoke such lyricism has seemed to many readers to miss everything beautiful or meaningful about Shakespeare's work – even though, of course, this particular beauty only emerges when a reader identifies with and tacitly accepts the social position the speaker is creating. To accept the speaker's idealization is to accept his categorization, the sort of romantic moment we saw in chapter two when Shakespeare's unique feelings become everyone's feelings. If, as sonnet 116 famously puts it, "love"

> is an ever fixèd mark
> That looks on tempests and is never shaken;
> It is the star to every wandering bark,
> Whose worth's unknown, although his height be taken

the speaker himself is in the ship looking up at the star. Despite the tentativeness of sonnet 116 – its endorsement and definition of love through negatives ("Let me not"; "love is not love"; "Love's not Time's fool"; "Love alters not") and the use of the subjunctive in the couplet ("If this be error") followed by more negatives ("I never writ, nor no man ever loved") – the effect of the sonnet is an endorsement and powerful articulation of an ideal, not a slippery undermining of that pronouncement. The concretization of a social position occurs when we no longer notice that the speaker and his language are in the boat.

Yet as Greene insists, such idealization is always internally divided: "poetry can never be idolatrously one and can never find the metaphor, the example, which knows no difference. The poet's real enemy is . . . the voice inside himself."[54] Fineman similarly describes the way the sonnets addressed to the young man "characteristically resist and conflictedly inflect their most ideal expressions of visionary unity, the way they chafe against the 'constancy' to which they are 'confined.'"[55] In sonnet 84, for instance, the young man appears less as a noble imaginary than as an irritating airhead or "dumb blond."[56] The youth appears as a character whose vanity challenges the "store" "immurèd" in the "confine," the ideal portrait, presented in the first quatrain.

> Who is it that says most which can say more
> Than this rich praise – that you alone are you,
> In whose confine immurèd is the store
> Which should example where you equal grew ?
> Lean penury within that pen doth dwell
> That to his subject lends not some small glory,
> But he that writes of you, if he can tell
> That you are you, so dignifies his story;
> Let him but copy what in you is writ,
> Not making worse what nature made so clear,
> And such a counterpart shall fame his wit,
> Making his style admirèd everywhere.
>   You to your beauteous blessings add a curse,
>   Being fond on praise, which makes your praises worse.

Like Spenser's lady in *Amoretti* 45, the youth is not paying sufficient attention to the idealized form being created for him. The effect is to undermine the self-sufficiency of the youth, his status as a noble object, and to set him as a subject amidst the very narrative of exchange (robbing, lending) the speaker is at pains to separate him from. Yet the materialization of the youth undermines the speaker's power as well, particularly as he tries to differentiate himself from other poets. He wants to set his verse apart from mere fawners who "lend" their subjects "some final glory" by admitting in the couplet the difference, the interest, which make this sonnet more than "lean penury." If the best poetry simply writes "That you are you" and copies "what in you is writ" (because it merely records the perfection of the youth), the speaker sets apart his own praise (as Fineman insists)[57] by specifically including a criticism of the youth – that he is "fond on praise." On the one hand, the poem *is* merely a reflection of the youth, and a truer one than that written by fawning poets, because it includes in its idealizing portrait the vanity of the young man. The answer to the opening question – "Who is it that says most, which can say more, / Then this rich praise" – is the speaker himself, who both presents an idealized lyric isolation ("most") and says "more" by admitting the youth's shortcomings in the couplet. On the other hand, such an addition "add[s] a curse" because the superiority of the speaker's verse depends upon his ability to include the very difference which lyric idealism seeks to exclude. Like Nature's loan in sonnet 4, the speaker's authority lies in his ability to admit "increase" into his portrait of the youth: the effort to create "rich praise," a profitable non-usurer. Yet the shortcomings of the youth make "your praises," that is, the speaker's poetry, "worse."

The effort to distinguish his verse from the rival poet undermines the social distinctions the sonnet seeks to make. Yet these poetic failures simultaneously demarcate, with great precision, the social position of the speaker. We should thus not only see the construction of nobility here as, in Murray Krieger's words, a "noble prehistory" or utopian nostalgia free from the vicissitudes of mere economics.[58] Instead, the desire to wrest nobility from the economic, and the continual failure of that desire, also socially distinguishes the speaker. While the mark of nobility in sonnet 4, for instance, is the ability to generate interest while concealing the usury involved – to employ, in other words, a mode of profit not associated with nobility to reinforce nobility – in sonnet 78 the speaker represents his loss of exclusive representation of the young man as a loss of his "use":

> So oft have I invoked thee for my Muse
> And found such fair assistance in my verse
> As every alien pen hath got my use
> And under thee their poesy disperse.

Rather than controlling the relation between himself and his youth / Muse as a monopoly which conceals its "use," the speaker has his "increase" stolen away from him. The lyric ideal of the youth is "dispersed," that is, dissipated, because it is, like interest, distributed. In relation to "every alien pen," the nobility of the youth comes to be seen as merely "use," as the interest the speaker is able to generate. The speaker is distinguished from his competition by his superior ability to generate interest. Yet the fact that the not-fair, not noble speaker *creates* interest – and, effectively, nobility itself – recasts that noble imaginary into an exchange economy which provoked the desire for it. The sonnets present an ideal through their ability to generate "increase," their ability to "loan" to the youth as lyric object qualities the youth as character does not necessarily possess. And the very fact that the project of creating an ideal is conceived of as an "acceptable audit," an audit which, in the final sonnet to the young man, "answered must be" (126.13), betrays the speaker's noble, lyric object as the product of the "use" the usurious speaker himself controls.

The speaker's desire to construct the youth as a noble, lyric object is thus always at cross-purposes: the failure, and success, of distinctions distinguishes the distinguisher. As sonnet 21 famously puts it, "I will not praise, that purpose not to sell." The immediate context for this remark is the speaker's disparaging of other poets who, "Stirred by a painted beauty," use "heaven itself for ornament." But of course the speaker himself also praises the youth. The final line of the poem tries to separate the speaker and his representation of the youth from the pack of would merchandisers (I will not praise because I do not intend to sell). But "I will not praise, that purpose not to sell" also means "I will not praise *unless* I intend to sell" – a sense reinforced by the proverb the line echoes ("He praises who wishes to sell").[59] The very language the speaker utilizes to distinguish the youth continually threatens to collapse back into the market narrative which it helps to create, and his own social position emerges as the expert best able to describe this imminent collapse.

Misuse, forswearing, and the dark lady

In the young man sonnets, the speaker's social distinction emerges from his ability to use his position in a narrative of exchange to promote a lyric ideal that, in turn, seeks to conceal the "use" and "increase" that produce such ideal "fairness" – a stable, imaginary noble status. In the dark lady sonnets, the speaker's position emerges instead from his capacity to label this narrative as feminine. He differentiates himself as he uses gender in addition to lyric objectification to separate the youth from the market. Like the authority of Mun's merchant-accountant, the speaker identifies femininity with "the kind of unlawfulness essential to the idea of a law-abiding market."[60] Unlike Mun, however, the speaker neither embraces a mode of representation that seeks to conceal its status as representation – what Poovey identifies as double entry bookkeeping or the putatively objective language of mathematics – nor entirely distances himself from the dark lady. Indeed, as often as he misogynistically demonizes her, he also identifies with her. In admiring the dark lady – an admiration which he himself puzzles over – the speaker betrays an admiration for the very social forces that he seeks to marginalize, demonize, and finally gain some control over.

In suggesting that the "demonization" of the dark lady contributes to the speaker's authority, I am again following Sedgwick's reading. She argues that the relations "between men" become sexually charged precisely as they create the opportunity to construct and consolidate social power. While women become conduits for male homosocial relations (figured most prominently as the "hell" of sonnets 135–136), they remain both literally and symbolically necessary for men to become men: "Only women have the power to make men less than men within this world. At the same time, to be fully a man requires having obtained the instrumental use of a woman, having *risked* transformation by her."[61]

As Poovey suggests, the identification of women with those p
the market which could not be controlled was central to the em
a new kind of authority within and over a newly conceptualize
By equating the dark lady with the narrative of change, exch
social mobility, the speaker attempts to extricate the young
that narrative by emphasizing his masculinity; but the speaker also
establishes himself as a kind of financial expert who is able to distinguish
the masculine and feminine parts of the economy. Such expertise emerges
as he "risks" identifying with the dark lady – that is, with a mutable
economy he cannot finally control.

As we have already seen, in sonnet 144 the speaker identifies the lady
not only as his "worser spirit"; he also identifies her as the agent which
disintegrates the static binaries that "suggest" and imaginatively stabilize
him. She is the "evil" of the psychomachia and ultimately responsible for
setting the narrative in motion. What that narrative finally involves is his
"bad angel" firing out his "good one." Behind the desire for a stable
identity defined by binaries lies a complex constellation of economic,
social, and political forces entangled in the problems of inflation and
the value of currency. In sonnet 134, which has become a sort of test case
for economically oriented readings of the *Sonnets*,[62] the speaker is even
more explicit in identifying the lady with the socially disruptive power of
such forces. While he pleads for the youth to become a profitable non-
usurer in sonnet 4 to "naturalize" and obscure the economic sources of his
social distinction, in sonnet 134 both the speaker and the youth are
"mortgaged" and generally in the debt of a true usurer, the dark lady
herself:

> So, now I have confessed that he is thine,
> And I myself am mortgaged to thy will,
> Myself I'll forfeit, so that other mine
> Thou wilt restore to be my comfort still.
> But thou wilt not, nor he will not be free,
> For thou art covetous, and he is kind;
> He learned but surety-like to write for me
> Under that bond that him as fast doth bind.
> The statute of thy beauty thou wilt take,
> Thou usurer that put'st forth all to use,
> And sue a friend came debtor for my sake;
> So him I lose through my unkind abuse.
>   Him have I lost, thou hast both him and me;
>   He pays the whole, and yet am I not free.

She is "covetous," a "usurer that put's forth all to use"; in sonnet 133,
which 134 builds on, she has "engrossed" (l. 6), that is, "bought up in

gross" (Kerrigan), "taken exclusive possession of" (Booth), "gained a monopoly" (Duncan-Jones) on the speaker's "next self," the youth. Her resolute financial determination will not permit the sort of mediated "use," profit used to reinforce social hierarchy, for which the speaker himself pleads. The first quatrain makes clear that the dark lady is in complete economic control, so that the only means the speaker has to make the youth "free" is to offer himself as "forfeit." Forfeit here carries a technical economic sense of property lost as a result of the mortgage of line one, and the second quatrain clarifies the social implications of this financial control. The dark lady's covetousness immediately calls the youth's social status into question. Since he is under her "bond," the youth cannot be "free" ("noble" or simply "not a serf") even though the speaker hints that the youth is by blood noble ("kind" – a sentiment also suggested in the couplet of sonnet 82: "And their gross painting might be better used / Where cheeks need blood; in thee it is abused"). In the speaker's presentation, the youth's nobility depends centrally on severing him from participation in the financial transactions the dark lady controls. The speaker's attempt to "forfeit" himself to make the youth "free" is in part an attempt to re-establish a nobility which has fallen into the control of a usurer. In refusing the speaker's forfeit, the dark lady effectively erases social stability, the creation of a new (if imaginary) social nobility. The result is that the speaker, like the youth, is "not free" (line 14) – not noble and under financial restraint to the dark lady.

The dark lady is consequently "unkind": her covetousness in line six means that she is not of the youth's "kind" – that is, noble, as in line 12 where her "abuse" of the speaker is "unkind." But the speaker, of course, is also "unkind"; the "unkind abuse" of line 12 is quite specifically his own. The youth "came debtor for my sake; / So him I lose through my unkind abuse"; he has taught the youth "but surety-like to write for me," an act which is "unkind" because it does not separate the youth from use. The speaker's abuse, and not only the dark lady's, has brought the youth into this financial arrangement. Their unkindness, in short, marks them as both of the same kind – not noble, but demarcated by their economic acumen.

As the argumentative length to which one must resort to make sense of this sonnet implies, the tacit identification between the speaker and the lady is nevertheless not much emphasized here. Instead, the speaker repeatedly depicts himself as under her power ("So, now I have confessed that he is thine, / And I myself am mortgaged to thy will"; "thou hast both him and me"). This confession nevertheless itself becomes a means by which he tries to extricate the youth, and himself, from her narrative. In emphasizing her power, the speaker more closely identifies the social disruptiveness of her social position with her gender – despite the clear implication that the masculine speaker himself is as responsible as she is for the youth not being "free." Much as in sonnet 84, the speaker both identifies himself with the social position of usurers and tries to conceal that identification as he endorses the youth's noble status and concedes narrative power to the lady. And much as in sonnet 144, the speaker associates the dark lady with the action which sets the relationship – financial and otherwise – in motion. The dark lady and her gender thus become identified with those forces – social and economic – which the speaker cannot control but which are necessary for him to have any authority at all.

Such a reading partially accounts for a sense of the speaker's attitude toward the dark lady as "not so much passionate devotion to a distantly cruel mistress as elaborate mockery of a woman who is no more than a sexual convenience"[63]; the "elaborate mockery" of her "misuse" of use, and the close identification of her voracious sexual appetite with this misuse, can be made to stand in for a wide variety of social disruptions. Yet it does not account for those moments of affection and identification we see throughout the dark lady section. By "affection" I mean desire for the dark lady not simply as a means to further the speaker's authority through his relationship with the young man (and all the construction of social positions that involves), but also an explicit desire for and identification with qualities she herself seems to possess (at least as far as the speaker represents her). Demonizing the dark lady and equating her with a narrative of social and economic disruption gives the speaker the lyric power to reinforce a noble imaginary. Why then does he seem to like her ? It is a question he asks himself repeatedly (in, for example, sonnets 139, 146, 147, 148, 149) and most explicitly in sonnet 150:

> O, from what power hast thou this powerful might
> With insufficiency my heart to sway ?
> To make me give the lie to my true sight
> And swear that brightness doth not grace the day ?
> Whence hast thou this becoming of things ill
> That in the very refuse of thy deeds
> There is such strength and warrantise of skill
> That in my mind thy worst all best exceeds ?
> Who taught thee how to make me love thee more,
> The more I hear and see just cause of hate ?
> O, though I love what others do abhor,
> With others thou shouldst not abhor my state.
>   If thy unworthiness raised love in me,
>   More worthy I to be beloved of thee.

The question of the dark lady's attractiveness is puzzling for the speaker because in asking it he is also seeking to identify precisely that "power," that social configuration, which both enables him to speak at all while provoking his desire for the young man as well: it "raised love in me." The dark lady's attractiveness lies in her "insufficiency," her "unworthiness," and her ability to make these things seem so desirable that, against his own reason, he finds that "brightness doth not grace the day" as much as she does. What is finally both most attractive and troubling about the dark lady is the extent to which her social position, and her power, are the same as the speaker's. She too is a member of the "we" in sonnet 1 that desires "increase" from "fairest creatures"; he, in turn, maintains the same "insufficiency" he finds in her – "others" seem to "abhor" his "state."

Yet as the gender difference implies, and as the speaker's confusion attests, this "we" is not a class consciousness; it may be a class-in-itself, but it is not a class-for-itself. Instead, we see here a process, not an integral class. To the extent that this process has a name, it is blackness, not bourgeois. In sonnet 127 he finds the lady's dark eyes so "becoming of their woe" that he sets himself amidst the socially level and undistinguished populace ("every tongue") that "says beauty should look" like she does:

> In the old age black was not counted fair,
> Or, if it were, it bore not beauty's name;
> But now is black beauty's successive heir,
> And beauty slandered with a bastard shame:
> For since each hand hath put on nature's power,
> Fairing the foul with art's false borrowed face,
> Sweet beauty hath no name, no holy bower,
> But is profaned, if not lives in disgrace.
> Therefore my mistress' eyes are raven black,
> Her eyes so suited, and they mourners seem
> At such who, not born fair, no beauty lack,
> Sland'ring creation with a false esteem.
>   Yet so they mourn, becoming of their woe,
>   That every tongue says beauty should look so.

The first quatrain sets up an alternative conception of heredity to the "fair" ideological apparatus established in the first seventeen sonnets. Black has become heir to beauty because "art's false borrowed face" has made true beauty indistinguishable from those who "no beauty lack" through their use of cosmetics and art. His mistress' eyes are consequently beautiful because their blackness allows them to mourn the demise of beauty, even as "every tongue says beauty should look" like her eyes. But of course, at the same time, her eyes aren't "born fair" either; they are *made* fair by "art's borrowed face": they are "so suited," that is, appareled, and "they mourners *seem*[.]" The sonnet and the speaker participate in the same social change from fair to black which is embodied in the dark lady herself, and which is suggested by the young man's failure to reproduce. The "old age" of fairness has been replaced, through the actions of the speaker, the dark lady, and (so to speak) the inaction of the young man, by a new process of social differentiation: blackness. Both he and she are "not born fair" – not born noble. Their social position is defined instead by its cosmetics, its art, and its ability to "put on nature's power." "*Every* tongue says beauty should look so" because "*every* tongue" endorses the socially mobile forces which allow them to speak at all.

Thus the speaker's celebration of his relationship with the dark lady in sonnet 138 is, at the same time, a celebration of their means of social distinction: their mutual and exemplary capacity to "lie" to and with each other. He praises their ability to imagine themselves not as static lyric ideals but as characters that they both recognize as fake. He plays "some untutored youth," and she portrays a woman who is true and just:

> When my love swears that she is made of truth
> I do believe her, though I know she lies,
> That she might think me some untutored youth,
> Unlearnèd in the world's false subtleties.
> Thus vainly thinking that she thinks me young,
> Although she knows my days are past the best,
> Simply I credit her false-speaking tongue;
> On both sides thus is simple truth suppressed.
> But wherefore says she not she is unjust ?
> And wherefore say not I that I am old ?
> O, love's best habit is in seeming trust,
> And age in love loves not to have years told.
> > Therefore I lie with her, and she with me,
> > And in our faults by lies we flattered be.

What defines their relationship here is his (and implicitly hers as well) ability to "credit her false-speaking tongue." "Credit" here picks up on the economic overtones of the source of the power of the dark lady and the speaker; for instance, it draws upon the same shifting locations of value embedded in "bad angels." Like "bad angels," this "credit" is a cultural and social phenomenon, an ability to manipulate and perform a variety of "habits" that closely resembles that performative power Shakespeare insistently and incessantly celebrates on stage. If in sonnet 23 the speaker claims to be like "an unperfect actor on the stage, / Who with his fear is put besides his part," in sonnet 138 they are both virtuoso actors.

The desire of the speaker for the dark lady should consequently be seen as a conflicted endorsement of his own social position: the capacity of his lyricism (his lying) to produce an ideal in the figure of the young man, and his ability to master the intricacies of the social forces embedded in the sequence's narrative. But while the speaker's power originates in his ability to perform within this narrative of social, economic, and political instability, the very fact of that instability simultaneously provokes a desire for social, political, and ontological stability – his desire for the young man and his hatred of the dark lady. The "dark age" of the dark lady sonnets is thus never subsequent to the "fair" age of the young man sonnets; it is instead, as Fineman repeatedly insists, the dialectical opposite of the same social forces that produce the "desire" of the "we" in sonnet 1. The speaker's demonization and feminization of narrative in the figure of the dark lady is intensely problematic precisely because it always also demonizes the speaker himself.

Only usurers write these sorts of sonnets. While the viciousness of sonnet 152 is a classic example of Renaissance misogyny, that hatred also emerges because of the uncomfortable similarity the speaker sees between himself and the dark lady:

> In loving thee thou knowst I am forsworn,
> But thou art twice forsworn, to me love swearing;
> In act thy bed-vow broke, and new faith torn
> In vowing new hate after new love bearing.
> But why of two oaths' breach do I accuse thee,
> When I break twenty ? I am perjured most,
> For all my vows are oaths but to misuse thee,
> And all my honest faith in thee is lost;
> For I have sworn deep oaths of thy deep kindness,
> Oaths of thy love, thy truth, thy constancy,
> And to enlighten thee gave eyes to blindness,
> Or made them swear against the thing they see;
>   For I have sworn thee fair – more perjured eye,
>   To swear against the truth so foul a lie.

The intense oscillation between who is worse, him or her, arises out of the same issues which the speaker celebrates in sonnet 138: they both lie. He concludes in the couplet that he, finally is worse, because his lie consisted of swearing she was "fair." Fair here again carries not only a sense of beauty but of social position – his ultimate "perjury" lies in swearing that the dark lady is noble. But, of course, while he twice claims to have done so (in 147 and 152), he has never sworn in the sonnets that she *is* "fair," only that she is beautiful despite not being "born fair." His perjury lies, rather, in swearing that the "thee" – and here "thee" might apply to the young man as much as to the dark lady – is noble and fair, for, as he makes abundantly clear throughout the sonnet, "all my vows are oaths but to misuse thee." "Misuse" means, as Kerrigan notes, revile, mistreat, slander, debauch, and deceive. But it also means "mis-use," the (mis) application of that "use" which the speaker's position in narrative generates in order to swear that "thee" is fair and noble. Nobility in this sequence is literally a lie. The speaker's claim that the dark lady is "true" or "kind" is not much different from his claim that the youth is "fair." Both originate in his compulsive capacity to deploy, in the service of a social imaginary of "fairness" and "kindness," the social and economic mobility of the narrative that instigates his desire – even though, or because, that capacity is undermined by the very fact that the "not fair" speaker utters it. And both of them are lies: the lady is no more "true" than the young man is "fair." Rather, they are both products of the speaker's mastery of the emerging economic field in which he exists. Consequently, he is, as Fineman famously maintains, a perjured "I" who is defined throughout the entire sequence by the contradiction between his desire to articulate and to produce a lyric ideal and the narrative which provokes, enables, and undermines that desire as a "lie." In the very act of swearing her fair – "For I have sworn" – the speaker is always also forsworn ("For [I have] sworn").[64]

This perjured eye, however, signals not only Fineman's "modern poetic subjectivity" but also social distinction. Like Spenser's speaker, this "I" distinguishes itself through an increasingly contingent procedure for making social distinctions. Yet it is a position which the speaker himself tends to try either to hide, by "naturalizing" it in the service of the production of a noble ideal, or to demonize, by associating it with the dark lady. As a term, class demarcates a way of socially distinguishing, but it does not demarcate a self-conscious group, a class-for-itself. Shakespeare's speaker does not want to be bourgeois any more than Spenser's speaker does. One desires a noble youth, the other desires to be a feudal lord, and both have internally contradictory attitudes toward the feminized transformative power that instigates their desires. Because their distinctive social position emerges out of their articulation of a noble imaginary, the social position of the speaker in Daniel, Spenser, and Shakespeare remains implicit and emergent. When we turn to Drayton's *Idea*, however, this position becomes more and more explicit as Drayton's speaker gradually ceases to apologize for himself. Rather than celebrating an imagined nobility, Drayton's speaker begins to celebrate his verse as "the true image" of his own mind.

Drayton and absolutism

Why does the sonnet sequence gradually fall from literary favor in the seventeenth century? After all, if the claims that I have been making for sonnet sequences are true – that they are a site for the creation of class as a new means of producing social distinction – shouldn't sequences have become a dominant genre as social relations in England continued to change, as class became an increasingly explicit social phenomenon? Tracing Drayton's changes to his sonnet sequences *Idea* helps to answer this question. While he composed the first version of his sequence at the height of Elizabethan sonneteering in 1594, Drayton repeatedly and substantially revised *Idea* over the next twenty-five years, publishing a final version in 1619.[1] The changes Drayton makes embody the shifting literary taste for sonnet sequences, but they also participate in the social transformations within which that taste emerges.[2] These changes are especially apparent in the models that Drayton chooses. Like other sonneteers, Drayton initially takes "diuine Sir Philip" as his principal model, but after 1603 he patterns his poetic voice less on Sidney and more on King James' status as what Jonathan Goldberg influentially describes as the "Poet-King" – James' capacity to maintain and create his monarchical authority in part by fashioning himself as a poet.[3] As a result of this shift, Drayton's sequence moves from articulating a noble imaginary – an Astrophil – to confronting the reconstruction of social space more explicitly. Invoking James as a model allows Drayton's speaker to follow royal precedent notoriously to challenge Jacobean policy.

In the process, Drayton participates in a contradiction central to absolutism itself – that the nobility, and especially the absolute monarch, become a general model for new conceptions of social position. As Michael McKeon suggests, the peculiar, contradictory movement of absolutism, its dependence upon conceptions of social distinction based in both juridical status and control of capital, provides the means for its own critique:

The dynamic tension that animates absolutism, and that is expressed in the tension between royal will and noble privilege, is the impulse to dissolve the limitations imposed by feudal social relations without also dissolving the implicit sanctions of feudal hierarchy. The impulse is unfulfillable . . . From this broad vantage point, the emergence of such [absolutist] doctrines can be seen to signal not the culminating triumph of absolute princely authority but the beginning of a process whereby the confident exercise of royal power becomes a more general model for the way in which diverse human exertions aim to reform society to alternative ideals.[4]

Absolutism is inherently contradictory because it represents both an enlargement of noble status and a model of social position based in class. These contradictions within absolutism date back in England at least a hundred years to the Tudor foundation of an absolutist state. They are readily apparent, for instance, in the complex relationship between Lok's speaker and Queen Elizabeth. The appropriation of Elizabeth's position as protector of the New Jerusalem by Lok's speaker functions very much like the maneuvers of Drayton's speaker. Likewise, the noble imaginaries constructed by Sidney, Spenser, and Shakespeare are always internally contradictory; they undermine noble ideals with the vocabulary they deploy to articulate them.

Tracing Drayton's changes consequently helps to clarify the operations of absolutism that are implicit in English sonnet sequences from the start. At the same time, Drayton's work demarcates the changing relations between sonnet sequences and absolutism. While absolutism is a social fact for several generations, it reaches something like critical mass in the reign of King James. James' exercise of royal authorship as specifically a Poet-King marks a culmination of absolutism as a general model of both a noble status and a writer authorizing himself in a market. The concept of the Poet-King puts unprecedented pressure on this relationship, and one result is that James' authority provides a pattern for those with an agenda often quite antagonistic to him. If the sonnet sequence could function successfully, if uneasily, with Elizabethan absolutism, such was not the case with James.

By using James as a model, Drayton makes his social position, and the means he uses to classify it, increasingly explicit. Such social distinction gradually overcomes the difficulties that epitomize the works of earlier sonneteers. Sequences by Lok, Daniel, Spenser, and Shakespeare repeatedly stage the struggle of a speaker to locate an authoritative position from which to speak, a self-defeating internal dynamic whereby a social authority based in class is deployed to create and to reinforce a noble imaginary. Spenser's speaker wants to use the social processes undermining feudal nobility in order to become a feudal lord; Shakespeare's speaker uses economic language to try to construct the illusory noble standing of the young man. By the 1619 version of *Idea*, this dynamic changes as Drayton's speaker locates and announces his own distinctive social and poetic authority – an "English straine," as he terms it in the opening sonnet of the 1619 *Idea*, embodied in his wide-ranging lyric voice. With James as his model, Drayton's speaker gradually absorbs the narrative of the sequence – a story of loss and lack of authority, of frustration and self-negation – into his own lyric power. By 1619, *Idea* tells the story of the formation of that lyric authority, retrospectively narrated by the speaker himself. The most striking difference between *Idea* and earlier sequences, then, is that the effort to find an authoritative social and literary position from which to speak is no longer imagined in relation to an idealized nobility – Sidney's "Astrophil," Spenser's lady, Shakespeare's young man. Instead, *Idea* repeatedly celebrates the changeableness of the speaker himself, the fact that, as the opening sonnet famously puts it, he "cannot long one Fashion intertaine." Drayton's speaker celebrates his location in a shifting, mutable world as the *source* of his literary and social authority.

Tracing the evolution of the changes to *Idea*, then, suggests that sonnet sequences gradually become less popular because class, the mode of social distinction the form facilitates, begins to attain a power which is no longer, as it was for earlier sonneteers, implicit and apologetic. Though sonnet sequences were published and reprinted after Drayton's 1619 *Idea*, sequences such as those by Wroth, Greville, or Donne are authorized by a variety of means previously only partially formed or non-existent – through new conceptions of authorship, through the book and book culture, through new conceptions of the economy, new organizations of sex and gender, and so on. The after-life of the sonnet sequence – Drayton's "English straine" – consequently lies in conceptions of poetry, authorship, and above all class which writers of earlier sequences labored to articulate, rather than in the continuation of the genre itself. And in this sense, Drayton's devotion to the sonnet sequence, which has almost always been depicted as backward-looking,[5] comes to seem very much forward looking, anticipating (and contributing to) some of the ground-work for a more wide-spread "English straine," the English Revolution, in the two decades after Drayton's death in 1631.[6]

Idea 1594–1599

Drayton's sequence first appeared in 1594 titled *Ideas Mirrour*, and almost no one has liked that particular manifestation very much, then or since. It begins in "Amour 1" by asking the lady to "Reade heere (sweet

Mayd) the story of my wo," but that story quickly turns by the second
line into "The drery abstracts of my endles cares."[7] What makes *Ideas
Mirrour* so boring? With his title, Drayton effectively dispenses with the
fiction that any real lady is being addressed, and this change signals a
more general issue.[8] It is not a problem of biography: we don't need to be
overly concerned with the name of a real woman because Drayton's title
suggests that he and his contemporaries did not much think about an
actual lady inspiring the poems. Instead, by abstracting his "endles
cares," Drayton's speaker cuts himself off from the social relationships –
amorous, economic, entrepreneurial, and so on – that other sequences
struggle to conceptualize. Much of the power of Spenser's *Amoretti*, for
instance, emerges less from the speaker's capacity to articulate his lady as
an ideal than from his overwhelming awareness of the difficulties that
imaginary embodies. The problem with *Ideas Mirrour* isn't that its idea is
bad, but that the world in which that idea might be situated is almost
non-existent. Drayton's work consequently resonates with Sidney's
insistence in *An Apology for Poetry* (which first appeared in print a year
after *Ideas Mirrour*) that "any understanding knoweth the skill of each
artificer standeth in that *Idea* or fore-conceit of the work, and not in the
work itself." But he seems to have missed much of the effect of narrative
in *Astrophil and Stella*, the crucial *poetic* function of Sidney's teasing
invitation of biographical readings. As Sidney suggests,

many of such writing as come under the banner of unresistible love, if I were a
mistress, would never persuade me they were in love; so coldly they apply fiery
speeches, as men that had rather hear lovers' writings . . . But let this be a
sufficient though short note, that we miss the right use of the material point of
poesy.[9]

For Sidney the persuasive power of love poetry lies in its relation to a
historical reality that grounds conventional abstractions – a "material
point" characteristically achieved in the dramatized narrative of a
sequence. Here is the paradox of Sidney's argument in the *Apology*: that
freely ranging in the zodiac of one's own wit, while liberating, always
must have a didactic function: the poet escapes the brazen world in order
to reorganize it via the imagination of a golden world. Otherwise, poetry
is frivolous and meaningless, the mere toy that Sidney worries so much
about.[10] In devoting himself to the abstracts of his cares at the expense of
a narrative relation with his putative mistress, Drayton's speaker "coldly"
applies "fiery speeches" and eliminates the "material point of poesy"; he
naively ignores, rather than transcends, the social relations he exists in.
As Marx would say three hundred years later, these are revolutions in the
mind, but not in the world. *Ideas Mirrour* remains socially and poetically

banal because the speaker never situates himself in relation to a specific historical situation; it lacks in large part the conspicuously public and political bravura of Drayton's later work.

Such pointless abstraction did not go unnoticed. By all indications, contemporary readers hated *Ideas Mirrour*. Joseph Hall mocked Drayton's boldness in *Virgidemiae* ("For he can tell how fury reft his sense, / And Phoebus fill'd him with intelligence"), and Sir John Davies ridiculed Drayton as "Poet Decius" for the presumption of "Amour 8", a sonnet which effectively claims to restructure the world of learning by adding a tenth worthy to the existing nine (hence the mocking "Decius").[11] As Davies implies, a sonnet as clunky as "Amour 8" hardly lives up to its own pretensions. Still, such criticisms also register some of the ambitiousness of Drayton's enterprise. The claim to "mirrour" "idea" itself is wildly presumptuous, and this poetic boldness becomes Drayton's most distinctive and admirable feature. For Kathleen Tillotson, one of Drayton's twentieth-century editors, "[i]t is almost as if Marlowe were writing sonnets."[12] Drayton's Marlovian brashness betrays a sense that in his decision to write sonnets there resides, despite the abstractions of the poems, a tacit understanding of stakes that, in 1594, he cannot quite articulate.

With his extensive revision of the work in 1599, Drayton starts making the material point of his poetry more explicit; that is, he begins thinking critically about the world in which his poetry exists. Rather than a tale of woe, the opening sonnet of 1599 claims that the "story" the sonnets will tell is the sportive ranging of an "active Muse," of one rejecting the abstract "whyning" of cold sonnets in favor of "the worlds right straine":

> Into these loues who but for passion lookes,
> At this first sight, here let him lay them by,
> And seeke elsewhere in turning other bookes,
> Which better may his labour satisfie.
> No far-fetch'd sigh shall euer wound my brest,
> Loue from mine eye, a teare shall neuer wring,
> Nor in ah-mees my whyning Sonets drest,
> (A Libertine) fantastiklie I sing;
> My verse is the true image of my mind,
> Euer in motion, still desiring change,
> To choyce of all varietie inclin'd,
> And in all humors sportiuely I range;
> My actiue Muse is of the worlds right straine,
> That cannot long one fashion entertaine.[13]

I have already considered the 1619 revision of this sonnet in some detail in the opening chapter, but this earlier version, marking a turning point in Drayton's work on his sequence, seems important enough that I hope it will be worth briefly going over similar ground again. Appearing as it does at the start of a sequence of sonnets, this poem initially invites the reader to see the work as a loose collection of lyrics, of momentary subjective fashions. This poetic ranging promises to be the "true image" of the speaker's mind: we who look "into these loues" will see not simply a display of poetic craftsmanship but a poetic self, a distinctive and fashionable personality that breaks free of the labored "ah-mees" of sonneteering. The poetic subject claims superiority because it is "Euer in motion, still desiring change" and consequently "of the worlds right straine." "Straine" here means primarily "a melody, tune" (*OED* 12); the speaker is singing a song in tune with the "world" in a way that "whyning Sonets" are not. Yet the authority of this "Libertine" subject also emerges from the ability of his "actiue Muse" to become part "of" the "worlds right straine." Here "straine" means "Offspring, progeny" (*OED* 4), of the same "lineage" (*OED* 5); like the world his Muse belongs to, the speaker "cannot long one fashion entertaine." This lyric authority recalls the "material point" of other sequences to enact a shifting world – for example, Daniel's figuring his sequence *Delia* as an account book in its opening sonnet. But the boldness of the 1599 *Idea* lies not simply in the ambitious authority of its lyric speaker (which was after all, apparent in the speaker of *Ideas Mirrour*) but rather in the attempt to build his lyric audacity and construct an alternative *narrative*, a story not of woe but of a poetic libertine in a changing world. Making this ambition explicit, whether or not it is successful, marks a decided turning point in the trajectory of the English sonnet sequence.

But "straine," of course, also carries a lingering sense of a correct ("right") social order in the world into which the poem and the speaker fit. Indeed, in setting himself off from "whyning Sonets," the speaker likewise erects a "right straine," that is somehow better than "passion." "[T]he worlds right straine" is thus a paradoxical desire to fit a lyric authority into a narrative "right straine" even as that authority, "To choyce of all varietie inclin'd," resists order generally. Again, we might finally call this tension itself a "straine," in the sense of a trial or hardship (*OED* 10.a) – a strain concerned with strains. The desire of the speaker is to be both "of the worlds right straine" *and* to be "ever in motion" to avoid the "ah-mees" of earlier sonnets. If the "story" of the sonnet is the speaker's sportive ranging, it is *also* a narrative of his position within and (re) creation of a "right straine."

As most readers have noticed, however, the narrative of woe is never entirely jettisoned; much whining remains throughout the sequence, not simply because thirty-one sonnets (some revised) remain from *Ideas*

Mirrour but because the speaker clearly does not entirely wish to dispense with such language. While Drayton's adherence to sonnet "ah-mees" is often seen as evidence of his failure as a poet, or his irredeemable Elizabethanism, we can begin initially to account for his devotion to the genre by considering the social ramifications of this "straine." As the historical specificity of "the *worlds* right straine" implies, his insistence on considering the relation between the formal poetic strain and the world in which it exists articulates more generally the question of the speaker's social position, his habitus. In highlighting a strain in poetic order, the sonnet points to a more general problem of making social distinctions, a problem compounded by Drayton's hesitation in deciding what things count in constructing a social hierarchy. Throughout the 1599 *Idea*, the speaker draws on poetic and social criteria. In "Sonet 3," the poem immediately following the equivocal opening declaration of subjective autonomy, Drayton's speaker inverts his emphasis on his own subjective ranging and tries to place himself into a literary trajectory, a "kind." This kind is an early version of the Protestant ideals that will become associated with the Spenserian poets.[14] But the question of social position complicates Drayton's championing of such Sidneyan ideals and their valorization of nobility. No sooner does his speaker invoke Sidney, Constable, and Daniel as precedents for his own efforts (and thereby undermine the distinctiveness of his own "actiue Muse") than the social implications of this "kind" creep in – speaking of (in particular) Sidney is like "Poore men" speaking of a "King":

> Many there be excelling in this kind,
> Whose well trick'd rimes with all inuention swell,
> Let each commend as best shall like his minde,
> Some *Sidney, Constable*, some *Daniell*.
> That thus theyr names familiarly I sing,
> Let none thinke them disparaged to be,
> Poore men with reuerence may speake of a King,
> And so may these be spoken of by mee;
> My wanton verse nere keepes one certaine stay,
> But now, at hand; then, seekes inuention far,
> And with each little motion runnes astray,
> Wilde, madding, iocund, and irreguler;
> Like me that lust, my honest mery rimes,
> Nor care for Criticke, nor regard the times.

"[T]his kind" suggests both a literary and a social order, but these orders are not necessarily mutually reinforcing. Coming as it does after "Sonet 2," "this kind" refers to the poetic Muse the speaker invokes in the previous sonnet, and it constructs a literary trajectory by tacitly claiming membership in the poetic family of Sidney, Constable, and Daniel: these poets create a "straine" of which the speaker wishes to be a part. And yet his insistence on his own libertine verse implicitly resists this "kind": after all, who are the whining sonneteers if not, at least, Sidney, Constable, and Daniel? This internal poetic contradiction in turn points to a social tension. Placing Constable and Daniel in the same "kind" as the nephew of the Earl of Leicester complicates social hierarchy by placing a poetic "kind" against a social one.[15] The social strain becomes even more explicit in the second quatrain, when the speaker equates his singing of this kind to the poor speaking of a king. The problem is that the speaker identifies with both the poor and the king, but his simile confounds the social organization it tries to reinforce. The king is set above "*Poore* men": what identifies these men is lack of wealth, rather than simply social status – they are "Poore," rather than vulgar or "the worser sort." The "kind" the king represents stands for "more wealth" as much as it does "more status"; conversely, the poetic "kind" Drayton's speaker constructs depends more on poetic wealth than familial status. What makes the speaker nervous about singing "familiarly," then, is the sense that such singing undermines familial, blood distinctions of status and replaces them with distinctions based on something else – poetic authority or wealth; and he is nervous about such distinctions because he desires both to be part of this "kind" and to distinguish himself – poetically and socially – from it.

These somewhat abstract implications attain a material specificity for Drayton's authorial identity in the final sonnets of the sequence, where the entire apparatus of "strain" is set within Drayton's well-documented difficulties securing a patron.[16] These sonnets make explicit the degree to which his poetic "kind," his "actiue Muse," depends upon the social status he tacitly resists in "Sonet 3." The last three sonnets of the 1599 *Idea* constitute a sort of greatest hits of patronage poems; Drayton lifts dedicatory sonnets from a variety of his earlier works and places them all at the end of the sequence.[17] The result is an abstraction of patronage itself, set against the authority of the speaker in "Sonet 2," that consistently situates him as powerless. The "ah mees" of "whyning Sonets" he so fervently resists at the start of the sequence come back at the end in the form of a quest for patronage.

In "Sonet 57" he asks Lucy, Countess of Bedford (whom Drayton eventually turned bitterly against)[18] to "grace this poore Muse of mine, / whose faith, whose zeale, whose life, whose all is thine." The speaker asks for no subject but Lucy, who is represented as an "essence" of the speaker's "chiefest good." Moreover, her power and virtue are hers by "blood," by "descent true" "which no fortune can depriue." Lucy's lineage sets her above the mutable world of "fortune" and wealth – precisely the world which the "active Muse" (now turned "*poore* Muse") of "Sonet 2" claims to reflect and embrace. In a striking negation of the work's opening proclamation, "To the Lady Anne Harington [. . .] Sonet 58" begins "Madam, my words *cannot* expresse my mind" (my emphasis), and it goes on to celebrate Lady Anne's personal integrity: "to your selfe say you are onely you." In the face of this self-replicating, static order, the speaker as panegyrist can only stand "dumbe":

> what should commend your modesty and wit,
> Is by your wit and modesty commended,
> And standeth dumbe, in most admiring it,
> And where it should begin, it there is ended.

Likewise, the last sonnet of the 1599 version, "To Sir Anthony Cooke," sharply curtails the freedom, changeableness, and autonomy of the poetic voice claimed at the beginning of the sequence. This sonnet was originally the dedication to *Ideas Mirrour* and appeared at the very beginning of the work.[19] Set within the 1599 edition, the poem virtually allegorizes the containment of the speaker's wandering by the social status he simultaneously seeks to obtain:

> Vouchsafe to grace these rude vnpolish'd rimes,
> which but for you had slept in sable night,
> And come abroad now in these glorious times,
> Can hardly brooke the purenes of the light.
> But sith you see their desteny is such,
> That in the world their fortune they must try,
> Perhaps they better shall abide the tuch,
> wearing your name their gracious liuery.
> Yet these mine owne, I wrong not other men,
> Nor trafique further then this happy Clime,
> Nor filch from *Portes* nor from *Petrarchs* pen,
> A fault too common in this latter time.
> Diuine Sir *Phillip*, I auouch thy writ,
> I am no Pickpurse of anothers wit.

The speaker's ambition is decidedly circumscribed, for though he invokes momentarily Desportes and Petrarch, he promises to "trafique [no] further than this happy Clime" of England. He briefly invokes the idea of a wider, more varied world of mercantile "trafique" and continental poetics, and perhaps even a tentative desire to move in such circles, but those worlds become instead a backdrop to the specific and local restriction of the speaker's ambition within "this happy Clime." Such restriction, such working within a very specific tradition, is similarly clear in the final couplet's quotation of Sidney's *Astrophil and Stella* 74.

Drayton's speaker here limits his own poetic authority by giving credit to
Sidney: Drayton's speaker is a pickpurse of no other wit *but* that of
"diuine Syr *Phillip*." Yet while he can pick Sidney's literary lineage, he
cannot steal Sidney's other lingering significance – his existence as an
ideal noble figure. Unlike the strain between poetic and social "kinds" in
"Sonet 3," here the bid for patronage and the invocation of literary
heritage are mutually reinforcing; both act to limit the "trafique" of the
speaker by placing him inside a poetic "desteny," a strictly delineated
narrative of failure that serves to reinforce the power of the patron and
the idealization of "diuine Syr *Phillip*" at the expense of the speaker's
own authority. His poems wear the "livery" of a superior lord. The initial
promise in "Sonet 2" of not only a distinctive lyric authority but a new
narrative of wandering collapses back into a mundane narrative of loss –
these final poems are nothing if not "whyning Sonets." This regression
back into (what the speaker imagines as) a sequence of "ah-mees" means
the momentary reinforcement of social distinction as a status based on
blood, like Lucy's "descent trew," rather than one based on something
else – the speaker's poetic "kind" and the distinction it signals.

His partial embrace of such a chaotic, thoroughly subjective world
view consequently betrays the speaker's *inability* to articulate an
alternative to "whyning sonets." The 1599 *Idea* is much like the
sequences by Spenser and Shakespeare, caught between the "traffique"
of a new form of social distinction and a determination or compulsion to
employ this new energy in the service of a noble imaginary. The poetic
authority he claims ultimately fails in the face of Lady Anne's "integrity,"
and his inability to completely imagine, represent, and describe "the
worlds right straine" in which he maintains authority forces him into a
position "still desiring change."

Yet this failure should not be taken as a containment of the speaker's
libertine energies by a newly organized feudal polity (here figured as the
patronage system) but rather as a rearticulation of the strain apparent
throughout the 1599 volume. The contradiction between poetic and
social authority in the sequence demonstrates a dialectic in which poetic
authority increasingly reacts against the very social structures which
promoted it in the first place. Indeed, Drayton places the entire sequence
itself amidst this contradiction between a reinforcement of social
hierarchy and an endorsement of a poetic authority which that hierarchy
generates out of itself. *Idea* was published in 1599 at the back of a revised
edition of Drayton's popular work *Englands Heroicall Epistles*. The
location of the sonnet sequence in relation to the *Epistles* sets in motion
the social contradiction between the speaker's desire for a poetic
authority set apart from "strains" and his desire to locate himself *in* a

strain.[20] In terms of both the content of the poems and their layout on the page it is very hard to tell if *Idea* is an extension of the *Epistles* or if it offers an alternative to the "heroicall" and largely aristocratic loves the *Epistles* celebrate. A sonnet (the absent "Sonet 1") between the *Epistles* and *Idea* articulates the problem:

> The worlds faire Rose, and *Henries* frosty fire,
> *Iohns* tyrannie; and chast *Matilda's* wrong,
> Th' inraged Queene, and furious *Mortimer*,
> The scourge of Fraunce, and his chast loue I sung;
> Deposed *Richard*, *Isabell* exil'd,
> The gallant *Tudor*, and fayre *Katherine*,
> Duke *Humfrey*, and old *Cobhams* haplesse child,
> Couragious *Pole*, and that braue spiritfull Queene,
> *Edward*, and that delicious London Dame,
> *Brandon*, and that rich dowager of Fraunce,
> *Surrey*, with his fayre paragon of fame,
> *Dudleys* mishap, and vertuous *Grayes* mischance;
> Their seuerall loues since I before haue showne,
> Now giue me leaue at last, to sing mine owne.

On the one hand, the speaker here takes responsibility for ordering and giving meaning to the "seuerall loues" ("I . . . haue showne") by summarizing the content of the *Epistles* – an authority similarly apparent in the "I" of the *Epistles'* elaborate scholarly notations.[21] But this declaration of poetic authority is undercut when he asks for "*leaue*" "to sing mine owne." "[A]t last," in this sense, means quite literally last in line, at the bottom of a social hierarchy. At the same time, however, "at last" is characteristically presumptuous. It implies, on the one hand, that the speaker's love is the end or realization of a historical movement; and on the other hand, it suggests a touch of belated irritation (finally!). The love expressed in *Idea* may be the speaker's "owne," but this declaration of possession is substantially tempered by the realization that his love is also the expression of a teleological historical unfolding of English heroical love. And yet, his determination to insist that this love is his *own* might reasonably be read as an assertion of independence from the very historical narrative he claims to be continuing.[22]

Idea 1600–1605

Both in its layout and its argument, then, the 1599 *Idea* articulates a strain between a poetic, lyric authority and a social narrative which makes the poetic voice possible but which that voice tends to resist. Though the 1599 revision of *Idea* remained the most substantial, Drayton continued to revise his sonnet sequence for the next twenty years, and eventually these revisions created a profoundly different work. Gradually, Drayton's speaker stops asking for leave to sing about himself. The narrative of the sequence – even the history of the revisions themselves – becomes the story of the speaker's authoritative ranging, not a tale of his failure. As many critics have noted, the sequence becomes increasingly satiric and dramatic over time, and this tendency itself suggests that the voice of the speaker becomes more and more stable and authoritative.[23] While most studies of Drayton try to explain these stylistic changes formally by describing the influence of other poets (the usual suspects are Shakespeare and Donne),[24] these changes, and the styles in which they are expressed, reflect shifting conceptions of social distinction in early seventeenth-century England. Rather than looking to Sidney for a noble ideal, the speaker looks to King James' "absolute" authority and begins to pattern his own lyric power on James as much as on Sidney. The result, however, is that the speaker begins to articulate a new mode of social distinction – class – which increasingly rivals that of the monarch.

This use of James as a model is apparent in an otherwise subtle revision in the 1600 edition of *Idea*. While the sequence remains largely the same as the 1599 *Idea* in terms of both its content, layout, and position following *Englands Heroicall Epistles*, Drayton adds at the start of the three patronage poems a new sonnet, numbered 62, addressed "*To the high and mighty Prince*, James, *King of Scots*," a panegyric which embodies Drayton's hopes and ambitions at the prospect of James' rule. Drayton's sonnet is in many ways characteristic of the poems addressed to James both a few years before and after his coronation (Drayton himself also published *To the Majestie of King James, A gratulatorie Poem* in 1603). In these panegyrics James is often figured as a Poet-King, a monarch whose power emerges, as Goldberg argues, through his ability to control discourse.[25] James himself cultivated this image; he had a humanist education and had been publishing poetry and other works since 1584 when he styled himself a "a prentice in the divine art of poesie."[26] But James' dual identity created several representational difficulties, both in the king's own verse as well as for those who wished to extol him. Writers wishing to praise James, as Curtis Perry argues, had "recourse to seemingly contradictory rhetorical gestures: they alternatively ally themselves with the king's authorial power, and express their unworthiness or inability to do so."[27]

What this means in relation to the 1599 *Idea* is that James becomes, for a moment at least, a figure whose social position and status as a poet promises to fulfill what the speaker in 1599 cannot: James both embodies poetic, subjective authority as well as literally embodying social order. In sonnet 62, lyric and narrative are reconciled as James' poetic authority becomes a story of social triumph, not failure:

> Not thy grave Counsells, nor thy Subjects love,
> Nor all that famous Scottish royaltie,
> Or what thy soveraigne greatnes may approve,
> Others in vaine doe but historifie,
> When thine owne glory from thy selfe doth spring,
> As though thou did'st, all meaner prayses scorne:
> Of Kings a Poet, and the Poets King,
> They Princes, but thou Prophets do'st adorne;
> Whilst others by their Empires are renown'd,
> Thou do'st enrich thy Scotland with renowne,
> And Kings can but with Diadems be crown'd,
> But with thy Laurell, thou doo'st crowne thy Crowne;
> That they whose pens, (even) life to Kings doe give,
> In thee a King, shall seeke them selves to live.[28]

Social order is emphasized as the speaker stresses that James descends from "all that famous Scottish royaltie"; James' "owne glory" stands as the culmination of a long historical narrative. At the same time, James' "owne glory from [him] selfe doth spring" through his capacity as a poet. This reconciliation of lyric and narrative authority is articulated in the chiasmus of "Of Kings a Poet, and the Poets King." Here is the position sought by Drayton's speaker – a poet who fits into or embodies the social order without losing lyric authority. Yet while the figure of James embodies both a social narrative and a poetic power, these two sources of authority are not, in the speaker's opinion, in any way equal. "[W]ith thy *Laurell*, thou doo'st crowne thy Crowne," he emphasizes. Poetry is much more than simply praise – it is *the* source of power which in turn bestows authority upon James himself, for the sonnet's metonymic "pens" give "life to Kings." While the phrase "Poets King" means that James is King of Poets, it also means that he is the king who belongs to poets. James' kingship is imagined not only as the paradigmatic instance of authorship, but as a space within which poets "shall seeke them selves to live."

As Perry suggests, such a formulation of the king's power also potentially undermines it. Drayton increasingly takes over James' position, and this appropriation is apparent in the gradual marginalization within the sequence of the sonnet to James. Initially, by situating the sonnet at the start of the patronage sonnets that end the sequence in 1600, Drayton effectively identifies the king with those patrons in front of whom Drayton's speaker can only stand dumb. Like Lady Anne, James is self-sufficient. Emulating James, however, enables Drayton to begin to change this dynamic. While Drayton made minor changes to *Idea* in 1603, publishing it as an appendage to *The Barons Warres*, in 1605 he published a significantly different version of the sequence in the first edition of his *Poems*. Rather than ending his sequence with the patronage poems, as he had done in the four previous versions of *Idea*, Drayton ends with "Truce gentle love, a parly now I crave," the sonnet that would continue to end the sequence from 1605 on. On the page following the final sonnet is an elaborate border and a new title, "Certaine other Sonnets to great *and worthy Personages*." All the patronage sonnets are thus grouped under a new heading and are separated off from, and not exactly part of, *Idea* itself. The 1605 *Poems* was, moreover, the first edition of Drayton's collected works, a book which unifies a variety of previously published works under the moniker, as the title page puts it, "Michaell Draiton, Esquire."[29] The separation of the patronage poems in the volume that first establishes Drayton as an author with a unified body of work is crucial: the public establishment of Drayton as an author coincides with the marking off of his own work from his dedicatory sonnets, the establishment of a public poetic voice apart from those sonnets which both provoked and stifled it. By marginalizing the sonnet to James, and in fact all the patronage sonnets, the speaker's authority becomes articulated independently of the sequence's social narrative; or rather, that narrative itself changes to become increasingly what the introductory sonnet to the 1599 edition promised it would be: the narrative of the emergence of a distinctive poetic and *social* identity.

Nevertheless, Drayton's poetic authority remains largely patterned after the social status which eluded him in his quest for patronage. As a result that authority is also set above the lower-class rabble of "the thronged Theaters" in a sonnet new in 1605, number 47:

> In pride of wit, when high desire of fame
> Gaue Life and Courage to my labouring pen,
> And first the sound and vertue of my name,
> Won grace and credit in the eares of men:
> With those the thronged Theaters that presse,
> I in the circuite for the Lawrell stroue,
> Where the full praise I freely must confesse,
> In heate of blood a modest minde might moue:
> With showts and claps at euerie little pawse,
> When the prowd round on euerie side hath rung,
> Sadly I sit vnmoue'd with the applawse,
> As though to me it nothing did belong:
> No publique glorie vainely I pursue,
> The praise I striue, is to eternize you.[30]

The turn away from vain "publique glory" associated with the public theater should naturally be viewed with some skepticism; the speaker is certainly not suddenly getting sentimental on us. The reason for such suspicion lies in what exactly it is he wants to "eternize" – who the "you" of the last line is. At such a contrived moment of sincerity, it's worth remembering that the "you" of the poem, the "idea," is poetry itself and, by extension, the poet; after all, the title *Idea* underscores Drayton's disinterest in any particular lady, and there are no quasi-autobiographical moments as there are for Sidney and Spenser. In his move to "eternize," the speaker is consequently making an even more aggressive and earnest grab for the poetic "Lawrell." His singular focus on poetic distinction erects itself as a sort of nobility, a status set against the "thronged Theatre," a valorization of what John Huntington calls "poetic fury," the embrace of poetry by writers from Marlowe to Chapman as a form of social distinction and cultural capital that is "nobler than nobility."[31] And yet this social position does not reinforce the existing social hierarchy as strictly a desire to become noble, for the speaker's longing for status comes almost entirely at the expense of a would be patron who he might otherwise "eternize." Even as he distances himself from the theater crowd, they provide him with "grace" and "credit" – both social status and an authority based in exchange. This authority is both literal – Drayton apparently made a living writing plays when he couldn't find a patron – and metaphoric; it provides a social distinction outside of patronage itself in the increasingly autonomous world of "credit." The difference between "In pride of wit" and, for instance, the address to Lady Anne Harrington is remarkable. Whereas in the face of Lady Anne's integrity, the speaker was unable to say anything, here his glory *emerges* out of his ability to eternize the object of the poem – his own poetry. The contradiction between the speaker's poetic ranging, his "actiue Muse," and the social world within which he operates, has disappeared.

This retrospective narration of the emergence of a lyric authority, of a speaker looking back over his life, has definite political consequences. In sonnet 51, the story of the speaker's coming into existence is also a history of England (and increasingly Britain), but it is a history which reacts quite explicitly against the policies of King James:

> Calling to minde since first my loue begunne,
> Th'incertaine times oft varying in their course,
> How things still vnexpectedly haue runne,
> As please the fates, by their resistlesse force:
> Lastly, mine eyes amazedly haue seene,
> *Essex* great fall, *Tyrone* his peace to gaine,
> The quiet end of that long-liuing Queene,
> This Kings faire entrance, and our peace with Spaine,
> We and the Dutch at length our selues to seuer.
> Thus the world doth, and euermore shall reele,

Yet to my goddesse am I constant euer;
How ere blind fortune turne her giddy wheele:
Though heauen and earth proue both to me vntrue,
Yet am I still inuiolate to you.

Historical events are here filtered through the "minde" of the speaker;
like "Into these Loves," the speaker's mind is seen as "of the worlds right
straine" – a precise reflector and embodiment of the material history that
he calls "to minde." Rather than searching for a place inside historical
events, historical events reside in him. As Norbrook notes, the incidents
mentioned in this sonnet – the fall of Essex, the death of Elizabeth, the
peace with Spain, the severing of connections with the Netherlands –
were all hot-button issues for the Spenserian poets. They chronicle a
move by James away from a pro-Protestant interventionist policy on the
continent towards a policy of strengthening ties with Spain where James
thought "the principles of order and degree were more firmly
maintained."[32] Against this sort of aristocratic "degree," Drayton's
speaker sets the "inuiolate" order of prophetic poetry, and, presumably,
the Elizabethan (and Sidnean) chivalric Protestant ideal that "fell," as far
as the Spenserians were concerned, with Essex. The speaker's "inviolate"
relation to poetry and his goddess are thus simultaneously an indictment
of James' foreign policy. And yet as we saw in sonnet 47, the possibility of
such a reaction against the king is made possible by a sense of status very
much *like* that of the king.

Consequently, the relation between poetic and monarchical authority
is dialectical rather than merely antagonistic; after all, both Drayton's
increasingly impudent political sounding off and his devotion to his Muse
were paradoxically made possible by his acquisition of Sir Walter Aston
as a reliable patron. This politically and poetically liberating effect of
Aston's patronage is clear in the dedicatory sonnet to the 1605 *Poems*,
"*To Sir Walter Aston, Knight of the honourable order of the Bath, and my
most worthy Patron*":

I will not strive m'inuention to inforce,
With needlesse words your eyes to entertaine,
T'obserue the formall ordinarie course
That euerie one so vulgarly doth faine:
　Our interchanged and deliberate choise,
Is with more firme and true election sorted,
Then stands in censure of the common voice,
That with light humor fondly is transported:
　Nor take I patterne of anothers praise,
Then what my pen may constantly avow,
Nor walke more publique nor obscurer waies

> Then vertue bids, and iudgement will allow;
> So shall my loue, and best endeuours serue you,
> And still shall studie, still so to deserue you.[33]

Far from the customary fawning of dedications – and even further from the dumb failure of Drayton's attempts at patronage in the 1599 *Idea* – this sonnet presents the meeting of equals. Aston's knighthood is virtually equated with his status as Drayton's patron; he is a worthy patron and a patron worthy of Drayton ("Our interchanged and deliberate choise"). They are both elevated over the "common voice" that "vulgarly doth faine." In little, Aston acts as a sort of absolute model to Drayton's pen which only avows what "vertue bids." Patronage, like absolutism, facilitates its own critique. Though he still needs Aston's monetary support, Drayton no longer depends upon nobility to authorize his writing; and while he sets his poetic status above "the common voice" (like the theater), that status is not the same as nobility.[34]

There are specific reasons Drayton could adopt such an attitude. Jean Brink suggests that "[s]ince Aston was less than twenty years old when he became Drayton's patron, he may not have minded Drayton's reputation for indiscretion and may have hired him as a secretary because he valued his learning."[35] In 1605, Drayton himself was over forty. Nevertheless, the ability of the speaker of *Idea* to position himself both above a vulgar throng and with a social position challenging that of the nobility points to a more general shift in the means of socially distinguishing; if poetry itself can come to represent a specific prophetic and explanatory power, this is because it increasingly embodies the values and voice of a new conception of social distinction. Yet class does not function here merely in opposition to status; it emerges out of, and is not always antagonistic to, the language of patronage and, more generally, the language of absolutism. Indeed, what is crucial to recognize here is that while Drayton's speaker begins to utilize explicitly class as a form of social distinction, he cannot be said to belong to a *particular* class. Class emerges in dialectical relation to absolutism, but it does not emerge as "a class in Marx's sense, that is, a group which is mobilized for common purposes, and especially against another class"[36] – for instance, the revolutionary "middle class" that historians of the English Revolution spent so many years trying to find. Drayton's speaker continues to desire to "serue" and "deserue" Aston and his patronage, but that very service articulates a new form of social power that challenges its model. The discourse of absolutism, intimately connected to the emergence of capitalism, enables socially ambiguous writers like Drayton to create an inviolate body that wields social power. At the same time, James, and to a lesser extent Elizabeth, are likewise prime examples of the sort of "inviolate" subjects that nascent capitalism produced. As I suggested in my overview of Elizabethan monetary policy in chapter six, the queen herself was a paradigmatic participant in the market. Similarly, James' discursive power emerges as he "prentices" *himself* to the "*Divine Art of Poesie*" in 1584 and invents a discursive, "absolute" persona in the public world of print. Class power models itself on James, but the king's absolutism itself is also produced out of a language of a social distinction gained through circulation of poetic capital. Shifts in social distinction do not flow in only one direction, dribbling down from nobles: if noble and monarchical poetic productions offer us a glimpse of the rhetorical strategies of court, they *also* depend upon non-noble "poetic" production. Drayton can successfully imitate King James because, at some level, James is imitating – apprenticed to – "divine" poets like Drayton.[37]

Idea 1619 and after

The social force of Drayton's lyric authority emerges most conspicuously in the 1619 folio edition of Drayton's complete works, a landmark publication in the history of English literature. Recognition of the importance of the volume itself does much to challenge a lingering sense of Drayton as a poet who outlived his time. Drayton's preface, a dedication to Aston, is characteristically unsubtle:

SIR, *These my few Poemes, the works of that Mayden Reigne, in the Spring of our Acquaintance, as it pleased you then to Patronize, as I singly set them forth: so now collected into this small Volume; I make the best Present, that my poore Abilitie is able to tender you: howsoever they may appeare to these more prodigious Dayes, I know not: but thus much I will say, to mine owne disadvantage, (should they hap to be unwelcome to these Times:) That they were the fruit of that Muse-nursing Season: before this frosty* Boreas *(I meane the worlds coldnesse) had nipt our flowery* Tempe; *that with his pestilencial Fogs is like utterly to poyson the* Pierean *Spring, doe not* Apollo *mightily protect it: before (I say) Hell had sent vp her black Furies, that in euery corner breathe their venome in the face of cleere Poesie: And, but that as shee is Diuine, her beauties be Immortal, or they had before this blasted her sweetnesse, and made her as ugly to the world, as they themselves are in the eyes of true Judgement and Vertue.*

Drayton's appeal to Elizabethan ideals ("that Mayden Reigne") and to the seriousness and importance of poetry itself constitutes an attack on James, and he goes on to compare James' reign to "this frosty *Boreas*" that kills "our flowery *Tempe*," "pestilencial Fogs" that will likely poison the "*Pieran* Spring," and Hell's "black furies" "that in euery corner breathe their venome in the face of cleere Poesie." The authority of poetic fury is set against the power of the monarch.

Like the folio in which it resides, the 1619 *Idea* looks forward into the seventeenth century by re-crafting the favorite genre of "that Mayden Reigne" into a new sense of authorship. Critics have typically argued that despite glimpses and hints of a "metaphysical," libertine poetic brilliance, the 1619 *Idea* reverts to an Elizabethan and anachronistic conception of "passion." Walter Davis classically suggests that the sequence is fundamentally about "the attempt to establish the uniqueness of individual experience and its failure, the attempt to escape from standard passionate suffering into a libertine pose and its failure, the attempt to range sportively inside an offhand fantastic style and its failure in returning to sighs and tears and all the rest of the Petrarchan panoply of emotions."[38] But as Brink argues, "[b]y 1619 [Drayton] was critically aware of convention and could explore and articulate the problems an artist faced in working in a conventional form."[39] The speaker whose love in 1599 could never exactly fit into the social order of "the worlds right straine" by 1619 uses his own authority to create a social order, and that order depends both on Drayton's authorial status and his continuing adherence to the genre of the sonnet sequence.[40] As a number of critics have noted, the Spenserian poets' embrace of pastoral maintained a similar political charge.[41] The implications of such protest, however, move outside of local policy disagreements; what is at stake here is a shift in the means of social legitimation itself, and not just a polemic in a political debate.[42] The 1619 folio begins with a declaration against "this frosty *Boreas*," sets a revision of *Idea* in its middle, and ends, notably, with pastoral. It is this adherence to a largely Elizabethan mode which paradoxically allows the sequence to point forward. In the 1619 *Idea*, the patronage sonnets are completely cut, and *Idea*'s relation to *Englands Heroicall Epistles* is transformed. "The World's faire Rose," retitled "A Catalogue of the Heroicall Loves," ends the *Epistles* (it is followed by "Finis"). *Idea*, in some sense the speaker's own love, is clearly differentiated by an elaborate title page facing the final sonnet of the *Epistles*.

More famously, Drayton revises the last four lines of "Into these Loves, who but for Passion lookes" (retitled "To The Reader Of These Sonnets") into the sharply focused sonnet familiar from anthologies, the version I considered in chapter one. In the 1599 edition, the last lines read

> To choyce of all varietie inclin'd,
> And in all humors sportiuely I range;
> My actiue Muse is of the worlds right straine,
> That cannot long one fashion entertaine.

In 1619 the lines are transformed:

> *And as thus to Varietie inclin'd,*
> *So in all Humors sportively I range:*
> *My Muse is rightly of the* English *straine,*
> *That cannot long one Fashion intertaine.*

While in 1599 lines eleven and twelve are simply an extension of the sorts of "ranging" already elaborated in the first ten lines, in 1619 they are the culmination of a specific logic: "And as . . . So." The speaker's general ranging in 1599 defined itself against the social order embodied in the patronage sonnets (even though the speaker sought similar status). But in 1619 he and his Muse are "*rightly* of the English straine"; the tentativeness of the speaker's location in, for instance, the English heroical loves of the *Epistles* is gone. Rather than fitting himself into a "right straine," he *embodies* the strain. "English" names the social distinction of changeableness itself.

The location of historical variety in the figure of the speaker likewise appears in the opening sonnet of 1619, where he claims to be "Like an adventurous Sea-farer" who retrospectively narrates the history which has produced him and placed him in the English strain. Like the representation of James in the patronage sonnet, the speaker reconciles lyric and narrative authority. Rather than gazing up at the idealized star from the boat, as in Shakespeare's sonnet 116, the story now belongs to, and the idealization resides in, the speaker himself:

> LIKE an adventurous Sea-farer am I,
> Who hath some long and dang'rous Voyage beene,
> And call'd to tell of his Discoverie,
> How farre he say'ld, what Countries he had seene,
> Proceeding from the Port whence he put forth,
> Shewes by his Compasse, how his Course he steer'd,
> When East, when West, when South, and when by North
> As how the Pole to ev'ry place was rear'd,
> What Capes he doubled, of what Continent,
> The Gulphes and Straits, that strangely he had past,
> Where most becalm'd, where with foule Weather spent,
> And on what Rocks in perill to be cast?
> Thus in my Love, Time calls me to relate
> My tedious Travels, and oft-varying Fate.

Despite the promise of an exotic narrator called upon by nothing less than Time itself to tell his "tedious Travels, and oft-varying Fate," the bulk of this sonnet is far from dramatic. Instead, it is decidedly practical, more concerned with wind patterns, compass readings, and dangerous rock formations than Othello's exotic "Anthropophagi, and men whose heads / Do grow beneath their shoulders."[43] In this sense, the poem appeals to men interested in the practical details of sea voyages. Consequently, the "adventurous Sea-farer" of the 1619 *Idea* remains as heroic as the "brave Heroique Minds" of Drayton's "To the Virginian Voyage," originally published in 1606 and reprinted in the 1619 folio. Like the seamen Drayton celebrates, the adventurous speaker of *Idea* becomes an embodiment of an Elizabethan spirit to "Honour still pursue" ("To the Virginian Voyage," line 3) and a rebuke to those who disdain such activities – particularly James himself, who was luke-warm at best at the prospects of colonialism.[44] After all, what Drayton's speaker tells those brave English seamen to expect to find in Virginia is poetry itself.[45] In the dedicatory sonnet to *Ideas Mirrour*, Drayton's speaker invokes a sense of world-wide ranging with the mercantile word "trafique" only to circumscribe that energy within the strictly defined confines of social hierarchy. In "Like an adventurous Sea-farer" that energy has become part of the ordering system of the speaker himself.

A principal source of this social power lies in Drayton's deployment of the "Elizabethanism" of the genre of the sonnet sequence. Sonnet 61, one of the most well-known of Drayton's sonnets, plays with an Elizabethan language of passion in support of an agenda, and a speaker, quite contemporary:

> SINCE ther's no helpe, Come let us kisse and part,
> Nay, I have done: You get no more of Me,
> And I am glad, yea glad withall my heart,
> That thus so cleanly, I my Selfe can free,
> Shake hands for ever, Cancell all our Vowes,
> And when We meet at any time againe,
> Be it not seene in either of our Browes,
> That We one jot of former Love reteyne;
> Now at the last gaspe, of Loves latest Breath,
> When his Pulse fayling, Passion speechlesse lies,
> When Faith is kneeling by his bed of Death,
> And Innocence is closing up his Eyes,
> Now if thou would'st, when all have given him over,
> From Death to Life, thou might'st him yet recover.

While the third quatrain's personification of Love, Passion, and Innocence comes close to sounding like the bad, abstract verse of *Ideas Mirrour*, the quatrain is literally surrounded by the speaker's colloquial voice which effectively places the over-wrought passion there for its own purposes. Rather than "reverting" to love, passionate and anachronistic language becomes part of his *current* persona.

Consequently, it makes sense that the 1619 *Idea* ends not with new poems but with old poems. Sonnet 62, also originally in *Ideas Mirrour*, becomes a living reminder of the speaker's connection to the glorious Elizabethan past:

> WHEN first I Ended, then I first Began,
> Then more I Traveld, further from my Rest,
> Where most I Lost, there most of all I Wan

And likewise, in the final sonnet of the sequence, first included in 1599, Elizabethan plaint is converted into an energetically defiant stance:

> TRUCE, gentle Love, a Parly now I crave,
> Me thinkes' long since first these Warres begun,
> Nor thou, nor I, the better yet can have:
> Bad is the Match, where neither partie wonne.
> I offer free Conditions of faire Peace,
> My Heart for Hostage that it shall remaine,
> Discharge our Forces, here let Malice cease,
> So for my Pledge thou give me Pledge againe.
> Or if no thing but Death will serve thy turne,
> Still thirsting for subversion of my state;
> Doe what thou canst, raze, massacre, and burne;
> Let the World see the utmost of thy hate:
> I send defiance, since if overthrowne,
> Thou vanquishing, the Conquest is mine owne.

Though the conceit of this poem is highly familiar,[46] placed in the powerful authorial presence of the 1619 folio, this sonnet is hardly commonplace. Like Donne's speaker (which the poem clearly echoes), he has become his own "state," and his rejection prompts him not to dejection, to "whyning Sonets," but to an open declaration of war. The strain between poetic lyricism and idealized nobility, so basic to the dynamics of previous sonnet sequences, is gone, replaced by a social position standing in tension with the world in which the folio itself exists; in other words, the strain, like the internal contradiction of absolutism, is externalized and set into the world. As Catherine Gray remarks of Katherine Philips' royalist poetry of the 1650s, this poem too "marks the shift . . . from monarchy as a matter of fact, to monarchy as a matter of public debate." In the sharp "defiance" of the final sonnet, "the English straine" of *Idea* similarly becomes a "political ideology"[47] that anticipates the more general, more intense social strain – the English Revolution – that unfolds over the next thirty years.

Sending "defiance" in the face of one who thirsts "for subversion of [his] state" is consequently prescient, but not necessarily in a strictly political way. In a revised reading in the second edition of *Poetry and Politics in the English Renaissance*, Norbrook clarifies and emphasizes a connection between Spenserians like Drayton and the English Revolution by arguing that the literary clubs that met at taverns near the bookstalls in St. Paul's (most famously in the *Mermaid*) constituted a Habermasian literary public sphere.[48] If this argument occasionally stresses the political import of poetry at the expense of its broader social impact, it nevertheless crucially places the literary activities of the early 1600s in the emergence of a public sphere that Norbrook details in *Writing the English Republic*.[49] A large part of the argument of this book has been that sonnet sequences are a place where class *happens*, even when (or if) such social changes may or may not happen in more conspicuously political forms. A bourgeois public sphere ultimately depends not only on sites of rational communication (taverns, salons, coffeehouses) but upon a rearrangement of social, and not just political, classification that facilitates such communicative action in the first place and shapes its meaning. Sonneteers might have more or less influence on high politics at any given moment; what they begin to acquire – relatively explicitly, by Drayton's 1619 folio – is cultural capital, a social distinctiveness that reflects and creates new social relations and whose social power in part depends, as Bourdieu stresses, on their purported political disinterest – their devotion to poetry itself as an instance of social truth. What is revolutionary in Drayton's work, finally, is not its capacity to represent a definite class or political interest (he seems to have liked King Charles),[50] but its capacity to register and enact new forms of social distinction – the conceptual groundwork which makes a specifically "bourgeois" public imaginable at all. Whatever the political causes and delineations of the bloodshed that would occur in the British Isles over the next twenty years,[51] Drayton's transformation of the sonnet sequence suggests that a social revolution was already taking place.

Afterword: Engendering class: Drayton, Wroth, Milton, and the genesis of the public sphere

In its valorization of changeableness, Drayton's 1619 *Idea* fundamentally alters the dynamic which informs the sequences of both Shakespeare and Spenser. Those works continually attempt to wrest themselves from the socially mutable effects of exchange they gender female: throughout *Amoretti and Epithalamion*, Spenser associates narrative change with femininity and lyric control with masculinity; likewise, Shakespeare's *Sonnets* attempt to keep separate the modes of social distinction associated with the young man and the dark lady by distinguishing between them in gendered terms. In claiming changeableness and fashion for himself, Drayton's speaker embraces the very contingency Spenser and Shakespeare associate with femininity and turns it into a masculine virtue.

Class itself, as a mode of producing social distinction, increasingly becomes gendered male. In the sixth sonnet of the 1619 *Idea*, Drayton's speaker creates his own masculine, classed authority in part by setting it against a feminized court:

> HOW many paltry, foolish, painted things,
> That now in Coaches trouble ev'ry Street,
> Shall be forgotten, whom no Poet sings,
> Ere they be well wrap'd in their winding Sheet?
> Where I to thee Eternitie shall give,
> When nothing else remayneth of these dayes,
> And Queenes hereafter shall be glad to live
> Upon the Almes of thy superfluous prayse;
> Virgins and Matrons reading these my Rimes,
> Shall be so much delighted with thy story,
> That they shall grieve, they liv'd not in these Times,
> To have seene thee, their Sexes onely glory:
> So shalt thou flye above the vulgar Throng,
> Still to survive in my immortall Song.[1]

The poem argues that the social distinction of poetic immortality trumps the transitory distinction of riding around in a Coach; as a result, the familiar sonnet trope of erecting the speaker's masculine power through the control of a feminized object is given a distinct social spin. On one hand, the poem appears as socially leveling. The speaker wants to eliminate the insular "Coaches" that "trouble ev'ry Street," and there is a very real social antagonism here, a hatred, or at least an attempt at disdain, for these "paltry, foolish, painted things" who seem to be courtiers and nobles as much as women. On the other hand, the speaker would make the poetic object even more exclusive than the coaches he derides. He constructs a new, nobler, poetic distinction by replacing the social status figured in the enclosed coaches with the insularity of a poetic object (sealed off from the mutability of time rather than the street). While the coaches zip about London, this object "flye[s] above the vulgar Throng," who now seem to include both the coaches and the lower orders. Nevertheless, this new distinction ends up looking quite a lot like the court and nobility it would reject; both the poem and the Coach want to escape the teeming hordes of a London street, and both are set in motion by feminizing an object. By gendering the "Coaches" female, the speaker can demonstrate his masculine control of a feminine object, but his social distinction always resembles the feminized object he claims to overcome: his poem becomes a coach. As a result, this new social distinction remains tenuous, a lyric moment of masculine control in a conspicuously public political struggle. The sonnet effectively begins, and perhaps ends, in the middle of street traffic; the speaker seems in danger of being run over by a coach. The result of such ambivalence is that, like Spenser and Shakespeare, the social authority of Drayton's speaker emerges as a masculinity trying to control the onslaught of feminine painted things. Unlike Spenser and Shakespeare, this class struggle is an explicit and public masculine pursuit.

Drayton's increasingly masculinized class authority contrasts sharply with what has recently become the most celebrated sonnet sequence composed in the early seventeenth century, Lady Mary Wroth's *Pamphilia to Amphilanthus*. Critical attention to Wroth has characteristically begun by emphasizing the apparent reversal in her sequence: the female, long the object against which the male speaker defines himself, becomes the subject and speaks, though her speech is notably limited. Wroth's work initially became a locus for criticism that sought to delineate the near-impossibility of female subjectivity in the Renaissance.[2] More recently, it has become a prime location for understanding the possibilities of female subjects in the period and for the shifting relations between subjects and gender.[3]

Though gender remains a crucial category for understanding *Pamphilia to Amphilanthus*, what is initially striking to me is less its reversal of gender positions (female object becomes female subject) but rather its unnerving and wholesale occupation of the position of noble imaginary: Pamphilia becomes a new Astrophil. It is certainly true, as Naomi J. Miller suggests, that Wroth's sequence "can be seen to be carving out a discursive space among early modern English figurations of gender within which she can associate the 'otherness' of women, previously seen as objects of desire, with both sexes configured anew as agents of passion."[4] Yet at the same time, Pamphilia's almost suffocating emphasis on her own constancy seizes the very social consistency so desired by previous sonneteers and turns it to her own social advantage. As Elizabeth Hanson remarks, the sequence's "avowed purpose is to prove the persona's constancy, to demonstrate that however long she may write and suffer she will never, ever change."[5] While earlier sequences continually stage their own struggle into discourse in the slow appearance of a new vocabulary to describe social relations, the emphasis on constancy in Wroth's sequence should be seen as in part a distinctly rear-guard action resolutely asserting the social power of noble privilege. Both William Kennedy and Rosalind Smith have suggested that Wroth is best grouped as a restrained member of the politically engaged Protestant poets seeking to support pro-Protestant policies through the idealization of Elizabethan forms and, in particular, of Sidney as a chivalric knight. Far from subordinated, Wroth was a political player. For Kennedy, Wroth's emphasis on Pamphilia's "forbearance," in contrast to Astrophil's "irresponsible behavior," "has nothing to do with any essentialized gender differences between Astrophil's masculine defiance and Pamphilia's feminine compliance. It rather involves a status-inflected devotion to higher causes."[6] Wroth's patrimony makes possible – in a way simply not available to almost any other contemporary sonneteer – her appropriation of the noble ideals associated with Astrophil. Unlike Daniel, Spenser, or Shakespeare, Lady Mary Wroth, like her father Robert Sidney, could claim effectively to *be* an Astrophil.

In the final sonnet of "A crowne of Sonetts dedicated to Love," for instance, Pamphilia quite explicitly disentangles herself from the very economic difficulties so central to other sonneteers:

> Except my hart which you beestow'd before,
> And for a signe of conquest gave away
> As worthles to bee kept in your choyse store
> Yett one more spotles with you doth nott stay.
>
> The tribute which my hart doth truly pay
> Is faith untouch'd, pure thoughts discharge the score
> Of debts for mee, wher constancy bears sway,
> And rules as Lord, unharm'd by envyes sore,

Yett other mischiefs faile nott to attend,
As enimies to you, my foes must bee;
Curst jealousie doth all her forces bend
To my undoing; thus my harmes I see.

Soe though in Love I fervently doe burne,
In this strange labourinth how shall I turne?[7]

[P90]

Like nearly every English sonnet speaker, Pamphilia figures her love as a financial debt that needs to be repaid. Unlike any other sonneteer – including Sidney – Pamphilia considers her account reconciled: "pure thoughts discharge the score / Of debts for me." Her constancy functions as the noble imaginary so many previous sonneteers tried to use to pay off their willing loans. It is as if Shakespeare's young man not only reproduced, but freed himself of the dark lady's mortgage. Pamphilia's tender for this transaction is her constancy; as she puts in the final lines of her final sonnet, "And thus leave off, what's past showes you can love, / Now lett your constancy your honor prove" (P103.13–14). "Honor" here needs to be read not only as sexual honor – her constancy in love, her fidelity, the classic locus of female honor – but also as the other traditional sense of honor, the one Astrophil returns to again and again: honor as the outward sign of an inner nobility, of nobility itself set apart from the mutabilities of worldly exchange. Her nobility is proven, in the sense of both tested and established. In a strictly political register, the poem might be read, in Smith's words, as Wroth "offering her Protestant legacy to the king";[8] at a more broadly construed social level, it is a claim, set inside a "crown" of sonnets, to define and control nobility itself.

At the same time, Pamphilia's vigorous seizure of a noble imaginary is inherently contradictory. If Drayton's idealization of Astrophil leads him to a concrete formulation of a social distinction tacitly antagonistic to the monarch, Wroth's gender has similarly paradoxical effects. As Pamphilia puts it in P90, "Yett other mischiefs faile not to attend" her insistence upon her own honorific constancy. In claiming a noble and feminine place that is constant, her appropriation of the noble imaginary helps make possible the reimagination of "female" as private and increasingly domestic. As several critics note, this gender configuration, distinct from the classical understanding of *oikos*, facilitates the discourse of social mobility over the next three centuries.[9] Even as Pamphilia claims for herself an unprecedented position of noble social power, that position helps to codify the emergence of a new, explicit language of class through the articulation of a modern sex/gender system. Her claim to use her constancy to pay off her debts results in a suffocating emphasis on her distance from the social world:

> When every one to pleasing pastimes hies
> Some hunt, some hauke, some play, while some delight
> In sweet discourse, and musique showes joys might
> Yett I my thoughts doe farr above thes prise.
>
> The joy which I take, is that free from eyes
> I sitt, and wunder att this daylike night
> Soe to dispose them-selves, as voyd of right;
> And leave true pleasure for poore vanities;
>
> When others hunt, my thoughts I have in chase;
> If hauke, my minde att wished end doth fly,
> Discourse, I with my spiritt tauke, and cry
> While others, musique choose as greatest grace.
>
> O God, say I, can thes fond pleasures move?
> Or musique bee butt in sweet thoughts of love?

[P 26]

As Hanson notes, the pursuits Pamphilia rejects are not particularly masculine (as some have tried to claim). Instead, "[w]hat's being rejected here is social activity of any kind."[10] Yet these "pleasing pastimes" are quite specifically *noble* social activities (these aren't sheep shearing festivals), and while the activities are not specifically gendered, the speaker is. The conspicuous separation of a female speaker from these noble activities is an early instance of a largely eighteenth-century phenomenon chronicled by McKeon: the correlation of inner virtue as distinctly feminine and "associated with the reformative power of domesticity." Pamphilia's emphasis on an internal, feminine constancy participates in a broad seventeenth-century renovation of patriarchy. As McKeon argues, throughout the seventeenth century the "family is increasingly distinguished from the state, while the component members of the family are increasingly distinguished from each other." As a result, the separation of the domestic family from the aristocratic, patriarchal rule of the state is inseparable from "the modern division of labor and class formation."[11] Women's work, for instance, becomes increasingly devalued as women's private idleness becomes a sign of social standing, and the "vertical" hierarchy of aristocratic value is replaced with a "horizontal" sexual differentiation. Sexual differentiation and class formation are consequently inextricably linked, so that "the early modern emergence of class is one crucial element in the historicization of patriarchy." By rejecting all social activity in favor of her feminine idleness and noble constancy, Pamphilia unwittingly helps to set in motion the ideology of the private feminine household, even though her political influence insures that she is no madwoman in the attic. Because her noble position permits her to reject any social activity, seizing her aristocratic position ends up helping to feminize this nascent private sphere.

The implications of this shift might be traced in a variety of seventeenth-century love lyrics – Rochester, Marvell, and Philips would be high on the list – but it is especially apparent in the work of Milton.[12] Milton's sonnets bring us back where we began in chapter two, for they, as much as any other works, were the models which Romantic writers used to develop the theory of lyric so dominant over the last two hundred years. In the unpublished sonnet "To the Lord General Cromwell, May 1652," for instance, Milton refigures the myth of Astrophil – the Protestant noble hero who reconciles social contradiction – in the figure of the "Lord General" himself.[13] The poet who half comically hid in his house "When the assault was intended to the City," but who nevertheless claimed extravagant powers for poetry, now emerges and openly confronts this "captain or colonel":[14]

> Cromwell, our chief of men, who through a cloud
>   Not of war only, but detractions rude,
>   Guided by faith and matchless fortitude
>   To peace and truth thy glorious way hast ploughed,
> And on the neck of crownèd Fortune proud
>   Hast reared God's trophies and his work pursued,
>   While Darwen stream with blood of Scots imbrued,
>   And Dunbar field resounds thy praises loud,
> And Worcester's laureate wreath; yet more remains
>   To conquer still; peace hath her victories
>   No less renowned than war, new foes arise
> Threat'ning to bind our souls with secular chains:
>   Help us to save free conscience from the paw
>   Of hireling wolves whose Gospel is their maw.

The resolution Cromwell offers is both realized – the Scots and the Covenanters have been defeated – and promised: "new foes arise." Milton places the imaginary position which will resolve social problems within the social problems themselves, rather than situating resolution in a place apart; it is as if Shakespeare set the young man in the "bark" of sonnet 116, or as if Astrophil were able to identify in the present tense with his Arcadian personality in sonnet 41. In part, the possibility of situating an ideal figure within a narrative history emerges from Milton's Protestantism. Cromwell here is a new version of Lok's Queen Elizabeth, offering protection to the godly and a realization of the New Jerusalem on earth.

But also like Lok, Milton defers satisfaction by stressing contemporary political crisis. The result is that the speaker himself comes to resemble the imaginary position: it is not only Cromwell but Milton's speaker who is "chief of men." Like Drayton's adventurous sea farer, we register the oft-varying fate of the world through this speaker's embrace of contingency itself. As Christopher Kendrick remarks of the speaker of *Areopagitica*, "a state of indecision, in which the individual is determined by his situation, is turned into a state of decisive empoweredness."[15] Milton's speaker is a conspicuously public and male speaker, and his power appears in this public demonstration of his private "free conscience."

This dynamic is similarly present in Milton's famous final sonnet, "Methought I saw my late espoused Saint," possibly written in the 1650s but not published till 1673:

> Methought I saw my late espousèd saint
>   Brought to me like Alcestis from the grave,
>   Whom Jove's great son to her glad husband gave,
>   Rescued from death by force though pale and faint.
> Mine as whom washed from spot of child-bed taint
>   Purification in the old Law did save,
>   And such, as yet once more I trust to have
>   Full sight of her in Heaven without restraint,
> Came vested all in white, pure as her mind:
>   Her face was veiled, yet to my fancied sight,
>   Love, sweetness, goodness, in her person shined
> So clear, as in no face with more delight.
>   But O as to embrace me she inclined,
>   I waked, she fled, and day brought back my night.

The traditional questions about this sonnet – is it really about Milton's wife, and if so, which one? – articulate at a misleadingly biographical level a more fundamental conceptual move: the speaker here is defined largely in relation to marriage as an institution which promises an emotional and ontological security to a subject conspicuously in the "night" of the world. The aristocratic imaginary, long the object of the unrequited desire of English sonnet speakers, has been replaced with a new imaginary – wedded bliss. Whereas Spenser's vision of wedded love in the *Epithalamion* remains fixated on idealized nobility, Milton's "espousèd saint" sets in motion a conceptual maneuver that facilitates the reconceptualization of sonnets in the nineteenth century as expressing a private erotic desire, a true, interior affect.

The roots of this new domestic imaginary are deep. Milton's sonnet invokes the *donna angelicata* tradition so important for Spenser. The "espousèd saint" here represents the speaker's relation to the "Full sight of . . . Heaven without restraint," much as Beatrice and (to a lesser extent) Laura represent for Dante and Petrarch a conduit to holiness itself. Dante's conception of Beatrice depends upon a system of resemblances; his relation to Beatrice is like his relation to God, and the microcosm of his love leads to the macrocosm of the universe. Milton's speaker, conversely, is situated in a structure of difference: his ultimate distance from God, the conceptual residue of Milton's Calvinist roots, manifests itself in a negative logic familiar from Lok. Heaven and the "espousèd saint" exist as a dream, a utopian product of his "night," a place where Greek myth and the "old law" effortlessly intermingle to create conceptual order. In short, the space of the "espousèd saint" functions in much the same way as the noble imaginary "Astrophil" did for earlier sonneteers: a resolution to, and a rearticulation of, their own anxious social position. Yet Milton's departure from the English tradition of an aristocratic imaginary is crucial: marriage, not nobility, becomes an object of desire. What has also conspicuously changed, a change especially apparent in light of Wroth's Pamphilia, is the gender of that imaginary. Rather than a masculine ideal of nobility, the object of desire in sonnets becomes transformed into a feminine private scene. The social position of the speaker is no longer defined in relation to a noble imaginary but rather in relation to a private (here, quite literally a dream) vision of married life. At this moment, when feminized privacy starts to become a relatively secure ideal, class becomes an explicit social force in tandem with a sex/gender system that will find its telos, as Fineman might remark, in the Freudian interpretation of such dreams.[16]

Milton's sonnets on Cromwell and "Methought I saw my late espousèd saint" participate in a new dialectic of subject formation and social distinction.[17] For the very public and political pronouncements of the Cromwell sonnet are facilitated by the conceptual private life of the speaker of the final sonnet. Milton's sonnets articulate what Habermas terms the "Bourgeois Public Sphere," the place of "private people who related to each other in it as a public." This public, reasonable relation conversely is "guided specifically by such private experiences as grew out of the audience-oriented subjectivity of the conjugal family's intimate domain."[18] "Bourgeois" for Habermas consequently does not mean that the participants in the public sphere are exclusively bourgeois or middle class,[19] but rather that the criteria for participation – one's social distinction – is based upon bourgeois categories. "The public sphere is a social space of critical debate available to all," suggests Harold Mah, adding that "this idea of universal access . . . presupposes that individuals seem in a fundamental sense undifferentiated or unmarked by acquired traits of wealth, status, or membership in groups."[20] Such a notion of the public stands in sharp opposition to early modern conceptions, in which, Habermas shows, "public" "was something like a status attribute," a representation of one's specific interests, not one's disinterest.[21] What defines participation in the public sphere is not one's status, in other words, but class: "bourgeois" for Habermas refers less to a specific group than to a process of social differentiation. Anyone who appears rational, objective, and disinterested can participate in public debate.

Yet the seeming disinterest promised by class, in opposition to status, sets in motion a dialectic we have already seen in chapter two. For disinterest itself marks a specifically interested social position, a position invested in appearing objective. "[T]he conjugal family's self-image of its intimate sphere," argues Habermas, "collided even within the conscious-ness of the bourgeoisie itself with the real functions of the bourgeois family," for "it was a private autonomy denying its economic origins . . . that provided the bourgeois family with its consciousness of itself."[22] Mah similarly remarks that "[t]he enabling condition of a successfully staged public sphere is the ability of certain groups to make their social or group particularity invisible so that they can then appear as abstract individuals and hence universal."[23] The public sphere requires, in other words, what Bourdieu calls "symbolic capital," in Carolyn Betensky's elegant phrase, "capital that says it is not capital."[24] This dialectic leads to some paradoxical implications. Because public participation depends upon denying any private interest, this putative disinterest evaporates when those "invisible" private origins fail: failure in the market place, or in "the lasting community of love on the part of two spouses," eliminates the possibility of participation in the public sphere.[25] Milton's final sonnet enacts the precariousness of the position Habermas speaks of, the sense that the failure to command the commodity and the wife is at the same time a failure in public life, a collapse of public position. We might say then that the "espousèd saint" appears to Milton's speaker with all the mysteriousness of a commodity relation, an elusive promise of possession such as we saw in Spenser's *Amoretti and Epithalamion* and which will, two hundred years later, become the center-piece of Marx's analysis of capital. Nevertheless, Milton's capacity lyrically to abstract this precariousness into a sonnet itself sets in motion the private authority – the control of goods – which authorizes his public position. The very fact of his private "interest" signals his universal, humane emotion that authorizes his public, political pronouncements. Conversely, his public position, for instance, his ability to give political advice to Cromwell, depends upon the suppression of the speaker's particular interests under the category of private.

In post-romantic terms, we might call this privacy "original, unconventional lyricism." For with this formation of the control of feminine privacy in the service of public, objective declaration we enter into the earliest explicit foundations of romantic lyricism. A primary means of displaying one's disinterest, one's universal humanity, after all, is the sort of emotion one finds celebrated in Romantic sonnets. Sonneteers from Smith to Wordsworth construct the romantic conception of lyric out of the poetic potential of masculine public authority – what Wordsworth called the "majestic harmony" of Milton's sonnets[26] – defined in relation to a female private domain. Milton's renovation of the English sonnet is a source of the dialectic of romanticism in which private emotions become everyone's emotions; the purported universality and disinterest of affect authorizes public social participation. Converted by Milton into a domestic scene, the noble imaginary is gradually transformed into, as we saw in chapter two, the bourgeois aristocracy of culture. It is consequently a formula which sets in motion a distinctly bourgeois vision of social position – not, again, the exclusive right of the bourgeoisie as a group, but rather a conceptual organization of social life called class.

Notes

1   SONNET SEQUENCES AND SOCIAL DISTINCTION

1. Gayatri Chakravorty Spivak, "Translator's Preface" to Jacques Derrida, *Of Grammatology, Corrected Edition*, trans. Spivak (Baltimore: The Johns Hopkins University Press, 1998), xiii.
2. Pierre Bourdieu, *Distinction: A Social Critique of the Judgement of Taste*, trans. Richard Nice (Cambridge, MA: Harvard University Press, 1984), 483.
3. Henry Lok, *Svndry Christian Passions Contained in two hundred Sonnets* (London: Richard Field, 1593), A4^r.
4. *The Works of Michael Drayton*, 5 vols. ed. J. William Hebel (Oxford: The Shakespeare Head Press, 1932–41), 2.310. All quotations of Drayton refer to this edition.
5. Although Gascoigne momentarily describes some sonnets as a sequence, the term "sonnet sequence" does not become a stable generic marker until the nineteenth century. See the discussion in chapter 2. On Gascoigne, see William T. Going, "Gascoigne and the Term 'Sonnet Sequence,'" *Notes and Queries* 1 (1954): 189–91.
6. On the social position of epic and romance, see David Quint, *Epic and Empire: Politics and Generic Form from Virgil to Milton* (Princeton: Princeton University Press, 1993); on the ties between Lucan's *Pharsalia* and a republican tradition see David Norbrook, *Writing the English Republic: Poetry, Rhetoric and Politics, 1627–1660* (Cambridge: Cambridge University Press, 1999).
7. See Michael R. G. Spiller, *The Development of the Sonnet: An Introduction* (London: Routledge, 1992), 11–27, who charts the murky emergence of sonnets and sonnet sequences out of Italian and Provençal traditions.
8. M. M. Bakhtin, "Epic and Novel: Toward a Methodology for the Study of the Novel," in *The Dialogic Imagination*, ed. Michael Holquist, trans. Caryl Emerson and Michael Holquist (Austin: University of Texas Press, 1981), 3.
9. For previous efforts to define sonnet sequences systematically, see Michael R. G. Spiller, *The Sonnet Sequence: A Study of Its Strategies* (New York: Twayne Publishers, 1997); T. P. Roche, *Petrarch and the English Sonnet Sequences* (New York: AMS Press, 1989); and Carol Thomas Neely, "The Structure of English Renaissance Sonnet Sequences," *ELH* 45 (1978): 359–89.
10. *The Winter's Tale*, 3.2.103–04, in *The Riverside Shakespeare*, ed. G. Blakemore Evans *et al.* (Boston: Houghton Mifflin, 1974).

11. Stephen Greenblatt, *Renaissance Self-Fashioning from More to Shakespeare* (Chicago: University of Chicago Press, 1980).
12. I cannot do justice to the complexity of Bourdieu's argument in this introduction, but for a representative, self-consciously funny example, see Bourdieu, *Distinction*, 482: "The classifying subjects who classify the properties and practices of others, or their own, are also classifiable objects which classify themselves (in the eyes of others) by appropriating practices and properties that are already classified (as vulgar or distinguished, high or low, heavy or light etc. – in other words, in the last analysis, as popular or bourgeois) according to their probable distribution between groups that are themselves classified. The most classifying and best classified of these properties are, of course, those which are overtly designated to function as signs of distinction or marks of infamy, stigmata, especially the names and titles expressing class membership whose intersection defines social identity at any given time – the name of a nation, a region, an ethnic group, a family name, the name of an occupation, an educational qualification, honorific titles and so on. Those who classify themselves or others, by appropriating or classifying practices or properties that are classified and classifying, cannot be unaware that, through distinctive objects or practices in which their 'powers' are expressed and which, being appropriated by and appropriate to classes, classify those who appropriate them, they classify themselves in the eyes of other classifying (but also classifiable) subjects, endowed with classificatory schemes analogous to those which enable them more or less adequately to anticipate their own classification."
13. For an overview of this familiar issue, see Richard Halpern, *The Poetics of Primitive Accumulation: English Renaissance Culture and the Genealogy of Capital* (Ithaca: Cornell University Press, 1991), 2–9. Throughout I am deeply influenced by the subtle rereading of Foucault and Althusser by Judith Butler, *The Psychic Life of Power: Theories in Subjection* (Stanford: Stanford University Press, 1997), 106–31; and by Slavoj Žižek's reading of Butler in *The Ticklish Subject: The Absent Centre of Political Ontology* (London: Verso, 1999), 247–312.
14. See Pierre Bourdieu, *Pascalian Meditations*, trans. Richard Nice (Stanford: Stanford University Press, 2000): "because habitus is . . . a product of a history, the instruments of construction of the social that it invests in practical knowledge of the world and in action are socially constructed, in other words structured by the world that they structure. It follows from this that practical knowledge is doubly informed by the world that it informs: it is constrained by the objective structure of the configuration of properties that the world presents to it; and it is also structured through the schemes, resulting from incorporation of the structures of the world, that it applies in selecting and constructing these objective properties . . . One can also say, following the same logic, that habitus helps to determine what transforms it" (148–49).
15. Giving a name – even one as elusive as "the *English* straine" – to this cultural phenomenon indicates Drayton's awareness that his work participates in a concern with "Englishness" at the Elizabethan fin-de-siècle, an issue which is outside the scope of this book. For a wide-ranging discussion of the connections between Petrarchism and nationalism, see William Kennedy, *The*

Site of Petrarchism: Early Modern National Sentiment in Italy, France, and England (Baltimore: The Johns Hopkins University Press, 2003). See also Richard Helgerson, *Forms of Nationhood: The Elizabethan Writing of England* (Chicago: University of Chicago Press, 1992), 14, who cites "Into these loves" as an example of the mobility of English national identity.

16. Christopher Pye, *The Vanishing: Shakespeare, the Subject, and Early Modern Culture* (Durham: Duke University Press, 2000), 7. Pye draws in particular on Ernesto Laclau and Chantal Mouffe, *Hegemony and Socialist Strategy: Toward a Radical Democratic Politics*, 2nd edn. (London: Verso, 2001).

17. My stress on the instability of social order, and on struggles over classification, differentiates my work from the recent turn to a "new materialism" in Renaissance studies. See Pye, *The Vanishing*, who remarks that the emphasis on "the empirical fact of multiplicity," on tracing "discursive instances" across a wide range of texts, tends "to answer an essentialist account of the subject with a positive account of the social domain," "as if the empirical fact of multiplicity might at once counter humanist universalism and acknowledge social difference, conveying something of the endlessly rich texture of historical society as such." In contrast, Pye stresses that "an analysis of the subject as socially determined needs to be as scrupulous in its questioning of the existence of society as a phenomenal category, as a given, as it is in its questioning of the existence of subjectivity as a given" (7). See also Étienne Balibar, *The Philosophy of Marx*, trans. Chris Turner (London: Verso, 1995), esp. 13–41. The problem with "all hitherto existing materialisms" for Marx, argues Balibar, was that they were all finally idealisms. In contrast, Marx's radical "materialist" turn in *The German Ideology* "resulted not so much in putting an end to idealism, but in installing the materialism/idealism dilemma – the perennial question of their difference – at the very heart of the theory" (27). The emphasis on "objects" in recent Renaissance criticism tends, as Balibar remarks of Marx's critique of "old materialism," to conceal "an idealist foundation" (25). For related sentiments, see Jonathan Gil Harris, "The New New Historicism's *Wunderkammer* of Objects," *European Journal of English Studies* 4. 3 (2000): 111–23. On the material turn, see for instance *Renaissance Culture and the Everyday*, ed. Patricia Fumerton and Simon Hunt (Philadelphia: University of Pennsylvania Press, 1998); and Ann Rosalind Jones and Peter Stallybrass, *Renaissance Clothing and the Materials of Memory* (Cambridge: Cambridge University Press, 2000).

18. For lists of sequences and discussions of criteria for counting them, see Roche, *Petrarch and the English Sonnet Sequences*; and Spiller, *The Development of the Sonnet*.

19. See Slavoj Žižek, *The Sublime Object of Ideology* (London: Verso, 1989): "This is probably the fundamental dimension of 'ideology': ideology is not simply a 'false consciousness,' an illusory representation of reality, it is rather this reality itself which is already to be conceived as 'ideological' – *'ideological' is a social reality whose very existence implies the non-knowledge of its participants as to its essence* – that is, the social effectivity, the very

reproduction of which implies that the individuals 'do not know what they are doing.' *'Ideological' is not the 'false consciousness' of a (social) being but this being itself in so far as it is supported by 'false consciousness'"* (21).

20. Joel Fineman, *Shakespeare's Perjured Eye: The Invention of Poetic Subjectivity in the Sonnets* (Berkeley: University of California Press, 1986), 22, 24. See also the very similar argument in Jonathan V. Crewe, *Trials of Authorship: Anterior Forms and Poetic Reconstruction from Wyatt to Shakespeare* (Berkeley: University of California Press, 1990), who locates doubleness in Wyatt's "craft," "a struggle for or against identification" that is "the condition of any Renaissance self, or of the Renaissance itself" (44).

21. The best current overview of the classic position is Gordon Braden, *Petrarchan Love and the Continental Renaissance* (New Haven: Yale University Press, 1999); see also William Kerrigan and Gordon Braden, *The Idea of the Renaissance* (Baltimore: The Johns Hopkins University Press, 1989), 157–89; and Leonard Wilson Forster, *The Icy Fire: Five Studies in European Petrarchism* (Cambridge: Cambridge University Press, 1969).

22. The seminal statement is by Arthur F. Marotti, "'Love is Not Love': Elizabethan Sonnet Sequences and the Social Order," *ELH* 49 (1982): 396–428. See also Roland Greene, *Unrequited Conquests: Love and Empire in the Colonial Americas* (Chicago: University of Chicago Press, 1999); Ilona Bell, *Elizabethan Women and the Poetry of Courtship* (Cambridge: Cambridge University Press, 1998); Lisa M. Klein, *The Exemplary Sidney and the Elizabethan Sonneteer* (Newark: University of Delaware Press, 1998); Kim F. Hall, *Things of Darkness: Economies of Race and Gender in Early Modern England* (Ithaca: Cornell University Press, 1995), 62–122; Nigel Smith, *Literature and Revolution in England 1640–1660* (New Haven: Yale University Press, 1994), 250–94; Patricia Fumerton, *Cultural Aesthetics: Renaissance Literature and the Practice of Social Ornament* (Chicago: University of Chicago Press, 1991), 67–110; Ann Rosalind Jones, *The Currency of Eros: Women's Love Lyric in Europe, 1540–1620* (Bloomington: Indiana University Press, 1990); Jane Hedley, *Power in Verse: Metaphor and Metonymy in the Renaissance Lyric* (University Park: Pennsylvania State University Press, 1988); Ann Rosalind Jones and Peter Stallybrass, "The Politics of *Astrophil and Stella*," *SEL* 24 (1984): 53–68; Patricia Parker, *Literary Fat Ladies: Rhetoric, Gender, Property* (London: Methuen, 1987), 126–54; Nancy Vickers, "Diana Described: Scattered Woman and Scattered Rhyme," *Critical Inquiry* 8 (1981): 265–79.

23. See for instance John Huntington, *Ambition, Rank, and Poetry in 1590s England* (Urbana: University of Illinois Press, 2001); Norbrook, *Writing the English Republic*; Louis A. Montrose, "Spenser's Domestic Domain: Poetry, Property, and the Early Modern Subject," in *Subject and Object in Renaissance Culture*, ed. Margreta de Grazia, Maureen Quilligan, and Peter Stallybrass (Cambridge: Cambridge University Press, 1996), 83–130; Patricia Parker, *Shakespeare from the Margins: Language, Culture, Context* (Chicago: University of Chicago Press, 1996); and Helgerson, *Forms of Nationhood*.

24. Steven W. May, *The Elizabethan Courtier Poets: The Poems and Their Contexts* (Columbia: University of Missouri Press, 1991).

25. William Kennedy, *Authorizing Petrarch* (Ithaca: Cornell University Press, 1994); Kennedy, *The Site of Petrarchism*, 3.

26. See Roland Greene, *Post-Petrarchism: Origins and Innovations of the Western Lyric Sequence* (Princeton: Princeton University Press, 1991). See also Gordon Braden, "Gaspara Stampa and the Gender of Petrarchism," *TSLL* 38. 2 (1996): 115–39, who criticizes "[r]eferences to Petrarchism in recent criticism (particularly English-language criticism)" that "often imply that we largely know what to make of it now" (115). The exhaustion of a tradition of epideictic poetry is a central thesis of Fineman, *Shakespeare's Perjured Eye*.

27. Diana E. Henderson, *Passion Made Public: Elizabethan Lyric Gender, and Performance* (Urbana: University of Illinois Press, 1995), 11. Lynn Enterline, *The Rhetoric of the Body from Ovid to Shakespeare* (Cambridge: Cambridge University Press, 2000), 36. See also Gordon Braden, *Petrarchan Love*; Elizabeth Hanson, "Boredom and Whoredom: Reading Renaissance Women's Sonnet Sequences," *The Yale Journal of Criticism* 10 (1997): 165–91; Naomi J. Miller, *Changing the Subject: Mary Wroth and Figurations of Gender in Early Modern England* (Lexington: University Press of Kentucky, 1996), 18–63; Heather Dubrow, *Echoes of Desire: English Petrarchism and Its Counterdiscourses* (Ithaca: Cornell University Press, 1995); Kennedy, *Authorizing Petrarch*; and Barbara L. Estrin, *Laura: Uncovering Gender and Genre in Wyatt, Donne, and Marvell* (Durham: Duke University Press, 1994). My understanding of early modern gender throughout is indebted to Katherine Eggert, *Showing Like a Queene: Female Authority and Literary Experiment in Spenser, Shakespeare, and Milton* (Philadelphia: University of Pennsylvania Press, 2000); Jennifer Summit, *Lost Property: The Woman Writer and English Literary History, 1380–1589* (Chicago: University of Chicago Press, 2000); Jonathan Goldberg, *Desiring Women Writing: English Renaissance Examples* (Stanford: Stanford University Press, 1997); Lorna Hutson, *The Usurer's Daughter: Male Friendship and Fictions of Women in Sixteenth-Century England* (London: Routledge, 1994); and Ann Baynes Coiro, "Writing in Service: Sexual Politics and Class Position in the Poetry of Aemilia Lanyer and Ben Jonson," *Criticism* 35 (1993): 357–76.

28. See Pierre Bourdieu, *Masculine Domination*, trans. Richard Nice (Stanford: Stanford University Press, 2001): "one has to confront a new paradox, entailing a complete revolution in the approach to 'women's history': do not the invariants which, beyond all the visible changes in the position of women, are observed in the relations of domination between the sexes require one to take as one's privileged object the historical mechanisms and institutions which, in the course of history, have continuously abstracted these invariants from history?" (4).

29. Greene, *Unrequited Conquests*, 4.

30. In contrast, see William Stull, "'Why Are Not *Sonnets* Made of Thee?' A New Context for the 'Holy Sonnets' of Donne, Herbert, and Milton," *Modern Philology* 80. 2 (1982): 129–35, who suggests that Henry Lok, Constable, Herbert, and Donne offer a religious alternative to the Petrarchan sonnet tradition.

31. The most compelling such account is Greene, *Post-Petrarchism*, 3–21, who describes the interaction of "ritual" and "fictional" modes in lyric. See my discussion in chapter two of Paul de Man, "Lyric and Modernity," in *Blindness*

and Insight: Essays in the Rhetoric of Contemporary Criticism (Minneapolis: University of Minnesota Press, 1971), 166–86; and Theodor W. Adorno, "On Lyric Poetry and Society," *Notes to Literature*, 2 vol., ed. Rolf Tiedemann, trans. Shierry Weber Nicholsen (New York: Columbia University Press, 1991), 2:37–54. See also Susan Stewart, "Preface to a Lyric History," in *The Uses of Literary History*, ed. Marshall Brown (Durham: Duke University Press, 1995), 199–218; Dubrow, *Echoes of Desire*, 28–35; Christopher Martin, *Policy in Love: Lyric and Public in Ovid, Petrarch, and Shakespeare* (Pittsburgh: Duquesne University Press, 1994); Teodolinda Barolini, "The Making of a Lyric Sequence: Time and Narrative in Petrarch's *Rerum vulgarium fragmenta*," *MLN* 104 (1989): 1–38; Sandra L. Bermann, *The Sonnet Over Time: A Study in the Sonnets of Petrarch, Shakespeare, and Baudelaire* (Chapel Hill: University of North Carolina Press, 1988); Patricia Parker, *Literary Fat Ladies*, 54–66; John Freccero, "The Fig Tree and the Laurel: Petrarch's Poetics," *Literary Theory/Renaissance Texts*, ed. Patricia Parker and David Quint (Baltimore: The Johns Hopkins University Press, 1986), 20–32; *Lyric Poetry: Beyond New Criticism*, ed. Chaviva Hosek and Patricia Parker (Ithaca: Cornell University Press, 1985); Adena Rosmarin, "Hermeneutics versus Erotics: Shakespeare's Sonnets and Interpretive History," *PMLA* 100 (1985): 20–37; M. L. Rosenthal and Sally M. Grall, *The Modern Poetic Sequence: The Genius of Modern Poetry* (Oxford: Oxford University Press, 1983); W. R. Johnson, *The Idea of Lyric: Lyric Modes in Ancient and Modern Poetry* (Berkeley: University of California Press, 1982); Nancy J. Vickers, "Diana Described"; Sharon Cameron, *Lyric Time: Dickinson and the Limits of Genre* (Baltimore: The Johns Hopkins University Press, 1979); James E. Miller, *The American Quest for a Supreme Fiction : Whitman's Legacy in the Personal Epic* (Chicago: University of Chicago Press, 1979); and Giuseppe Mazzotta, "The *Canzoniere* and the Language of the Self," *SP* 75 (1978): 271–96.

32. For a contemporary articulation of this position, see Helen Vendler, *The Art of Shakespeare's Sonnets* (Cambridge, MA: Belknap Press, 1997): "Contemporary emphasis on the participation of literature in a social matrix balks at acknowledging how lyric, though it may *refer to* the social, remains the genre that directs its *mimesis* toward the performance of the mind in *solitary* speech. Because lyric is intended to be voiceable by anyone reading it, in its normative form it deliberately strips away most social specification (age, regional location, sex, class, even race). A social reading is better directed at a novel or a play: the abstraction desired by the writer of, and the willing reader of, normative lyric frustrates the mind that wants social fictions or biographical revelations" (1–2). Vendler's objections are fully anticipated by Adorno, "On Lyric Poetry and Society."

33. This view finds its most extreme embodiment in archetypal and numerological accounts of sequences. See for example Alastair Fowler, *Triumphal Forms: Structural Patterns in Elizabethan Poetry* (Cambridge: Cambridge University Press, 1970), 174–97, who suggests that we view the sonnets of a sequence as stanzas rather than discrete poems.

34. *Dear Mr. Rossetti: The Letters of Dante Gabriel Rossetti and Hall Caine 1878–1881*, ed. Vivien Allen (Sheffield: Sheffield Academic Press, 2000), 176.

35. See Bourdieu, *Distinction*, 485–500.

36. Fredric Jameson, *The Political Unconscious: Narrative as a Socially Symbolic Act* (Ithaca: Cornell University Press, 1981), 79.
37. I gloss over many substantial disagreements here. For an overview, see the collection of exchanges by Ernst Bloch, George Lukács, Bertolt Brecht, Walter Benjamin, and Theodor Adorno, *Aesthetics and Politics* (New York: Verso, 1980).
38. Žižek, *The Sublime Object of Ideology*, 11.
39. See in this regard especially Judith Butler, *Bodies That Matter: On the Discursive Limits of "Sex"* (New York: Routledge, 1993).
40. On Bourdieu's ties to a Marxist tradition, see the introduction to *Reading Bourdieu on Society and Culture*, ed. Bridget Fowler (Oxford: Blackwell, 2000), 1–21.
41. On Bourdieu's reception, see Loic J. D. Wacquant, "Bourdieu in America: Notes on the Transatlantic Importation of Social Theory," in *Bourdieu: Critical Perspectives*, ed. Craig Calhoun, Edward LiPuma, and Moishe Postone (Chicago: University of Chicago Press, 1993), 235–62; John Guillory, "Bourdieu's Refusal," *MLQ* 58.4 (1997): 367–98. and Daniel Simeoni, "Anglicizing Bourdieu," in *Pierre Bourdieu: Fieldwork in Culture*, ed. Nicholas Brown and Imre Szeman (Lanham, MD: Rowman and Littlefield, 2000), 65–86. Bourdieu is in turn sharply critical, even dismissive, of Butler in *Masculine Domination*, viii. Butler reads Bourdieu as a closet structuralist in "Performativity's Social Magic," in *Bourdieu: A Critical Reader*, ed. Richard Shusterman (Oxford: Blackwell, 1999), 113–28; Despite these differences, see the connections between them made by Terry Lovell, "Thinking Feminism With and Against Bourdieu," in *Reading Bourdieu*, 27–48.
42. I follow especially Pierre Bourdieu, "Social Space and the Genesis of 'Classes,'" *Language and Symbolic Power*, ed. John B. Thompson, trans. Gino Raymond and Matthew Adamson (Cambridge, MA: Harvard University Press, 1991), 229–51.
43. Bourdieu, "Social Space and the Genesis of 'Classes,'" 238.
44. Mary Poovey, "The Social Constitution of 'Class': Toward a History of Classificatory Thinking," in *Rethinking Class: Literary Studies and Social Formations*, ed. Wai Chee Dimock and Michael T. Gilmore (New York: Columbia University Press, 1994), 15; Bourdieu, "Social Space and the Genesis of 'Classes,'" 233. On the renewed emphasis on the historical construction of class and its relation to literature, see Rita Felski, "Nothing to Declare: Identity, Shame, and the Lower Middle Class," *PMLA* 115 (2000): 33–45; James Holstun, *Ehud's Dagger: Class Struggle in the English Revolution* (London: Verso, 2000); Fredric Jameson, "Marx's Purloined Letter," in *Ghostly Demarcations: A Symposium on Jacques Derrida's* Specters of Marx (London: Verso, 1999), 26–67; Mary Poovey, *A History of the Modern Fact: Problems of Knowledge in the Sciences of Wealth and Society* (Chicago: University of Chicago Press, 1998); Wai Chee Dimock, *Residues of Justice: Literature, Law, Philosophy* (Berkeley: University of California Press, 1996); Michael McKeon, "Historicizing Patriarchy: The Emergence of Gender Difference in England, 1660–1760," *Eighteenth-Century Studies* 28 (1995): 295–322; Rosemary Kegl, *The Rhetoric of Concealment: Figuring Gender and Class in Renaissance Literature* (Ithaca: Cornell University Press,

1994); John Guillory, *Cultural Capital: The Problem of Literary Canon Formation* (Chicago: University of Chicago Press, 1993); Halpern, *The Poetics of Primitive Accumulation*; Mary Poovey, *Uneven Developments: The Ideological Work of Gender in Mid-Victorian England* (Chicago: University of Chicago Press, 1988); McKeon, *The Origins of the English Novel*; and Christopher Kendrick, *Milton: A Study in Ideology and Form* (London: Methuen, 1986). Throughout I am indebted to the rethinking of class generally by Bourdieu, "Social Space and the Genesis of 'Classes'"; Balibar, *The Philosophy of Marx*; Ellen Meiksins Wood, *The Pristine Culture of Capitalism: A Historical Essay on Old Regimes and Modern States* (London: Verso, 1991); *Bringing Class Back In: Contemporary and Historical Perspectives*, ed. Scott G. McNall, Rhonda F. Levine, and Rick Fantasia (Boulder: Westview Press, 1991); Henri Lefebvre, *The Production of Space*, trans. Donald Nicholson-Smith (Oxford: Blackwell, 1991), 68–168; Jürgen Habermas, *The Structural Transformation of the Public Sphere: An Inquiry into a Category of Bourgeois Society*, trans. Thomas Burger with the assistance of Frederick Lawrence (Cambridge, MA: MIT Press, 1989); Joan Wallach Scott, "On Language, Gender, and Working-Class History," *Gender and the Politics of History* (New York: Columbia University Press, 1988), 53–67; Ellen Meiksins Wood, *The Retreat from Class: A New "True" Socialism* (Cambridge: Cambridge University Press, 1986); and Jürgen Habermas, "Introduction: Some Difficulties in the Attempt to Link Theory and Praxis," *Theory and Practice*, trans. John Viertel (Boston: Beacon Press, 1973), 1–40.

45. "Resemblance" is a term associated with Foucault's account of the episteme of the sixteenth century. See Michel Foucault, *The Order of Things: An Archaeology of the Human Sciences*, 1970 (New York: Vintage, 1994), 17–30. See also Michael Hardt and Antonio Negri, *Empire* (Cambridge, MA: Harvard University Press, 2000), 69–92, who describe the replacement of a "medieval form of transcendence" (83) with a "plane of immanence" (71). On the transition from "status" to "class," throughout I follow in particular McKeon, *The Origins of the English Novel*, 131–75; McKeon, "Historicizing Patriarchy"; Habermas, *The Structural Transformation of the Public Sphere*, 1–26; Halpern, *The Poetics of Primitive Accumulation*; Albert O. Hirschman, *The Passions and the Interests: Political Arguments for Capitalism before Its Triumph* (Princeton: Princeton University Press, 1977); and Lawrence Stone, *The Crisis of the Aristocracy 1558–1641* (Oxford: Oxford University Press, 1967).

46. Brenner, "The Origins of Capitalist Development: A Critique of Neo-Smithian Marxism," *New Left Review* 104 (July/August 1977): 25–92, 83. See also Robert Brenner, "Bourgeois Revolution and Transition to Capitalism," in *The First Modern Society: Essays in English History in Honour of Lawrence Stone*, ed. A. L. Beier, David Cannadine, and James M. Rosenheim (Cambridge: Cambridge University Press, 1989), 271–304, 280; *The Brenner Debate: Agrarian Class Structure and Economic Development in Pre-Industrial Europe*, ed. T. H. Aston and C. H. E. Philpin (Cambridge: Cambridge University Press 1985); Brenner, "The Social Basis of Economic Development," in *Analytical Marxism*, ed. John Roemer (Cambridge: Cambridge University Press, 1986), 23–53; Brenner, *Merchants and Revolution: Commercial Change, Political Conflict, and London's Overseas Traders,*

1550–1653 (Princeton: Princeton University Press, 1993), particularly the Postscript, 638–716. Brenner especially builds upon the argument of Maurice Dobb, *Studies in the Development of Capitalism* (London: Routledge and Kegan Paul, 1946), who stresses that capitalism emerges endogenously from feudalism. Dobb is famously critiqued by Paul Sweezy, who tends to stress external factors in the emergence of capitalism. On the "Sweezy-Dobb Debate," see *The Transition from Feudalism to Capitalism*, ed. R. H. Hilton (London: Verso, 1976). For an ardent defense of and succinct introduction to Brenner, see Ellen Meiksins Wood, *The Origin of Capitalism: A Longer View*, 1999 (London: Verso, 2002), 50–121. See also the important criticisms of *Merchants and Revolution* by Perry Anderson, "Maurice Thomson's War," *London Review of Books*, 4 November 1993. See also Richard Lachmann, *From Manor to Market: Structural Change in England, 1536–1640* (Madison: University of Wisconsin Press, 1987); Robert DuPlessis, *Transitions to Capitalism in Early Modern Europe* (Cambridge: Cambridge University Press, 1997); and Richard Lachmann, *Capitalists in Spite of Themselves: Elite Conflict and Economic Transitions in Early Modern Europe* (Oxford: Oxford University Press, 2000).

47. Robert Brenner, "Feudalism," in *The New Palgrave: Marxian Economics*, ed. John Eatwell, Murray Milgate, and Peter Newman (New York: W. W. Norton, 1990), 170–85, 184. See also Habermas, *The Structural Transformation of the Public Sphere*, who stresses that "[o]n the one hand this [early] capitalism stabilized the power structure of a society organized in estates, and on the other hand it unleashed the very elements within which this power structure would one day dissolve" (15); and Hirschman, *The Passions and the Interests*, who remarks that "[t]o portray a lengthy ideological change or transition as an endogenous process is of course more complex than to depict it as the rise of an independently conceived, insurgent ideology concurrent with the decline of a hitherto dominant ethic. A portrayal of this sort involves the identification of a sequence of concatenated ideas and propositions whose final outcome is necessarily hidden from the proponents of the individual links, at least in the early stages of the process; for they would have shuddered – and revised their thinking – had they realized where their ideas would ultimately lead" (4–5).

48. See the similar argument by Elizabeth Hanson, *Discovering the Subject in Renaissance England* (Cambridge: Cambridge University Press, 1998): "by the time epistemic assumptions are held with sufficient consciousness and consistency to receive philosophical treatment they have long been used by people in highly contingent and untheorized ways to negotiate myriad local crises and opportunities in economic, social, and institutional life" (3). Marx makes a similar point in his discussion of the fetishism of commodities in *Capital: A Critique of Political Economy*, 3 vols. trans. Samuel Moore and Edward Aveling (New York: The Modern Library, 1906): "The characters that stamp products as commodities, and whose establishment is a necessary preliminary to the circulation of commodities, have already acquired the stability of natural, self-understood forms of social life, before man seeks to decipher, not their historical character, for in his eyes they are immutable, but

their meaning" (1:87). On the concept of class before "classes," see E. P. Thompson, "Eighteenth-century English Society: Class Struggle Without Class?" *Social History* 3 (1978): 133–65.

49. See McKeon, "Historicizing Patriarchy." See also Susan Dwyer Amussen, *An Ordered Society: Gender and Class in Early Modern England* (New York: Blackwell, 1988).

50. Eggert, *Showing Like a Queen*, 9–10.

51. Poovey, *Uneven Developments*, 58, 60.

52. Thomas Laqueur, *Making Sex: Body and Gender from the Greeks to Freud* (Cambridge, MA: Harvard University Press, 1990). See also Stephen Orgel, *Impersonations: The Performance of Gender in Shakespeare's England* (Cambridge: Cambridge University Press, 1996); and McKeon, "Historicizing Patriarchy."

53. Lok, *Svndry Christian Passions*, pp. A5^r–A6^v.

54. Parker, *Shakespeare from the Margins*, 21, 22.

55. Such problems similarly inform the two most famous efforts to order Elizabethan England into "sorts," William Harrison's *The Description of England* and Sir Thomas Wilson's *The State of England anno Dom. 1600*. As Holstun, *Ehud's Dagger*, remarks, "[p]remodern systems of status are always, among other things, ways of thinking about, reproducing, and even transforming class relations" (100). See also the discussion of these "perceptions of the social order" in Keith Wrightson, *English Society 1580– 1680* (London: Hutchinson, 1982), 17–38; *The Middling Sort of People: Culture, Society, and Politics in England, 1550–1800*, ed. Jonathan Barry and Christopher Brooks (New York: Palgrave Macmillan, 1994); and Wrightson, "Estates, degrees, and sorts: Changing Perceptions of Society in Tudor and Stuart England," in *Language, History and Class*, ed. Penelope J. Corfield (Oxford: Basil Blackwell, 1991), 30–52.

56. On Lok's familial relations, see the discussion of his mother Anne in chapter 1. On Lok's connections with James VI's court, see the introduction to *New Poems by James I of England From a Hitherto Unpublished Manuscript (ADD. 24195) in the British Museum*, ed. Allan F. Wescott (New York: Columbia University Press, 1911).

2   POST-ROMANTIC LYRIC: CLASS AND THE CRITICAL APPARATUS OF SONNET CONVENTIONS

1. Jacques Derrida, *Dissemination*, trans. Barbara Johnson (Chicago: University of Chicago Press, 1981), 99.

2. Fredric Jameson, *Postmodernism, or, the Cultural Logic of Late Capitalism* (Durham: Duke University Press, 1991), 3.

3. The origination of the term "sonnet sequence" was first noticed by William T. Going, "The Term *Sonnet Sequence*," *MLN* 62 (1947): 400–02; and Going, "Gascoigne and the Term 'Sonnet Sequence,'" *Notes and Queries* 1 (1954): 189–91. Figures for the nineteenth-century production of sonnets and sequences are from William T. Going, *Scanty Plot of Ground: Studies in the Victorian Sonnet* (The Hague and Paris: Mouton, 1976), 34–35.

4. *The Norton Anthology of English Literature, Vol. 1B, The Sixteenth Century, The Early Seventeenth Century*, 7th edn. Stephen Greenblatt et al. (New York: W. W. Norton and Co., 2000), 916–17.
5. The term unrequitedness comes from Roland Greene, *Unrequited Conquests: Love and Empire in the Colonial Americas* (Chicago: University of Chicago Press, 1999). Greene goes on to note that "[w]e live in a culture still heavily invested in Romantic notions about literature, and one of the most powerful of these is that lyric poetry is personal by nature, and social or political only occasionally, indirectly, at removes." Though New Historicism has partially challenged this understanding, "it has come signally short where lyric poetry is concerned . . . recent historicist interpretations of lyric poems are silently beholden to the logic – some would say the tyranny – of that twentieth-century invention, the personalist close reading, which prefers the fictions of personal experience to the social or the cultural, let alone the cross-cultural" (2–3).
6. Lawrence Manley, *Convention 1500–1750* (Cambridge, MA: Harvard University Press, 1980), 3. Manley goes on to note that "[t]he contradiction of the individual with a world of predetermined codes and values is part of our post-Romantic heritage. Although this confrontation was in certain ways anticipated in antiquity, the utter incompatibility of a collective order with the individual was not then seriously at issue. Rather, within the framework of an order-centered and collectively minded world, the principal concern was with the difference between natural patterns and social ones, between those which were universal or permanent and those which were merely arbitrary or temporary . . . If it seems impossible for us to imagine such a world, or to understand it as more than the temporary domination of a specific social code over the minds of individuals, we should remember that neither are we conscious of ourselves as individuals except through opposition to collective order . . . Our opposition to convention is in this respect a post-Romantic issue" (8).
7. See Natalie M. Houston, "Valuable by Design: Material Features and Cultural Value in Nineteenth-Century Sonnet Anthologies," *Victorian Poetry* 37 (1999): 243–72: "the sonnet was, by the end of the nineteenth century, increasingly seen as an object of study for those readers who desired cultural capital – culture that could, in the form of the sonnet, be easily memorized and exchanged" (249). See also Jennifer Wagner, *A Moment's Monument: Revisionary Poetics and the Nineteenth-Century English Sonnet* (Madison and Teaneck: Fairleigh Dickinson University Press; London: Associated University Presses, 1996), 113–28, a detailed study of the emergence of sonnet literature in the nineteenth century. Throughout I also rely on John Guillory, *Cultural Capital: The Problem of Literary Canon Formation* (Chicago: University of Chicago Press, 1993); and Barbara M. Benedict, *Making the Modern Reader: Cultural Mediation in Early Modern Literary Anthologies* (Princeton: Princeton University Press, 1996).
8. Loïc J. D. Wacquant, "The Structure and Logic of Bourdieu's Sociology," in Pierre Bourdieu and Wacquant, *An Invitation to Reflexive Sociology* (Chicago: University of Chicago Press, 1992), 1–59, 40–41, 42.
9. Ellen Meiksins Wood, *The Pristine Culture of Capitalism: A Historical Essay on Old Regimes and Modern States* (London: Verso, 1991). In her succinct definition, the Bourgeois Paradigm is a "dominant paradigm of progress and

historical change" which can be expressed "by a few simple oppositions: rural
vs urban, agriculture vs commerce and industry, communal vs individual,
unreason (magic, superstition, even religion) vs reason, status vs contract,
coercion vs freedom, and, above all, aristocracy vs bourgeoisie . . . The
principle of movement between these polarities of ancient and modern is, in
one form or another, the progressive development of human knowledge,
reason or, more specifically, technology; but these developments tend to take
the shape, within a general framework of rising and falling classes, of a
triumphant bourgeoisie, the bearer of knowledge, innovation and progress –
and, ultimately, the bearer of capitalism and liberal democracy" (3). Wood
goes on to argue that "this model implies that there is a *natural* course of
capitalist development . . . and probably also that the evolution of capitalism
was inevitable" (2). As a result, "the identification of 'capitalism' with
'bourgeoisie' has brought with it a tendency to regard the capitalist system, its
characteristic activities, motivations and imperatives, as little more than an
extension of these apparently ageless social forms. Capitalism [appears as]
simply more trade, more markets, more towns, and, above all, a rising 'middle
class'" (7). Wood closely follows Robert Brenner, "Bourgeois Revolution and
Transition to Capitalism," in *The First Modern Society: Essays in English
History in Honour of Lawrence Stone*, ed. A. L. Beier, David Cannadine, and
James M. Rosenheim (Cambridge: Cambridge University Press, 1989), 271–
304. See also Wood, *The Origin of Capitalism: A Longer View*, 1999 (London:
Verso, 2002).

10. See Pierre Bourdieu, *Distinction: A Social Critique of the Judgement of Taste*,
    trans. Richard Nice (Cambridge, MA: Harvard University Press, 1984),
    especially chapter 1, "The Aristocracy of Culture."

11. Paul de Man, "Lyric and Modernity," in *Blindness and Insight: Essays in the
    Rhetoric of Contemporary Criticism* (Minneapolis: University of Minnesota
    Press, 1971), 166–86, 185–86.

12. On these terms, see M. H. Abrams, *The Mirror and the Lamp* (New York:
    W. W. Norton, 1958).

13. See Arthur F. Marotti, "'Love is Not Love': Elizabethan Sonnet Sequences
    and the Social Order," *ELH* 49 (1982): 396–428.

14. See Guillory, *Cultural Capital*, for a lengthy historicization of the position of
    de Man and his version of deconstruction in the canonization of theory: "the
    de Manian oeuvre [is] . . . a discourse that registers at the heart of its
    terminology the historical moment of the fusion of the university teacher's
    autonomous 'professional activity' with the technobureaucratic organization
    of intellectual labor. Within the larger discourse of 'theory,' rhetorical
    reading has the important symptomatic function of figuring a rapprochement
    with the institutional conditions of criticism, by acknowledging the loss of
    intellectual autonomy as a theory of linguistic determination – at the same
    time that autonomy is continually reinvested in the figure of the master
    theorist" (259).

15. Theodor Adorno, "On Lyric Poetry and Society," *Notes to Literature*, 2 vols.,
    ed. Rolf Tiedemann, trans. Shierry Weber Nicholsen (New York: Columbia
    University Press, 1991), 2 : 37–54, 40.

16. De Man, "Lyric and Modernity," 185.

17. Adorno, "On Lyric Poetry and Society," 45, 38–39.
18. See the description of "over-rapid historicization" in Slavoj Žižek, *The Sublime Object of Ideology* (London: Verso, 1989): "if over-rapid *universalization* produces a quasi-universal Image whose function is to make us blind to its historical, socio-symbolic determination, over-rapid *historicization* makes us blind to the real kernel which returns as the same through diverse historicizations/symbolizations" (50, my italics). Nineteenth-century criticism "universalized" sonnets by producing a "quasi-universal Image," but twentieth-century "over-rapid historicization" has blinded us to the *form*, the "real kernel" of these works.
19. Derrida, *Dissemination*, 168.
20. Samuel Johnson, *Lives of the English Poets*, 3 vols., ed. George Birkbeck Hill (Oxford: Clarendon Press, 1905), 1:169–70.
21. Jonathan Brody Kramnick, *Making the English Canon: Print-Capitalism and the Cultural Past, 1700–1770* (Cambridge: Cambridge University Press, 1998), 107–36. See also Benedict, *Making the Modern Reader*, 153–81; and Lawrence Lipking, *The Ordering of the Arts in Eighteenth-Century England* (Princeton: Princeton University Press, 1970).
22. Charlotte Smith, "Preface to the First Edition," *Elegiac Sonnets*, 4th ed. (London: Dodsley, Gardner, and Bew, 1786), iii. Quoted in Stuart Curran, *Poetic Form and British Romanticism* (Oxford: Oxford University Press, 1986), 30. My account of the sonnet in early romanticism largely follows Curran, 29–55.
23. *Petrarca: A Selection of Sonnets From Various Authors with an Introductory Dissertation on the Origin and Structure of the Sonnet*, ed. George Henderson (London: C. and R. Baldwin, 1803), xvii, xxxiv.
24. Samuel Taylor Coleridge, "Introduction to the Sonnet," *Poems on Various Subjects, 2nd ed., to which are now added Poems by Charles Lamb and Charles Lloyd* (Bristol: J. Cottle; London: Robinsons, 1797), 71. Quoted in Curran, *Poetic Form*, 36–37.
25. Henderson, *Petrarca*, xx–xxii.
26. Coleridge, "Introduction to the Sonnet," quoted in Curran, *Poetic Form*, 36.
27. Anne Janowitz, *Lyric and Labour in the Romantic Tradition* (Cambridge: Cambridge University Press, 1998), 13. Janowitz is reacting to, on the one hand, a humanist tradition of Romantic scholarship and, on the other hand, the deconstruction and historicization of the humanist sense. For the former, see for example Frank Kermode, *Romantic Image* (London: Routledge and Kegan Paul, 1957); Harold Bloom, *Poetry and Repression: Revisionism from Blake to Stevens* (New Haven: Yale University Press, 1975). For the latter, see for example Paul de Man, *The Rhetoric of Romanticism* (New York: Columbia University Press, 1984); Jerome McGann, *The Romantic Ideology* (Chicago: University of Chicago Press, 1980); and Marjorie Levinson, *Wordsworth's Great Period Poems* (Cambridge: Cambridge University Press, 1986). For a critique similar to Janowitz's which deals specifically with Wordsworth's sonnets, see William H. Galperin, *Revision and Authority in Wordsworth: The Interpretation of a Career* (Philadelphia: University of Pennsylvania Press, 1989).

28. Adela Pinch, *Strange Fits of Passion: Epistemologies of Emotion, Hume to Austen* (Stanford: Stanford University Press, 1996), 7.
29. Guillory, *Cultural Capital*, 92.
30. William Wordsworth, "Essay, Supplementary to the Preface (1815)," in *William Wordsworth*, ed. Stephen Gill (Oxford: Oxford University Press, 1984), 640–62, 657–58.
31. Henderson, *Petrarca*, ix.
32. *Laura: or An Anthology of Sonnets, (On the Petrarchan Model,) and Elegiac Quatuorzains: English, Italian, Spanish, Portuguese, French, and German; Original and translated; Great part never before publisht. With A Preface, Critical and Biographic; Notes, and Index. In Five Volumes*, ed. Capel Lofft (London: B. and R. Crosby and Co., 1814), cl–cli.
33. Cf. Paul Fussell, *Poetic Meter and Poetic Form*, rev. ed. (New York: Random House, 1979), whose commentary on the differences between the "Petrarchan" and "Shakespearean" sonnet is representative of this tradition. Lurking in Fussell's purely formalist language are complex questions of nationalist and social criteria: "Although the basic action of both Petrarchan and Shakespearean sonnets is similar, it is the proportioning that makes the immense difference between them. Both present and then 'solve' problems, the Petrarchan form in its octave and sestet, the Shakespearean in its comparatively hypertrophied initial twelve lines and then in its couplet. In the Petrarchan sonnet the problem is often solved by reasoned perception or by a relatively expansive and formal meditative process, for the sestet allows enough room for the undertaking of prudent, highly reasonable kinds of solutions. But in the Shakespearean sonnet, because resolution must take place within the tiny compass of a twenty-syllable couplet, the 'solution' is more likely to be the fruit of wit, or paradox, or even a quick shaft of sophistry, logical cleverness, or outright comedy . . . there remains something ineffably witty about the form of the Shakespearean sonnet, something that distinguishes it essentially as a form from the Petrarchan" (122).
34. See Houston, "Valuable by Design," 247; and Wagner, *A Moment's Monument*, 121.
35. *Sonnets of Three Centuries: A Selection including many examples hitherto unpublished*, ed. T. Hall Caine (London: Elliot Stock, 1882), xi.
36. Gary Taylor, *Reinventing Shakespeare: A Cultural History, From the Restoration to the Present* (Oxford: Oxford University Press, 1989), 156. See also Margreta de Grazia, *Shakespeare Verbatim: The Reproduction of Authenticity and the 1790 Apparatus* (Oxford: Clarendon Press, 1991); and Peter Stallybrass, "Editing as Cultural Formation," in *Shakespeare's Sonnets: Critical Essays*, ed. James Schiffer (New York: Garland, 1999), 75–88.
37. See de Grazia, *Shakespeare Verbatim*, 152.
38. Pinch, *Strange Fits of Passion*, 170. See also de Grazia, *Shakespeare Verbatim*, 132–76; and Adena Rosmarin, "Hermeneutics versus Erotics: Shakespeare's Sonnets and Interpretive History," *PMLA* 100 (1985): 20–37.
39. Eve Kosofsky Sedgwick, *Between Men: English Literature and Male Homosocial Desire* (New York: Columbia University Press, 1985), remarks that *The Princess* legitimates the bourgeois family by "tracing [it] back to aristocratic origins in feudal society" (124).

40. Sidney Lee, *A Life of William Shakespeare* (New York: Macmillan, 1898), 101, 123.

41. Lee's edition has been supplemented by *English and Scottish Sonnet Sequences of the Renaissance*, ed. Holger M. Klein (New York: Olms, 1984).

42. Cf. Jonah Siegel, "Among the English Poets: Keats, Arnold, and the Placement of the Fragments," *Victorian Poetry* 37 (1999): 215–31. Lee's scholarly emphasis participates in what Siegel describes as a shift in the criteria for the construction of anthologies: "Recognition of the breadth of the field of English letters, and of the related developments of specialized study of its various periods makes it imperative that a variety of specialists (or even specialized sensibilities) be employed [in choosing material for an anthology]" (217).

43. *Elizabethan Sonnets Newly Arranged and Indexed*, ed. Sidney Lee (New York: E. P. Dutton, 1904), xii. Throughout my comments on Lee are indebted to Janet H. MacArthur, *Critical Contexts of Sidney's* Astrophil and Stella *and Spenser's* Amoretti, English Literary Studies Monograph Series 46 (University of Victoria, 1989), 14–22, who also importantly emphasizes the connections between Lee's assessments of sonnet sequences and his need to defend and create English as a discipline.

44. Lee, *Elizabethan Sonnets*, ix–x.

45. See Joel Fineman, *Shakespeare's Perjured Eye: The Invention of Poetic Subjectivity in the Sonnets* (Berkeley: University of California Press, 1986).

46. Lee, *Elizabethan Sonnets*, cx.

47. See the discussion of the American Arts and Crafts movement in T. J. Jackson Lears, *No Place of Grace: Antimodernism and the Transformation of American Culture 1880–1920* (New York: Pantheon, 1981). Ruskin's formative statement of aestheticism is *The Renaissance*. On Arnold's contradictory stances, particularly as they pertain to T. H. Ward's anthology *The English Poets*, for which Arnold wrote the general introduction, see Siegel, "Among the English Poets." On Wilde, see especially Rebecca Laroche, "The Sonnets on Trial: Reconsidering *The Portrait of Mr. W. H.*," in *Shakespeare's Sonnets: Critical Essays*, 391–409.

48. [C. W. Russell], "Critical History of the Sonnet," part 1, *The Dublin Review* n. s. 27 (1876): 407–08; quoted in *Sonnets of This Century*, ed. William Sharp (London: Walter Scott, 1887), xxix.

49. Wagner, *A Moment's Monument*, 127. See also Wagner, 128: "the sonnet is not as primary an arena for politics in the late nineteenth century as it had been previously. The 'value' attributed to sonnets now is based more on the formal transcendence of the commonplace or 'actual world' than, say, on the urgency of voice that trumpets forth an imaginative and political Truth."

50. Linda Dowling, *The Vulgarization of Art: The Victorians and Aesthetic Democracy* (Charlottesville: University Press of Virginia, 1996), ix, xii. See also Lawrence Klein, *Shaftesbury and the Culture of Politeness: Moral Discourse and Cultural Politics in Early Eighteenth-Century England* (Cambridge: Cambridge University Press, 1994).

51. Dowling, *The Vulgarization of Art*, xiii.

52. Bourdieu, *Distinction*, 7, 241. Dowling, *The Vulgarization of Art*, attempts to distance herself from Bourdieu's conception of the aesthetic, which she sees as simply "mystification."

53. *Sonnets of This Century*, xxxvi.

54. *A Treasury of English Sonnets from the Original Sources with Notes and Illustrations*, ed. David M. Main (Manchester: Alexander Ireland, 1880). Cf. Guillory, *Cultural Capital*, who remarks that in the nineteenth century "[a]s the school becomes the exclusive agent for the dissemination of High Canonical works, replacing the quasi-educational institutions, the coffee-houses, literary clubs, and salons of eighteenth-century literacy – the realm of the bourgeois public sphere – the prestige of literary works as cultural capital is assessed according to the *limit* of their dissemination, their relative exclusivity" (133).

55. *Dear Mr. Rossetti: The Letters of Dante Gabriel Rossetti and Hall Caine 1878–1881*, ed. Vivien Allen (Sheffield: Sheffield Academic Press, 2000), 178. Dates for the letters are usually but not always reliable, and comments on sonnets and titles for the anthology are scattered throughout.

56. *Dear Mr. Rossetti*, 178, 185.

57. On the relations between format and social position in anthologies, see Benedict, *Making the Modern Reader*.

58. Charles Tomlinson, *The Sonnet: Its Origins, Structure, and Place in Poetry with Original Translations from the Sonnets of Dante, Petrarch, etc. and Remarks on the Art of Translating* (London: John Murray, 1874), 73–74.

59. Stallybrass, "Editing as Cultural Formation," 86.

60. *An English Garner in gatherings from Our History and Literature*, 8 vols., ed. Edward Arber (London: E. Arber, 1877–1897), 1:484.

61. Sidney Lanier, *Shakspere and His Forerunners: Studies in Elizabethan Poetry and its Development from Early English*, 2 vols. (New York: Doubleday, Page and Co., 1902), 1: 246–47.

62. *Elizabethan Sonnet-Cycles*, 4 vols., ed. Martha Foote Crow (London: Kegan Paul, Trench, Trübner, 1896), 1: v, vi, viii, ix–x.

63. See Janet G. Scott, *Les Sonnets Élisabéthains: Les Sources et L'Apport Personnel* (Paris: Librairie Ancienne Honoré Champion, 1929); Lu Emily Pearson, *Elizabethan Sonnet Conventions* (Berkeley: University of California Press, 1933); Lisle Cecil John, *The Elizabethan Sonnet Sequences: Studies in Conventional Conceits* (New York: Columbia University Press, 1938).

64. Guillory, *Cultural Capital*, 134–75.

65. Among the vast literature on Donne, see in this regard especially T. S. Eliot, "The Metaphysical Poets," in *Selected Essays* (New York: Harcourt, Brace and World, 1960), 241–50; and Donald Guss, *John Donne, Petrarchist: Italian Conceits and Love Theory in the Songs and Sonnets* (Detroit: Wayne State University Press, 1966).

66. J. W. Lever, *The Elizabethan Love Sonnet* (London: Methuen, 1956), 277. See also Hallett Smith, *Elizabethan Poetry: A Study in Conventions, Meaning, and Expression* (Cambridge, MA: Harvard University Press, 1952); C. S. Lewis, *English Literature of the Sixteenth Century Excluding Drama: The Completion*

of The Clark Lectures Trinity College, Cambridge 1944 (Oxford: Oxford University Press, 1954); and J. B. Leishman, *Themes and Variations in Shakespeare's Sonnets* (New York: Hutchinson, 1961).

67. Lever, *The Elizabethan Love Sonnet*, 275. In Lever's conversion of nationalism to archetype lies an origin of the continuing critical fascination with "structures" in sonnet sequences – from numerological calendars to prayer manuals – that is surely one of the odder features of twentieth-century sonnet criticism. See for example Alastair Fowler, *Triumphal Forms* (Cambridge: Cambridge University Press, 1970); Thomas P. Roche, Jr., *Petrarch and the English Sonnet Sequences* (New York: AMS Press, 1989); and Tom W. N. Parker, *Proportional Form in the Sonnets of the Sidney Circle: Loving in Truth* (Oxford: Oxford University Press, 1998).

68. Leishman, *Themes and Variations in Shakespeare's Sonnets*, 11, 69, 89, 91. The tradition of viewing Shakespeare as an inheritor of, rather than a departure from, Petrarch has been strongly voiced recently in the work of Gordon Braden – especially "Shakespeare's Petrarchism," in *Shakespeare's Sonnets: Critical Essays*, 163–83. Specifically citing Leishman as the best model for "Shakespearean *Quellenforschung*," Braden stresses that "Shakespeare's anomaly is also a return to origins" (170). As his recurrent invocation of Jacob Burckhardt's *The Civilization of the Renaissance in Italy* suggests, Braden's criticism reiterates the still powerful nineteenth-century view of sonnets, and the Renaissance generally, as the starting point for individuality and middle-class identity. See the trajectory of English Petrarchism traced in William Kerrigan and Gordon Braden, *The Idea of the Renaissance* (Baltimore: The Johns Hopkins University Press, 1989), 157–89; and Braden, *Petrarchan Love and the Continental Renaissance* (New Haven: Yale University Press, 1999).

69. Smith, *Elizabethan Poetry*, v, 150–51, 131.

70. Lewis, *English Literature of the Sixteenth Century*, 490–91.

71. Lewis, *English Literature of the Sixteenth Century*, 502, 503.

72. G. K. Hunter, *John Lyly: The Humanist as Courtier* (London: Routledge and Kegan Paul, 1962), 7.

73. Marotti, "'Love is Not Love'." Studies of Sidney include Richard B. Young, "English Petrarke: A Study of Sidney's *Astrophel and Stella*," in *Three Studies in the Renaissance: Sidney, Jonson, Milton* (New Haven: Yale University Press, 1958), 1–88; John Buxton, *Sir Philip Sidney and the English Renaissance* (London: Macmillan, 1954); Robert L. Montgomery, Jr., *Symmetry and Sense: The Poetry of Sir Philip Sidney*. 1961 (reprint Westport: Greenwood Press, 1969); David Kalstone, *Sidney's Poetry: Contexts and Interpretations* (Cambridge: Harvard University Press, 1965); Neil L. Rudenstine, *Sidney's Poetic Development* (Cambridge, MA: Harvard University Press, 1967); and Roger Howell, *Sir Philip Sidney: The Shepherd Knight* (London: Hutchinson, 1968).

74. See Perry Anderson, *Lineages of the Absolutist State* (London: New Left Books, 1974), and the critique of the "Nairn–Anderson Thesis" by Wood, *The Pristine Culture of Capitalism*, 11–17.

75. Jones and Stallybrass, "The Politics of *Astrophil and Stella*," 55. Jones and Stallybrass are responding specifically to Richard McCoy's distinction between public and private in *Sir Philip Sidney, Rebellion in Arcadia* (New Brunswick: Rutgers University Press, 1979).
76. Jameson, *Postmodernism*, 181–217. For similar readings of New Historicism, see Jonathan Crewe, *Hidden Designs: The Critical Profession and Renaissance Literature* (New York: Methuen, 1986), 70–88; Halpern, *The Poetics of Primitive Accumulation*, 1–15; Richard McCoy, "Lord of Liberty: Francis Davison and the Cult of Elizabeth," in *The Reign of Elizabeth I: Court and Culture in the Last Decade*, ed. John Guy (Cambridge: Cambridge University Press, 1995), 212–28; David Simpson, *The Academic Postmodern and the Rule of Literature: A Report on Half-Knowledge* (Chicago: University of Chicago Press, 1995); and Richard Halpern, *Shakespeare Among the Moderns* (Ithaca: Cornell University Press, 1997), 15–50.
77. See Jameson, *Postmodernism*, who regards "the ostensible subjects of [new historicist] essays – the Other and value – as pretexts for the montage in question rather than as 'concepts' in their own right" (191).
78. Jones and Stallybrass, "The Politics of *Astrophil and Stella*," 63.
79. Ibid.
80. Patricia Fumerton, *Cultural Aesthetics: Renaissance Literature and the Practice of Social Ornament* (Chicago: University of Chicago Press, 1991), 87, 109.
81. See for example Kim F. Hall, *Things of Darkness: Economies of Race and Gender in Early Modern England* (Ithaca: Cornell University Press, 1995), 62–122; and Patricia Parker, "Rhetorics of Property: Exploration, Inventory, Blazon," in *Literary Fat Ladies: Rhetoric, Gender, Property* (New York: Methuen, 1987), 126–54.
82. Fineman, *Shakespeare's Perjured Eye*, 47. Roland A. Greene, *Post-Petrarchism: Origins and Innovations of the Western Lyric Sequence* (Princeton: Princeton University Press, 1991), 4.
83. See the discussion by Slavoj Žižek, "Class Struggle or Postmodernism? Yes, please!" in Judith Butler, Ernesto Laclau, and Slavoj Žižek, *Contingency, Hegemony, Universality: Contemporary Dialogues on the Left* (London: Verso, 2000), 90–135.

3   "AN ENGLISHE BOX": CALVINISM AND COMMODITIES IN ANNE LOK'S *A MEDITATION OF A PENITENT SINNER*

1. *Sermons of John Calvin, upon the Songe that Ezechias made after he had bene sicke, and afflicted by the hand of God, conteyned in the 38. Chapiter of Esay. Translated out of Frenche into Englishe* (London: John Day, 1560). All further citations refer to the microfilm of the British Library copy. A note on spelling: there is no critical consensus on how to spell Lok's name. "Lock," "Locke," and "Lok" are the major variants. I employ "Lok" because that is the spelling encountered most frequently with other members of her family. In quotations I have retained the spelling employed by other scholars.

2. She is so identified in the *Dictionary of National Biography* entry for her son Henry Lok.

3. See Patrick Collinson, "The Role of Women in the English Reformation Illustrated by the Life and Friendships of Anne Locke," in *Godly People: Essays on English Protestantism and Puritanism* (London: The Hambledon Press, 1983), 273–87.

4. Roland Greene, "Ann Lock's Meditation: Invention Versus Dilation and the Founding of Puritan Poetics," in *Form and Reform in Renaissance England: Essays in Honor of Barbara Kiefer Lewalski*, ed. Amy Boesky and Mary Thomas Crane (Newark: University of Delaware Press, 2000), 153–70, 165.

5. Greene, "Ann Lock's Meditation," 153.

6. See Collinson, "The Role of Women." See also Susanne Woods, "Ann Lock and Aemilia Lanyer: A Tradition of Protestant Women Speaking," in *Form and Reform in Renaissance England*, 171–84; *The Collected Works of Anne Vaughan Lock*, ed. Susan Felch (Tempe: Arizona Center for Medieval and Renaissance Studies, 1999); Michael R. G. Spiller, "A Literary 'First': the Sonnet Sequence of Anne Locke (1560)" *Renaissance Studies* 11 (1997): 41–55; Susan Felch, "'Deir Sister': The Letters of John Knox to Anne Vaughan Lok," *Renaissance and Reformation* 19.4 (1995): 47–68; Margaret Hannay, "'Unlock my lipps': the *Miserere mei Deus* of Anne Vaughan Lok and Mary Sidney Herbert, Countess of Pembroke," in *Privileging Gender in Early Modern England*, ed. Jean R. Brink (Kirksville, MO: Sixteenth Century Journal Publishers, 1993), 19–36; Margaret P. Hannay, "'Strengthning the walles of . . . Ierusalem': Anne Vaughan Lok's Dedication to the Countess of Warwick," *ANQ* 5 (1992): 71–75; Susanne Woods, "The Body Penitent: a 1560 Calvinist Sonnet Sequence," *ANQ* 5 (1992): 137–40; Michael R. G. Spiller, *The Development of the Sonnet: An Introduction* (London: Routledge, 1992), 92–3; T. P. Roche, *Petrarch and the English Sonnet Sequences* (New York: AMS Press, 1989), 155–57; Elaine V. Beilin, *Redeeming Eve: Women Writers of the English Renaissance* (Princeton: Princeton University Press, 1987); and Kathy Lynn Emerson, *Wives and Daughters: The Women of Sixteenth Century England* (Troy, NY: Whitston Publishing, 1984). On women's writing in the period, see for example Joyce L. Irwin, *Womanhood in Radical Protestantism, 1525–1675* (New York: Edwin Mellen, 1979); Linda Woodbridge, *Women and the English Renaissance: Literature and the Nature of Womankind 1540–1620* (Urbana: University of Illinois Press, 1984); *Silent But for the Word: Tudor Women as Patrons, Translators, and Writers of Religious Works*, ed. Margaret Hannay (Kent: Kent State University Press, 1985); Beilin, *Redeeming Eve*; Ann Rosalind Jones, *The Currency of Eros* (Bloomington: Indiana University Press, 1990); *Women, Texts and Histories 1575–1760*, ed. Clare Brant and Diane Purkiss (New York: Routledge, 1992); Barbara Kiefer Lewalski, *Writing Women in Jacobean England* (Cambridge, MA: Harvard University Press, 1993); Patricia Crawford, *Women and Religion in England, 1500–1720* (London: Routledge, 1993); Susan M. Felch, "The Rhetoric of Biblical Authority: John Knox and the Question of Women," *Sixteenth-Century Journal* 24.6 (1995): 805–22; and *Women and Literature in Britain 1500–1700*, ed. Helen Wilcox (Cambridge: Cambridge University Press, 1996). On the psalm tradition, see Anne Lake Prescott,

"Evil tongues at the court of Saul: the Renaissance David as a slandered courtier," *JMRS* 12 (1991): 163–86; Roland Greene, "Sir Philip Sidney's Psalms, the Sixteenth-Century Psalter, and the Nature of Lyric," *SEL* 30 (1990): 19–40; Prescott, "King David as a 'Right Poet': Sidney and the Psalmist," *ELR* 19.3 (1989): 131–51; Rivkah Zim, *English Metrical Psalms: Poetry as Praise and Prayer 1535–1601* (Cambridge: Cambridge University Press, 1987); Hannay, "'Unlock my lipps'"; and Barbara Lewalski, *Protestant Poetics and the Seventeenth-Century Religious Lyric* (Princeton: Princeton University Press, 1979).

7. For critiques of the critical uses to which Renaissance women's writings have been put, see Jonathan Goldberg, *Desiring Women Writing: English Renaissance Examples* (Stanford: Stanford University Press, 1997); Elizabeth Hanson, "Boredom and Whoredom: Reading Renaissance Women's Sonnet Sequences," *The Yale Journal of Criticism* 10 (1997): 165–91; Diana E. Henderson, *Passion Made Public: Elizabethan Lyric Gender, and Performance* (Urbana: University of Illinois Press, 1995); and Ann Baynes Coiro, "Writing in Service: Sexual Politics and Class Position in the Poetry of Aemilia Lanyer and Ben Jonson," *Criticism* 35 (1993): 357–76. New Historicism has been particularly effective at breaking down the sharp distinctions between religious and literary outlooks. A collection on seventeenth-century "religious" verse (*New Perspectives on the Seventeenth-Century English Religious Lyric*, ed. John R. Roberts [Columbia and London: University of Missouri Press, 1994]) constantly calls "religion" as a category into question. For instance, in "The Poetry of Supplication: Toward a Cultural Poetics of the Religious Lyric" (75–104) Michael C. Schoenfeldt begins by noting that "[i]t is ironic that readers have tended to interpret the seventeenth-century religious lyric in deliberate isolation from social and cultural forces, since the early seventeenth-century practitioners of the devotional lyric . . . were themselves so profoundly aware of the social dimensions of their work" (75).

8. The best biography of Lok remains Collinson's "The Role of Women in the English Reformation." See also Spiller, "A Literary 'First,'" for a list of editions of her work which synthesize biographical material, and *The Collected Works of Anne Vaughan Lock*, xvi–xxxvi. On Stephen Vaughan see W. C. Richardson, *Stephen Vaughan Financial Agent of Henry VIII*, Louisiana State University Studies, Social Science Series Number Three (Baton Rouge: Louisiana State University Press, 1953); David Daniell, *William Tyndale: A Biography* (New Haven: Yale University Press, 1994), 4, 155, 174–222, 372; J. F. Mozley, *William Tyndale* (London: Society for Promoting Christian Knowledge, 1937), 187–320; Penry Williams, *The Tudor Regime* (Oxford: Clarendon Press, 1979), 62–70, 190; and G. D. Ramsey, *The City of London in International Politics at the Accession of Elizabeth Tudor* (Manchester: Manchester University Press, 1975), 33–80, who details the role of the Merchant Adventurers and the responsibilities of Vaughan and his later successor Thomas Gresham. On the Mercers and Merchant Adventurers see D. C. Coleman, *The Economy of England 1450–1750* (Oxford: Oxford University Press, 1977), 48–68. On Henry Brinkelow and the Cromwellian apologists see John King, *English Reformation Literature: The Tudor Origins of the Protestant Tradition* (Princeton: Princeton University Press,

1982), 44–56. On Sir William Lok and Michael Lok, see the respective entries in *The Dictionary of National Biography*. Kenneth R. Andrews, *Trade, Plunder and Settlement: Maritime Enterprise and the Genesis of the British Empire, 1480–1630* (Cambridge: Cambridge University Press, 1984) details the involvement of Michael Lok and other Loks in maritime voyages, especially that of Frobisher; see also Katherine Duncan-Jones, *Sir Philip Sidney, Courtier Poet* (New Haven: Yale University Press, 1991), 223–29 on Michael Lok's relation to Sidney and Frobisher's voyages. On Edward Dering see Patrick Collinson, *The Elizabethan Puritan Movement* (Berkeley: University of California Press, 1967); Collinson, "A Mirror of Elizabethan Puritanism: The Life and Letters of 'Godly Master Dering,'" in *Godly People*, 289–324; Peter Lake, *Moderate Puritans and the Elizabethan Church* (Cambridge: Cambridge University Press, 1982), 16–24; and Peter C. Herman, *Squitter-wits and Muse-haters: Sidney, Spenser, Milton and Renaissance Antipoetic Sentiment* (Detroit: Wayne State University Press, 1996), 25–68. On Lok and Knox see Collinson, "The Role of Women"; Susan M. Felch, "'Deir Sister': The Letters of John Knox to Anne Vaughan Lok," *Renaissance and Reformation* 19 (1995): 47–68; and Felch, "The Rhetoric of Biblical Authority." On Henry Lok see Roche, *Petrarch and the English Sonnet Sequences*. I am also indebted to Felch's introduction to *The Collected Works of Anne Vaughan Lock*. My sincere thanks to Professor Felch for allowing me to see her manuscript.

 9. Robert Weimann, *Authority and Representation in Early Modern Discourse*, ed. David Hillman (Baltimore: The Johns Hopkins University Press, 1996), 5, 29, 67.
10. Greene, "Sidney's Psalms," 23.
11. Norman Jones, *The Birth of the Elizabethan Age: England in the 1560s* (Cambridge: Blackwell, 1993), 49.
12. Hannay, "'Strengthning the walles of . . . Ierusalem,'" 72. Gary Waller, *English Poetry of the Sixteenth Century* (New York: Longman, 1986), notes that "for Protestants of the sixteenth century, poetry was not something that could be separated from the godly pursuit of a Protestant state" (95). Similarly, Prescott argues that post-Reformation readers viewed David as "something like a Renaissance anti-court poet" ("Evil tongues at the court of Saul," 165).
13. Jones, *The Birth of the Elizabethan Age*, 17–47. See also his *Faith by Statute: Parliament and the Settlement of Religion 1559* (London: Royal Historical Society, 1982), which details the parliamentary and political maneuvering necessary for the "Anglican Settlement." Jones, like all historians of the period, builds upon Patrick Collinson's seminal works. See in particular *The Elizabethan Puritan Movement*; *Archbishop Grindal 1519–1583: The Struggle for a Reformed Church* (London: Jonathan Cape, 1979); *The Religion of Protestants: The Church in English Society 1559–1625* (Oxford: Clarendon Press, 1982); and *Godly People*.
14. Lake, *Moderate Puritans*, notes that called before the Star Chamber in 1573 to comment upon Thomas Cartwright's controversial book, Dering assured the interrogators that "princes have full authority over all ecclesiastical and

civil persons and equally over both to punish the offenders or give praise to the well doers," but his firm belief in evangelical preaching became clear when he added that "in the church there is no lawgiver but Christ Jesus" (20).

15. Jones, *The Birth of the Elizabethan Age*, 61.

16. *Of the markes of the chil-dren of God, and of their comforts in afflictions. To the faithfull of the Low Countrie. By John Taffin.* Overseene againe, and augmented by the Author, and translated out of French by Anne Prowse (London: Thomas Orwin, 1590), A4 – A5.

17. See the introduction to *The Culture of English Puritanism, 1560–1700*, ed. Christopher Durston and Jacqueline Eales (New York: St. Martin's Press, 1996), 1–31, especially 10. Max Weber famously attempted to forge an alliance between Calvinism and the "spirit of capitalism" in *The Protestant Ethic and the Spirit of Capitalism*, 1930 (London: Routledge, 1992). Both the strengths and weaknesses of this position are articulated by R. H. Tawney, *Religion and the Rise of Capitalism: A Historical Study* (Holland Memorial Lectures, 1922) (New York: Harcourt, Brace and Company, 1926).

18. See generally King, *English Reformation Literature*; and David Norbrook, *Poetry and Politics in the English Renaissance* (London: Routledge and Kegan Paul, 1984), 32–90. On the "plain style" and its origins in medieval, didactic, non-aristocratic verse see Douglas L. Peterson, *The English Lyric from Wyatt to Donne: A History of the Plain and Eloquent Styles* (Princeton: Princeton University Press, 1967), 3–38; and Yvor Winters, "The 16th Century Lyric in England. A Critical and Historical Reinterpretation," in *Elizabethan Poetry: Modern Essays in Criticism*, ed. Paul J. Alpers, (Oxford: Oxford University Press, 1967), 93–125.

19. Spiller, "A Literary 'First,'" 49.

20. Alexandra Halasz, "Wyatt's David," in *Rethinking the Henrician Era: Essays on Early Tudor Texts and Contexts*, ed. Peter C. Herman (Urbana: University of Illinois Press, 1994), 198. Halasz is responding in particular to Stephen Greenblatt's influential rendering of "the circumstances that shape the psalmic voice" (197) and the fashioning of "inwardness" in Henry's court. See also Greenblatt, *Renaissance Self-Fashioning from More to Shakespeare* (Chicago: University of Chicago Press, 1980), 115–56.

21. Spiller, "A Literary 'First,'" 49.

22. Crane, *Framing Authority*, 170. See also Wendy Wall, *The Imprint of Gender: Authorship and Publication in the English Renaissance* (Ithaca: Cornell University Press, 1993), 23–30, who argues that Tottel's uses "an aristocratic value to criticize an aristocratic practice" (27); and Arthur Marotti, *Manuscript, Print, and the English Renaissance Lyric* (Ithaca: Cornell University Press, 1995), 212–28, who like Crane notes that Tottel "reverses the received notions of gentle and ungentle" (215).

23. *Tottel's Miscellany, 1557–1587*, ed. Hyder Edward Rollins (Cambridge, MA: Harvard University Press, 1928–1929), 2.

24. Crane, *Framing Authority*, 170, 168.

25. Wall, *The Imprint of Gender*, 26.

26. On commodities and the value they acquire through circulation, see Karl Marx, *Capital: A Critique of Political Economy*, trans. Samuel Moore and Edward Aveling (New York: Charles H. Kerr, 1906), 41–162.

27. Weimann, *Representation and Authority*, 2.
28. See the entry for Catherine Willoughby, the duchess of Suffolk, in Emerson, *Wives and Daughters*, 245–46.
29. Lok translates four sermons Calvin delivered on 5, 6, 15, and 16 November 1557 at Geneva. She may well have heard them in person, but her copy text seems to be not the manuscript version of the text but rather an early copy of a revision published in French in 1562. See Felch, *The Collected Works of Anne Vaughan Lock*.
30. On Calvin's "anxiety," see William J. Bouwsma, *John Calvin: A Sixteenth-Century Portrait* (Oxford: Oxford University Press, 1988), 9–65.
31. On the Hegelian term "negation," see Theodor Adorno's comments in an interview with Ernst Bloch in Ernst Bloch, *The Utopian Function of Art and Literature: Selected Essays*, trans. Jack Zipes and Frank Mecklenburg (Cambridge, MA: MIT Press, 1988): "[U]topia is essentially in determined negation, in the determined negation of that which merely is, and by concretizing itself as something false, it always points at the same time to what should be. Yesterday you [Bloch] quoted Spinoza in our discussion with the passage, 'Verum index sui et falsi' [The true is the sign of itself and the false]. I have varied this a little in the sense of the dialectical principle of the determined negation and have said, Falsum – the false thing – index sui et veri [The false is the sign of itself and the correct]. That means that the true thing determines itself via the false thing, or via that which makes itself falsely known. And insofar as we are not allowed to cast the picture of utopia, insofar as we do not know what the correct thing would be, we know exactly, to be sure, what the false thing is." Adorno puts this concept somewhat more succinctly earlier: "One may not cast a picture of utopia in a positive manner" (10–12).
32. Greene, "Ann Lock's Meditation," 164.
33. *The Geneva Bible: A Facsimile of the 1560 Edition*, introduction by Lloyd E. Berry (Madison: University of Wisconsin Press, 1969).
34. *Original Letters Relative to the English Reformation: Written During the Reigns of King Henry VIII, King Edward VI, and Queen Mary: Chiefly from the Archives of Zurich* (Cambridge: The Parker Society, 1846), 55.
35. Summit, *Lost Property*, 167.

4　"NOBLER DESIRES" AND SIDNEY'S *ASTROPHIL AND STELLA*

1. On the possible connection between Lok and the Sidneys, see Margaret P. Hannay, "'Unlock my lipps': the *Miserere mei Deus* of Anne Vaughan Lok and Mary Sidney Herbert, Countess of Pembroke," in *Privileging Gender in Early Modern England*, ed. Jean R. Brink (Kirksville, MO: Sixteenth Century Journal Publishers, 1993), 19–36.
2. William Kerrigan and Gordon Braden, *The Idea of the Renaissance* (Baltimore: The Johns Hopkins University Press, 1989), 170.
3. See for example Catherine Bates, *The Rhetoric of Courtship in Elizabethan Language and Literature* (Cambridge: Cambridge University Press, 1992), 45–88; Patricia Fumerton, *Cultural Aesthetics: Renaissance Literature and the*

Practice of Social Ornament (Chicago: University of Chicago Press, 1991); Katherine Duncan-Jones, *Sir Philip Sidney, Courtier Poet* (New Haven: Yale University Press, 1991); Maureen Quilligan, "Sidney and His Queen," in *The Historical Renaissance: New Essays on Tudor and Stuart Literature and Culture*, ed. Heather Dubrow and Richard Strier (Chicago: University of Chicago Press, 1988), 171–96; Clark Hulse, "Stella's Wit: Penelope Rich as Reader of Sidney's Sonnets," in *Rewriting the Renaissance: The Discourse of Sexual Difference in Early Modern Europe*, ed. Margaret W. Ferguson, Maureen Quilligan, and Nancy J. Vickers (Chicago: University of Chicago Press, 1986), 272–86; Ann Rosalind Jones and Peter Stallybrass, "The Politics of *Astrophil and Stella*," *SEL* 24 (1984): 53–68; Gary Waller, "The Rewriting of Petrarch: Sidney and the Languages of Sixteenth-Century Poetry," in *Sir Philip Sidney and the Interpretation of Renaissance Culture*, ed. Gary F. Waller and Michael D. Moore (Totowa, NJ: Barnes and Noble, 1984), 69–83; Arthur F. Marotti, "'Love is not Love': Elizabethan Sonnet Sequences and the Social Order," *ELH* 49 (1982): 396–406; Alan Sinfield, "Sidney and Astrophil," *SEL* 20 (1980): 25–41; Richard McCoy, *Sir Philip Sidney, Rebellion in Arcadia* (New Brunswick: Rutgers University Press, 1979); Alan Sinfield, "Astrophil's Self-Deception," *Essays in Criticism* 28 (1978): 1–18; and Louis Adrian Montrose, "Celebration and Insinuation: Sir Philip Sidney and the Motives of Elizabethan Courtship," *Renaissance Drama* 8 (1977): 3–35.

4. The "imperial Sidney" is the title of chapter four in Roland Greene, *Unrequited Conquests: Love and Empire in the Colonial Americas* (Chicago: University of Chicago Press, 1999), 171–93. See also Allan Stewart, *Philip Sidney: A Double Life* (London: Pimlico, 2000); Roger Kuin, "Querre-Muhua: Sir Philip Sidney and the New World," *Renaissance Quarterly* 51 (1998): 549–85; Lisa M. Klein, *The Exemplary Sidney and the Elizabethan Sonneteer* (Newark: University of Delaware Press, 1998); John Michael Archer, "Slave-Born Muscovites: Racial Difference and the Geography of Servitude in *Astrophil and Stella* and *Love's Labour's Lost*," in *Playing the Globe: Genre and Geography in English Renaissance Drama*, ed. John Gillies and Virginia Mason Vaughan (Madison, NJ: Fairleigh Dickinson University Press, 1998), 154–75; and Mary Thomas Crane, *Framing Authority: Sayings, Self, and Society in Sixteenth-Century England* (Princeton: Princeton University Press, 1993).

5. See Greene, *Unrequited Conquests*, who remarks that "[w]hile [mid-century] poets participated in the international project of domesticating Petrarchan humanism to several vernaculars and using it to think intermittently through many of the European and transatlantic issues of the age, Sidney theorizes and practices a more systematic poetry of affairs from within a worldview conditioned by the rivalry of two great powers, England and Spain" (171).

6. Crane, *Framing Authority*, 190.

7. William Kennedy, *The Site of Petrarchism: Early Modern National Sentiment in Italy, France, and England* (Baltimore: The Johns Hopkins University Press, 2003), 171. Part three argues that the "writings of Philip, Mary, and Robert Sidney, William Herbert, and Mary Wroth. . . express an idealized vision of the nation which totemizes noble families and their allegiance to aristocratic values" (170–71).

8. Stewart, *Philip Sidney*, 44.

9. In *The Poems of Sir Philip Sidney*, ed. William A. Ringler, Jr. (Oxford: Clarendon Press, 1962), Ringler notes that while Sidney "appears to have allowed the songs of *Astrophil and Stella* to circulate," "the sonnets he kept close" (ix). "In the hundreds of poems lamenting his death that were written at the universities and by men of letters elsewhere, [Sidney] was frequently referred to in general terms as a poet, but few of the writers showed direct acquaintance with his specific works" (lxii).

10. See *The Reign of Elizabeth I: Court and Culture in the Last Decade*, ed. John Guy (Cambridge: Cambridge University Press, 1995).

11. All quotations of *Astrophil and Stella* are from Ringler, *The Poems of Sir Philip Sidney*.

12. Maureen Quilligan, "Sidney and His Queen," 191. See also John Huntington, *Ambition, Rank, and Poetry in 1590s England* (Urbana: University of Illinois Press, 2001), who notes the intimate connection between noble privilege and the leisure time required for the liberal arts "which tends to express itself in the ability to squander wealth" (20).

13. David Kalstone, *Sidney's Poetry: Contexts and Interpretations* (Cambridge, MA: Harvard University Press, 1965), 131.

14. Jonathan Crewe, *Hidden Designs: The Critical Profession and Renaissance Literature* (New York: Methuen, 1986), 85.

15. Throughout my account of the fictionality of Astrophil's lyricism draws on Roland A. Greene, *Post-Petrarchism: Origins and Innovations of the Western Lyric Sequence* (Princeton: Princeton University Press, 1991), 63–108.

16. On Astrophil's debt to Aristotle, see Richard B. Young, "English Petrarke: A Study of Sidney's *Astrophel and Stella*," in *Three Studies in the Renaissance: Sidney, Jonson, Milton* (New Haven: Yale University Press, 1958), 5–88.

17. John Freccero, "The Fig Tree and the Laurel: Petrarch's Poetics," in *Literary Theory / Renaissance Texts*, ed. Patricia Parker and David Quint (Baltimore: The Johns Hopkins University Press, 1986), 20–32, 21.

18. See Michael McKeon, *The Origins of the English Novel, 1600–1740* (Baltimore: The Johns Hopkins University Press, 1987), 162–67.

19. McKeon, *The Origins of the English Novel*, 131.

20. Slavoj Žižek, *The Sublime Object of Ideology* (London: Verso, 1989), 162, 164.

21. For allusions to the Riches, see especially sonnets 9, 24, 33, 35, 37, and 79 and songs 5, 8, and 9; for puns on Sidney's name see particularly sonnets 22, 41, 49, 84; for clear allusions to political events see at the very least sonnets 3, 5, 8, 9, 21, 23, 24, 27, 28, 29, 30, 83, 103, 105.

22. Kalstone, *Sidney's Poetry*, 137.

23. Ringler, *The Poems of Sir Philip Sidney*, 461.

24. See Nona Fienberg, "The Emergence of Stella in *Astrophil and Stella*," *SEL* 25 (1985): 5–19: "[*Astrophil and Stella*] does not remain wholly imprisoned in its narcissism. Instead, the speaker self-consciously attempts to confront a 'real' Stella, who is not only a symbol for his political ambitions, his social standing, and his text" (5).

25. The *OED* cites Ascham in the *Scholemaster* : "If a yong ientleman be demure and still of nature, they say, he is simple and lacketh witte." Ascham means to advocate seriousness, but the sense of affectation and coyness – the more modern

sense – is explicitly present as early as Shakespeare's *Antony and Cleopatra* 4.15.27–29, where Cleopatra considers the horrible possibility of becoming captured: "Your wife Octavia, with her modest eyes,/And still conclusion, shall acquire no honour/Demuring upon me." *Antony and Cleopatra*. The Arden Shakespeare, ed. M. R. Ridley (New York: Methuen, 1954), 183–84.

26. On the shift in tone in the sequence, see especially Ronald Levao, *Renaissance Minds and Their Fictions* (Berkeley: University of California Press, 1985), 175. The question of despair at the end of the sequence has largely troubled readers intent on finding what they take to be a validation of Protestant moralism and a turn away from physical to divine love. This expectation itself rests on generic assumptions about how a sequence ought to end. A. C. Hamilton, *Sir Philip Sidney: A Study of His Life and Works* (Cambridge: Cambridge University Press, 1977), argues that the sequence's "'ending' departs radically from the ending of any earlier sonnet sequence" (104). Alan Sinfield, *Literature in Protestant England 1560–1660* (Totowa, NJ: Barnes and Noble, 1983), likewise adopts these generic assumptions and ties them to a fairly monolithic view of Protestantism and sexuality: "*Astrophil and Stella* is a notable puritan-humanist poem, taking the sonnet sequence, which often fudged the problem of sexual passion, and giving it an ethical implication consonant with protestantism" (60).

27. See Katherine Duncan-Jones, *Sir Philip Sidney: Selected Poems* (Oxford: Clarendon Press, 1973); and Duncan-Jones, *Sir Philip Sidney*. The Oxford Authors (Oxford: Oxford University Press, 1989).

28. Cf. Young, "English Petrarke," who argues that "[b]y the end of the sequence . . . [Astrophel] has discovered himself as part of the convention . . . Sonnet 108, then, is not conclusive in the sense of a complete resolution, but that very fact constitutes its dramatic function. It concludes the portrait of the conventional lover and the definition of the genre, ending the sequence with the acceptance of a frustration that can have no end" (88).

29. Tho[mas] Nashe, "Somewhat to reade for them that list," *Syr P. S. His Astrophel and Stella Wherein the excellence of sweete Poesie is concluded. . .* (London: Thomas Newman, 1591), sig. A3ᵛ.

30. Dominic Baker-Smith, "'Great Expectation': Sidney's Death and the Poets," in *Sir Philip Sidney: 1586 and the Creation of a Legend*, ed. Jan Van Dorsten, Dominic Baker-Smith, and Arthur Kinney (Leiden: E. J. Brill/Leiden University Press, 1986), 86.

31. *A Catalogue of the Royal and Noble Authors of England*, 1 (1758), 163–64, quoted in W. A. Ringler, "Sir Philip Sidney: The Myth and the Man," in Van Dorsten, Baker-Smith, and Kinney, *Sir Philip Sidney*, 4. On Sidney's temper and relation to Catholicism, see Duncan-Jones, *Sir Philip Sidney*, esp. 21–23 and 124–27.

32. On the lurking presence of King Philip in *Astrophil and Stella*, see Greene, *Unrequited Conquests*, 171–93.

33. Baker-Smith, "Great Expectation," 86.

34. On the creation of the Sidney legend and its relation to contemporary politics, see the two volumes of essays which emerged from the two conferences in Los Angeles and Leiden marking the quatercentenary of Sidney's death: *Sir Philip Sidney's Achievements*, ed. M. J. B. Allen, Dominic Baker-Smith, Arthur

Kinney, with Margaret M. Sullivan (New York: AMS Press, 1990); and Van Dorsten, Baker-Smith, and Kinney, *Sir Philip Sidney*. Quilligan, "Sidney and His Queen," conversely emphasizes that Sidney himself is responsible for his own myth: "it is useful to realize that poets still author, if not the entirety of their political lives, then at least the most powerful legends about them" (192).

35. Richard Helgerson, *The Elizabethan Prodigals* (Berkeley: University of California Press, 1976), 124–25, 127. Matthew Roydon, "An Elegie, or friends passion, for his Astrophil," *The Phoenix Next (1593)*, ed. Hyder Edward Rollins (Cambridge, MA: Harvard University Press, 1931), 13, quoted in Helgerson, *The Elizabethan Prodigals*, 124.

36. Raphael Falco, *Conceived Presences: Literary Genealogy in Renaissance England* (Amherst: University of Massachusetts Press, 1994), 56–59.

37. See Huntington, *Ambition, Rank, and Poetry in 1590s England*, 13. Huntington argues that Roydon's elegy for Sidney "advocates a poetic ideal that is contrary to the one Sidney himself stood for" (7; see also 112–15).

38. Iohn Harington, *Orlando Fvrioso in English Heroical Verse* (London: Richard Field, 1591), sig. L4ᵛ.

39. *The English Works of Giles Fletcher, the Elder*, ed. Lloyd E. Berry (Madison: University of Wisconsin Press, 1964), 75.

40. See Steven W. May, *The Elizabethan Courtier Poets: The Poems and Their Contexts* (Columbia: University of Missouri Press, 1991), 224.

41. All quotations of Daniel are from *Samuel Daniel: Poems and a Defense of Ryme*, ed. Arthur Colby Sprague (Cambridge, MA: Harvard University Press, 1930).

42. H. R. Woudhuysen, *Sir Philip Sidney and the Circulation of Manuscripts 1558–1640* (Oxford: Clarendon Press, 1996), 376–83. Woudhuysen examines the evidence surrounding the involvement of both Daniel and Harington (among others) in the publication of *Astrophil and Stella* in 1591. See also Margaret P. Hannay, *Philip's Phoenix: Mary Sidney, Countess of Pembroke* (New York: Oxford University Press, 1990), 116–19, on the relation of Daniel to the Countess of Pembroke.

5 "SO PLENTY MAKES ME POORE": IRELAND, CAPITALISM, AND CLASS IN
   SPENSER'S *AMORETTI AND EPITHALAMION*

1. David J. Baker, *Between Nations: Shakespeare, Spenser, Marvell, and the Question of Britain* (Stanford: Stanford University Press, 1997), 78. See also James Fleming, "A View from the Bridge: Ireland and Violence in Spenser's *Amoretti*," *Spenser Studies* 15 (2001): 135–64; Rebecca Ann Bach, *Colonial Transformations: The Cultural Production of the New Atlantic World, 1580–1640* (New York: Palgrave, 2000), 37–65; Judith Owens, "The Poetics of Accommodation in Spenser's *Epithalamion*," *SEL* 40 (2000): 41–62; Andrew Murphy, *But the Irish Sea Betwixt Us: Ireland, Colonialism, and Renaissance Literature* (Lexington: University Press of Kentucky, 1999), 60–96; the essays in *Spenser Studies* 12 (1991) (which actually appeared in 1998); Christopher Highley, "The Royal Image in Elizabethan Ireland," in *Dissing Elizabeth: Negative Representations of Gloriana*, ed. Julia M. Walker (Durham: Duke University Press, 1998), 60–76; Andrew Hadfield, *Edmund Spenser's Irish*

Experience: Wilde Fruit and Salvage Soyl (Oxford: Clarendon Press, 1997); Christopher Highley, *Shakespeare, Spenser, and the Crisis in Ireland* (Cambridge: Cambridge University Press, 1997); Willy Maley, *Salvaging Spenser: Colonialism, Culture and Identity* (New York: St. Martin's Press, 1997); *Spenser's Life and the Subject of Biography*, ed. Judith H. Anderson, Donald Cheney, and David A. Richardson (Amherst: University of Massachusetts Press, 1996); Andrew Hadfield, *Literature, Politics, and National Identity* (Cambridge: Cambridge University Press, 1994), 170–201; *Representing Ireland: Literature and the Origins of Conflict, 1534–1660*, ed. Brendan Bradshaw, Andrew Hadfield, and Willy Maley (Cambridge: Cambridge University Press, 1993); Richard A. McCabe, "Edmund Spenser, Poet of Exile," *Proceedings of the British Academy* 80 (1993): 73–103; Annabel Patterson, *Reading Between the Lines* (Madison: University of Wisconsin Press, 1993), 80–116; Richard Rambuss, *Spenser's Secret Career* (Cambridge: Cambridge University Press, 1993); Julia Reinhard Lupton, "Home-Making in Ireland: Virgil's Eclogue I and Book VI of *The Faerie Queene*," *Spenser Studies* 8 (1990): 119–45; and *Spenser and Ireland: An Interdisciplinary Perspective*, ed. Patricia Coughlan (Cork: Cork University Press, 1989). On "hybridity" as a key theoretical term, see Andrew Hadfield, "English Colonialism and National Identity in Early Modern Ireland," *Éire-Ireland* 28 (1993): 69–86; and Homi K. Bhabha, "Introduction: Narrating the Nation" and "DissemiNation: Time, Narrative, and the Margins of the Modern Nation," in *Nation and Narration*, ed. Homi K. Bhabha (London: Routledge, 1990), 1–7 and 291–322.

2. Louis A. Montrose, "Spenser's Domestic Domain: Poetry, Property, and the Early Modern Subject," in *Subject and Object in Renaissance Culture*, ed. Margreta de Grazia, Maureen Quilligan, and Peter Stallybrass (Cambridge: Cambridge University Press, 1996), 120. "Spenser's Domestic Domain" revises in particular Montrose's "The Elizabethan Subject and the Spenserian Text," in *Literary Theory/Renaissance Texts*, ed. Patricia Parker and David Quint (Baltimore: The Johns Hopkins University Press, 1986), 303–40. See also Michael C. Schoenfeldt, "The Poetry of Conduct: Accommodation and Transgression in *The Faerie Queene*, Book 6," in *Enclosure Acts: Sexuality, Property, and Culture in Early Modern England*, ed. Richard Burt and John Michael Archer (Ithaca: Cornell University Press, 1994), 151–69, who emphasizes that as "[t]he son of a clothmaker, Spenser was acutely aware of the necessity of accommodating himself to the demands of the social hierarchy" and that his "career delineates an ascent from lowly origins to noble aspirations" (152, 153).

3. Edmund Spenser, *The Faerie Queene*, ed. A. C. Hamilton (New York: Longman, 1977), 737.

4. Maureen Quilligan, *Milton's Spenser: The Politics of Reading* (Ithaca: Cornell University Press, 1983), 40.

5. All quotations of *Amoretti and Epithalamion* are from *The Yale Edition of the Shorter Poems of Edmund Spenser*, ed. William A. Oram, *et al.* (New Haven: Yale University Press, 1989).

6. See Paul Alpers, "Pastoral and the Domain of Lyric in Spenser's *Shepheardes Calendar*," *Representations* 12 (1996): 83–100; Alpers in turn is responding in particular to Montrose's earlier essay, "Of Gentlemen and Shepherds: The Politics of Elizabethan Pastoral Form," *ELH* 50 (1983): 41–59.

7. On Spenser's property acquisition, see Alexander C. Judson, *The Life of Edmund Spenser*, in *The Works of Edmund Spenser: A Variorum Edition*, 11 vols. (Baltimore: The Johns Hopkins Press, 1932–57), 8:84–137; and Willy Maley, *A Spenser Chronology* (Lanham, MD: Barnes and Noble Books, 1994). Spenser was granted a lease (we do not know from whom) in 1581 on Anniscorthy, an estate in County Wexford, which he immediately sold. Quite possibly he used the money in 1582 to buy an old Augustinian monastery at New Ross in County Wexford, from Lord Mountgarret, of Ballyragget, Kilkenny; Spenser sold this estate by 1584 to Sir Anthony Colclough, of Tintern, Wexford. In January 1582 Grey gave Spenser a house in Dublin, and in August 1582 Spenser was granted an estate called New Abbey in county Kildare. The lease to New Abbey was passed to Thomas Lambyn on 17 February 1589, and on 22 May Spenser obtained possession of Kilcolman. Kilcolman had originally been assigned in 1587 to Andrew Reade, an undertaker from Southampton, as part of the Munster plantation, but Spenser made an arrangement whereby the estate would become his if none of Reade's relatives moved there by Whitsuntide 1589. The estate passed to Spenser on 22 May 1589; on 26 October 1590 it legally became Spenser's property.

8. Julia Reinhard Lupton, "Mapping mutability: or, Spenser's Irish plot," in *Representing Ireland*, 97–98. See also Elizabeth Fowler's subtle discussion of the contradictory use of legal traditions to justify English occupation of Ireland, "The Failure of Moral Philosophy in the Work of Edmund Spenser," *Representations* 51 (1995): 47–76.

9. Sir John Davies, *A Discovery of the True Causes why Ireland was never entirely Subdued* (London, 1612), quoted Lupton, 97, and in Nicholas Canny, *The Elizabethan Conquest of Ireland: A Pattern Established, 1565–76* (New York: Barnes and Noble Books, 1976), 135.

10. Edmund Spenser, *A View of the Present State of Ireland . . . in 1596*, ed. W. L. Renwick (Oxford: Oxford University Press, 1970), 158.

11. Michael MacCarthy-Morrogh, *The Munster Plantation: English Migration to Southern Ireland, 1583–1641* (Oxford: The Clarendon Press, 1986), 226. Nicholas Canny notes that this discourse of a superior and more efficient use of "the bounty with which God had provided them was employed by every European colonizing power" ("Identity Formation in Ireland," in *Colonial Identity in the Atlantic World, 1500–1800*, ed. Nicholas Canny and Anthony Pagden [Princeton: Princeton University Press, 1987], 173).

12. Canny, *The Elizabethan Conquest*, 131. Canny also notes that Sidney's primary means "for reducing the feudal areas of Ireland to obedience . . . under the rule of English law was the creation of provincial councils modeled on those in the north of England and the marches of Wales" (93).

13. Davies to Salisbury, 1 July 1607, *Calendar of State Papers Irish, 1606–8*, 213; quoted in Canny, *The Elizabethan Conquest*, 131.

14. Baker, 81.

15. Cf. Lisa Jardine, "Encountering Ireland: Gabriel Harvey, Edmund Spenser, and the English Colonial Ventures," in *Representing Ireland*, 70: "there seems to be a remarkable match between Spenser's *leaving* the site of Elizabethan power, and his developing, in *The Faerie Queene*, the quintessential *figurative* version of that imperial power. Was it perhaps easier to develop the fantastic ideal away from the reality of Elizabethan court life, but where the ' cult' was an ideological necessity?"

16. See Richard Helgerson, *Forms of Nationhood: The Elizabethan Writing of England* (Chicago: University of Chicago Press, 1992), who notes that "[v]oyages to Russia, Turkey, and the East Indies were primarily the work of the merchants. Gentlemen, particularly west-country gentlemen connected to the Gilberts and Raleighs, dominated the attempts at western planting" (171).

17. Pauline Henley, *Spenser in Ireland* (Cork: Cork University Press, 1928), 64–65. See MacCarthy-Morrogh, *The Munster Plantation*, Tables 1 and 2 (291–94), for a complete list of planters. Canny notes that by the early seventeenth century the planters were disliked by English officials, who "were particularly scornful of the titles that had come within the reach of this group by means of their ill-gotten gains" and who suggested "that the social inadequacies of Ireland could be attributed as much to the shortcomings and failures of the New English themselves as to the innate barbarism of the native population" ("Identity Formation in Ireland," 183, 185).

18. See David Lee Miller, "Spenser and the Gaze of Glory," in *Edmund Spenser's Poetry*, 3rd ed., ed. Hugh Maclean and Anne Lake Prescott (New York: W. W. Norton, 1993), 756–64, who suggests that "[t]he same forces of historical change that made status more attainable for 'new men' (or for the 'new Poet') under the Tudor monarchs, also rendered status *as such* less secure: they tended to erode the illusion that the social and economic hierarchy was transcendent, unchanging, and divinely ordained" (761).

19. See Richard Lachmann, *Capitalists in Spite of Themselves: Elite Conflict and Economic Transitions in Early Modern Europe* (Oxford: Oxford University Press, 2000). See also Jonathan Dewald, *The European Nobility 1400–1800* (Cambridge: Cambridge University Press, 1996), who challenges Lawrence Stone's influential assertion of an aristocratic "crisis" and argues instead that European nobles continually adapted to new economic and social conditions and thereby maintained their dominance: "by 1600 [lordship of a demesne] had ceased to be a critical economic resource for most French nobles, and it had effectively disappeared from England much earlier." While "this transformation of the nature of property itself was a serious blow, which damaged or even destroyed [the] . . . economic position [of some aristocratic families] . . . most proved more resilient in the face of change . . . [and] overall the group retained its economic dominance of the countryside; in some places it tightened that dominance" (76–77).

20. As Frank Whigham points out, Richard Mulcaster, headmaster of the Merchant Taylors' School, was "aware by 1581 of the dangers of [the] overproduction" of educated young gentlemen. Mulcaster noted " [t]o have so many gaping for preferment, as no gulf hath store enough to suffice, and to let them roam helpless, whom nothing else can help, how can it be but that such shifters must needs shake the very strongest pillar in that state where

they live, and loiter without living?" *Ambition and Privilege: The Social Tropes of Elizabethan Courtesy Theory* (Berkeley: University of California Press, 1984), 15. On the impact of schools like the Merchant Taylors', see Halpern, *The Poetics of Primitive Accumulation*, 19–60; and Mary Thomas Crane, *Framing Authority: Sayings, Self, and Society in Sixteenth-Century England* (Princeton: Princeton University Press, 1993).

21. J. W. Lever, *The Elizabethan Love Sonnet* (London: Methuen, 1956), 96.
22. Louis Martz, "The *Amoretti*: 'Most Goodly Temperature,'" in *Form and Convention in the Poetry of Edmund Spenser: Selected Papers from the English Institute*, ed. William Nelson (New York: Columbia University Press, 1961), 146–68. Reprinted in *Edmund Spenser's Poetry*, 2nd edition, ed. Hugh Maclean (New York: W. W. Norton, 1982), 723–28, 724.
23. O. B. Hardison, Jr., "*Amoretti* and the *Dolce Stil Novo*," *ELR* 2 (1972): 208–16.
24. In emphasizing the lady's resistance to the speaker's efforts at objectification, I am building on the work in particular of Jacqueline T. Miller, who argues that the female poetic object in lyrics of this period is far from silent, particularly in her capacity as reader of the poem. See *Poetic License: Authority and Authorship in Medieval and Renaissance Contexts* (Oxford: Oxford University Press, 1986), 121–75; and " 'What may words say': The Limits of Language in *Astrophil and Stella*," in *Sir Philip Sidney and the Interpretation of Renaissance Culture: The Poet in His Time and Ours*, ed. Gary F. Waller and Michael D. Moore (Totowa, NJ: Barnes and Noble, 1984), 95–109.
25. Kim F. Hall, *Things of Darkness: Economies of Race and Gender in Early Modern England* (Ithaca: Cornell University Press, 1995), 82. Jonathan Sawday, *The Body Emblazoned: Dissection and the Human Body in Renaissance Culture* (New York: Routledge, 1995), contrasts the blazon in the *Epithalamion* with sonnet 15 and concludes that "the woman became arrayed as an object of consumption for other men, flaunted before an audience as something not only there to be looked upon, but eaten. And with the similes of fruit and flowers, came the evocation of a mercantile world, for she was displayed before an audience which was addressed (and constructed) as part of a thriving metropolitan commercial culture" (199). Bach, *Colonial Transformations*, while not specifically stressing the blazon, similarly argues that "[i]n a way Spenser's actual experience in Ireland did not, the love lyric enabled the poet to effect a conquest in the face of rebellion; and the lyric representation of conquest was predicated on a feminization of Ireland . . . The sequence thus participates in an English personification of Ireland as a subservient woman" (41). See also Nancy Vickers, "Diana Described: Scattered Woman and Scattered Rhyme," *Critical Inquiry* 8 (1981): 265–79; Vickers, "'The blazon of sweet beauty's best': Shakespeare's *Lucrece*," in *Shakespeare and the Question of Theory*, ed. Patricia Parker and Geoffrey Hartman (New York and London: Methuen, 1985), 95–115; Patricia Parker, "Rhetorics of Property: Exploration, Inventory, Blazon," in *Literary Fat Ladies: Rhetoric, Gender, Property* (London and New York: Methuen, 1987), 126–54; and Hannah Betts, " 'The Image of this Queene so quaynt': The Pornographic Blazon 1588–1603," in *Dissing Elizabeth*, 153–84.

26. See Eve Kosofsky Sedgwick, *Between Men: English Literature and Male Homosocial Desire* (New York: Columbia University Press, 1985).

27. See David Lee Miller, "Spenser and the Gaze of Glory," emphasizes that "[i]n apprehending Spenser . . . we too [as readers] are captivated by the phenomenon of spectacle: an image of ourselves informs the way we choose to read" (757); and Jonathan Goldberg's comments concerning the authorship of *The Lay of Clorinda* in *Sodometries: Renaissance Texts, Modern Sexualities* (Stanford: Stanford University Press, 1992), 81–101.

28. Judson, *The Life of Edmund Spenser*, 166, 169. Most of what is known about Elizabeth Boyle is synthesized in Judson 166–75, but see also Mary Anne Hutchinson's entry for the "Boyle family" in *The Spenser Encyclopedia*, ed. A.C. Hamilton *et al.* (Toronto: University of Toronto Press, 1990), 109, which also draws on Nicholas Canny, *The Upstart Earl: A Study of the Social and Mental World of Richard Boyle First Earl of Cork 1566–1643* (Cambridge: Cambridge University Press, 1982).

29. See Anne Lake Prescott, "The Thirsty Deer and the Lord of Life: Some Contexts for *Amoretti* 67–70," *Spenser Studies* 6 (1985): 33–76; and Reed Way Dasenbrock, *Imitating the Italians: Wyatt, Spenser, Synge, Pound, Joyce* (Baltimore: The Johns Hopkins University Press, 1991).

30. See in particular Jonathan V. Crewe, *Trials of Authorship: Anterior Forms and Poetic Reconstruction from Wyatt to Shakespeare* (Berkeley: University of California Press, 1990), 36–45, whose reading of "Whoso list" in many ways anticipates my understanding of Spenser.

31. See the discussion in Heather Dubrow, *Echoes of Desire: English Petrarchism and Its Counterdiscourses* (Ithaca: Cornell University Press, 1995), 76–81. See also Lisa M. Klein, *The Exemplary Sidney and the Elizabethan Sonneteer* (Newark: University of Delaware Press, 1998), 208–12; Klein, "'Let us love, dear love, lyk as we ought': Protestant Marriage and the Revision of Petrarchan Loving in Spenser's *Amoretti*," *Spenser Studies* 10 (1992): 109–37; John King, *Spenser's Poetry and the Reformation Tradition* (Princeton: Princeton University Press, 1990), 161–63; Joseph Loewenstein, "Echo's Ring: Orpheus and Spenser's Career," *ELR* 16 (1986): 287–302; Richard Helgerson, *Self-Crowned Laureates: Spenser, Jonson, Milton, and the Literary System* (Berkeley: University of California Press, 1983); Carol V. Kaske, "Spenser's *Amoretti and Epithalamion* of 1595: Structure, Genre, and Numerology," *ELR* 8 (1978): 271–95; G. K. Hunter, "Spenser's *Amoretti* and the English Sonnet Tradition," in *A Theatre for Spenserians*, ed. Judith M. Kennedy and James A. Reither (Toronto: University of Toronto Press, 1973), 124–44; A.R. Cirillo, "Spenser's *Epithalamion*: The Harmonious Universe of Love," *SEL* 8 (1968), 20; Wolfgang Clemen, "The Uniqueness of Spenser's *Epithalamion*," in *The Poetic Tradition: Essays on Greek, Latin, and English Poetry*, ed. D.C. Allen and Henry T. Rowell (Baltimore: The Johns Hopkins University Press, 1968), 92; A. Kent Hieatt, *Short Time's Endless Monument: The Symbolism of the Numbers in Edmund Spenser's Epithalamion* (New York: Columbia University Press, 1960); and C.S. Lewis, *English Literature in the Sixteenth Century* (Oxford: Clarendon Press, 1954), 373. Catherine Bates, *The Rhetoric of Courtship in Elizabethan Language and Literature* (Cambridge: Cambridge University Press, 1992), suggests that the

anacreontic poems which immediately follow the *Amoretti* provide an "alternative" yet "conventional" ending – "poems which testify to the poet's unchanged state as a resigned and suffering victim of love" (148).

32. Richard Rambuss, "Spenser's Lives, Spenser's Careers," in *Spenser's Life and the Subject of Biography*, 15. Rambuss builds on work begun in his *Spenser's Secret Career*. In describing Spenser's new inwardness as "domestic" rather than "private," Montrose similarly seeks to overcome a critical "binary" between private/public in descriptions of Spenser's late work that "privilege[s] privacy as the source of meaning, value, solace" apart from the public world of politics. The domestic domain is "not a place apart from the public sphere so much as it is the nucleus of the social order, the primary site of subjectification" ("Spenser's Domestic Domain," 95–96). See also Owens, "The Poetics of Accommodation in Spenser's *Epithalamion*"; Miller's deconstruction of the closure of the *Epithalamion* in *Poetic License*, 171–74, and especially note 81, 216–17; Loewenstein, "Echo's Ring"; and Joseph Loewenstein, "Spenser's Retrography: Two Episodes in post-Petrarchan Bibliography," in *Spenser's Life and the Subject of Biography*, 99–130.

33. Pierre Bourdieu, "Social Space and Symbolic Space," trans. Gisele Sapiro, in *Practical Reason: On the Theory of Action* (Stanford: Stanford University Press, 1998), 11.

34. Montrose, "Spenser's Domestic Domain," 114–15.

35. Thomas M. Greene, "Spenser and the Epithalamic Convention," *Comparative Literature* 9 (1957): 220–21.

36. Cf. G. K. Hunter, "Spenser's *Amoretti*," 126: "[t]he excellence of the *Epithalamion* derives in part from Spenser's capacity in this poem to use the facts of real life as a framework upon which, by mythological and biblical parallels, he throws what a later age was to call the colouring of imagination – the sense of a sacramental occasion, representative of human destiny, at once this wedding and all weddings, and not only all weddings but all sanctifications of fertility." Here is the privileging of privacy which Montrose's reading critiques.

37. Montrose, "Spenser's Domestic Domain," 115.

38. Greene, "Echo's Ring," p. 223. Montrose similarly associates the emergence of capitalism with the rise of the bourgeoisie: "Spenser's motives were undoubtedly to affirm his status as a gentleman rather than to assert his place in the vanguard of the bourgeoisie. Nevertheless, we may see in some of the thematic preoccupations of his later poetry, adumbrations of those values and aspirations that came increasingly to characterize the lives of the middling sort and the culture of mercantile capitalism" ("Spenser's Domestic Domain," 97). See David Lee Miller's sense that Montrose's essay, despite its "most responsible historicist" argument, occasionally "forget[s] uncertainties" as the text is subordinated to "personal and historical circumstance" ("The Earl of Cork's Lute," in *Spenser and the Subject of Biography*, 162–63).

39. See Robert Brenner, *Merchants and Revolution: Commercial Change, Political Conflict, and London's Overseas Traders, 1550–1653* (Princeton: Princeton University Press, 1993), who argues that new agricultural structures produced more efficiently, providing the disposable income to sustain the ever-growing desire for the consumer goods increasingly imported by the recently

established far-distance companies. By stressing that the emergent companies thrived on imports bought with the newly available disposable income enjoyed by landlords, Brenner effectively resituates these merchants as a sign, rather than a cause, of capitalism in England: "what made possible the new trades' extraordinary long-term growth and continuing high profits over more than a century was the remarkable secular rise of domestic demand for imports in England, as well as the growth of the reexport trades with Europe" (650).

40. Miller, *Poetic License,* 172.
41. See Loewenstein, "Echo's Ring," 288: "The barest argument of the tornata is that this song is intended to compensate for the poet's lack of wealth."
42. See Miller, *Poetic License*, 172: "The word *one* added to the repeated phrase in this line emphasizes the circumscribed scope of the poet's present aspiration. He knows that in a short time his one day will be over, and it is up to him to make the most of it."

6 "TILL MY BAD ANGEL FIRE MY GOOD ONE OUT": ENGENDERING ECO-NOMIC EXPERTISE IN SHAKESPEARE'S *SONNETS*

1. See especially David Hawkes, *Idols of the Marketplace: Idolatry and Commodity Fetishism in English Literature, 1580–1680* (New York: Palgrave, 2001), 95–114; Peter C. Herman, "What's the Use ? Or, The Problematic of Economy in Shakespeare's Procreation Sonnets," in *Shakespeare's Sonnets: Critical Essays*, ed. James Schiffer (New York: Garland, 2000), 263–83; Theodore B. Leinwand, *Theatre, Finance and Society in Early Modern England* (Cambridge: Cambridge University Press, 1999), 107–09; John B. Mischo, "'That use is not forbidden usury': Shakespeare's Procreation Sonnets and the Problem of Usury," in *Subjects on the World's Stage: Essays on British Literature of the Middle Ages and the Renaissance*, ed. David G. Allen and Robert A. White (Newark: University of Delaware Press, 1995), 262–79; Thomas M. Greene, "Pitiful Thrivers: Failed Husbandry in the Sonnets," in *Shakespeare and the Question of Theory*, ed. Patricia Parker and Geoffrey Hartman (New York: Methuen, 1985), 230–44.
2. Claims about the originality and unconventionality of Shakespeare's *Sonnets* are too numerous to mention; see the discussion in chapter 2. On Shakespeare's relation to an "exhausted" poetic tradition, see Joel Fineman, *Shakespeare's Perjured Eye: The Invention of Poetic Subjectivity in the Sonnets* (Berkeley: University of California Press, 1986).
3. Mary Poovey, "Accommodating Merchants: Accounting, Civility, and the Natural Laws of Gender," *differences* 8.3 (1996): 1–2. See also Linda Woodbridge's discussion of double-entry bookkeeping schools around the Globe theater in "Introduction," *Money and the Age of Shakespeare*, ed. Linda Woodbridge (New York: Palgrave, 2003), 1–18.
4. All quotations of the *Sonnets* are from *The Sonnets and A Lover's Complaint by William Shakespeare*, ed. John Kerrigan (London: Penguin, 1995).
5. *Shakespeare's Sonnets*, ed. Katherine Duncan-Jones. The Arden Shakespeare (London: Thomas Nelson, 1997), note to sonnet 144.

6. Eve Kosofsky Sedgwick, *Between Men: English Literature and Male Homosocial Desire* (New York: Columbia University Press, 1985), 31.
7. Fineman, *Shakespeare's Perjured Eye*, 26, 25.
8. Valerie Traub, "Sex without Issue: Sodomy, Reproduction, and Signification in Shakespeare's Sonnets," in Schiffer, *Shakespeare's Sonnets*, 431–53, 442. Margreta de Grazia makes a similar point in "The Scandal of Shakespeare's Sonnets," in Schiffer, *Shakespeare's Sonnets*, 89–112, 97. On Malone's edition, see de Grazia, *Shakespeare Verbatim: The Reproduction of Authenticity and the 1790 Apparatus* (Oxford: Oxford University Press, 1991).
9. Cf. Heather Dubrow, "'Incertainties now crown themselves assur'd': The Politics of Plotting Shakespeare's Sonnets," in Schiffer, *Shakespeare's Sonnets*, 113–33. Dubrow usefully spells out the possibilities for reading opened up by the rejection of Malone's division, but she never questions the lyric subject and the social position that the division concretizes. Because she continues to emphasize that "most of the Sonnets are internalized meditations" (123), Dubrow's interrogation of Malone's division is predicated upon retaining the post-romantic lyric position which the division helped to create. Dubrow similarly emphasizes the *Sonnets'* lyricism in *Captive Victors: Shakespeare's Narrative Poems and Sonnets* (Ithaca: Cornell University Press, 1987). For similar understandings of Dubrow, see Traub, "Sex without Issue"; and Olga L. Valbuena, "'The dyer's hand': The Reproduction of Coercion and Blot in Shakespeare's Sonnets," in Schiffer, *Shakespeare's Sonnets*, 325–45.
10. Sedgwick, *Between Men*, emphasizes at the start of her chapter that "Marx's warning [in the *Grundrisse*] about the 'developed, or stunted, or caricatured form etc.' in which historically decontextualized abstractions are apt to appear should be prominently posted at the entrance [to her chapter]" (29). On Fineman's attenuated understanding of sonnet history, see Gordon Braden, "Shakespeare's Petrarchism," in Schiffer, *Shakespeare's Sonnets*, 163–83.
11. See the notes in Kerrigan, *The Sonnets and A Lovers Complaint*, and Stephen Booth, *Shakespeare's Sonnets* (New Haven: Yale University Press, 1977). Duncan-Jones, *Shakespeare's Sonnets*, summarizes the other traditional view of the line: "there is presumably both an analogy with animals being smoked out of their holes or lairs and a suggestion that the man will sooner or later be venereally infected by the woman; cf. also the proverb 'One fire (heat) drives out another'" (404).
12. See the similar comments by James R. Siemon, "Dreams of Fields: Early Modern (Dis) Positions," in *Historicism, Psychoanalysis, and Early Modern Culture*, ed. Carla Mazzio and Douglas Trevor (New York: Routledge, 2000), 36–58. Siemon draws in particular on Bourdieu's critique of Foucauldian structuralism and Marxist reflection theory in "Principles for a Sociology of Cultural Works," in *The Field of Cultural Production*, ed. Randal Johnson (New York: Columbia University Press, 1993), 176–91.
13. On the "transformative power" of the emergent market, see Jean-Christophe Agnew, *Worlds Apart: The Market and the Theater in Anglo-American Thought, 1550–1750* (Cambridge: Cambridge University Press, 1986), 53. As Douglas Bruster points out in reaction to Agnew, "[r]ather than a 'proxy

form' of the market, however (the word here implies substitution, and in doing so confers upon the stage a privileged position in relation to the 'real' market), London's playhouses were, of course, actual markets." *Drama and the Market in the Age of Shakespeare* (Cambridge: Cambridge University Press, 1992), 9.

14. See Barbara Correll, "Scene Stealers: Autolycus, *The Winter's Tale* and Economic Criticism," in *Money and the Age of Shakespeare*, 53–65, who stresses the need for "a more politically invested post-structuralism that does not lose sight of the relations between signifying practices and social relations" (61–62).

15. S.T. Bindoff, *The Fame of Sir Thomas Gresham*. Neale Lecture in English History (London: Jonathan Cape, 1973), 25 note 3. Bindoff notes that "there is little or no foundation for the often sweeping claims of [Gresham's alleged influence on the English recoinage], which are usually based on nothing more than his inclusion of a plea for a sound currency in his letter of 1558 to Elizabeth, a plea which many of his contemporaries would have made." Bindoff, 28–29, Note 18. See also Stanford E. Lehmberg, *Sir Walter Mildmay and Tudor Government* (Austin: University of Texas Press, 1964): "in point of fact the recoinage was advocated by diverse people – merchants, governmental officials, even the Queen herself – and it was carried through by no single administrator but rather by a group of the government's financial officers" (60); and F.R. Salter, *Sir Thomas Gresham* (London: Leonard Parsons,1925), 38, who notes that the concept that debased coins drive out those with higher bullion content had been articulated by Oresme, Bishop of Lisieux in the 14th century, Copernicus, and possibly others as well.

16. Karl Marx, *Ökonomisch-philosophische Manuskripte (1844)*, in *Marx/Engels Gesamtausgabe* (Glashütten im Taunus: Verlag Detlev Auvermann, 1970), 1: 3: 81. On the naturalization and moralization of economics in the nineteenth century, see also Elaine Freedgood, "Banishing Panic: Harriet Martineau and the Popularization of Political Economy," in *The New Economic Criticism: Studies at the Intersection of Literature and Economics*, ed. Martha Woodmansee and Mark Osteen (New York: Routledge, 1999), 210–28.

17. Henry Dunning Macleod, *The Theory and Practice of Banking* 2nd ed. (London: Longmans, Green, Reader, and Dyer, 1866), 218–19.

18. Bindoff, *The Fame of Sir Thomas Gresham*, 6–7.

19. Cf. Herman, "What's the Use ?," who emphasizes that the *Sonnets* "explore the subjectivity resulting when the speaker is no longer defined by either courtly values . . . or Neoplatonic philosophy . . . but by the marketplace" (264). I cannot agree with Herman's humanist sense that "the Sonnets register the dehumanization implicit in an ideology of commodity," since that "ideology" comes in this period to constitute what "humanity" means at all.

20. Michel Foucault, *The Order of Things: An Archeology of the Human Sciences*, 1970 (New York: Vintage, 1994), 175.

21. D. M. Palliser, *The Age of Elizabeth: England under the later Tudors 1547–1603*, Second Edition (London: Longman, 1992), 154.

22. Norman Jones, *The Birth of the Elizabethan Age: England in the 1560s* (Oxford: Blackwell, 1993), 230; 229.

23. On this debasement, see J. D. Gould, *The Great Debasement: Currency and the Economy in Mid-Tudor England* (Oxford: Clarendon Press, 1970); and C. E. Challis, *The Tudor Coinage* (Manchester: Manchester University Press, 1978).

24. Palliser, *The Age of Elizabeth*, notes that "dearth" referred to both shortage of goods and an increase in the money supply "although they were uneasily aware that it did not fully apply to the latter" (154).

25. See John William Burgon, *The life & times of Sir Thomas Gresham, knt., founder of the Royal exchange; including notices of many of his contemporaries*, 2 vols. (London: E. Wilson, 1839), 1: 484. See also the five letters concerning the recoinage printed in *Tudor Economic Documents: Being Select Documents Illustrating the Economic and Social History of Tudor England*, 3 vols., ed. R. H. Tawney and Eileen Power (London: Longmans, Green and Co., 1924), 2: 193–203.

26. Jones, *The Birth of the Elizabethan Age*, 233.

27. Lehmberg, *Sir Walter Mildmay*, 61–62.

28. Jones, *The Birth of the Elizabethan Age*, 236–37.

29. G. D. Ramsay, *The City of London in International Politics at the Accession of Elizabeth Tudor* (Manchester: Manchester University Press, 1975), vii. See also Ramsay, *The Queen's Merchants and the Revolt of the Netherlands* (Manchester: Manchester University Press, 1986); and Wallace MacCaffrey, *The Shaping of the Elizabethan Regime* (Princeton: Princeton University Press, 1968), 268–90.

30. Quoted in Lehmberg, *Sir Walter Mildmay*, 63. Mildmay is here criticizing the granting of special licenses to "some covetous men" who offered "great sommes of mony" to the Queen in order to be able to import "from the Low Countreyes certeyne wares, the restreynt notwithstanding."

31. See Mary Poovey, *A History of the Modern Fact: Problems of Knowledge in the Sciences of Wealth and Society* (Chicago: University of Chicago Press, 1998), 69; Richard Halpern, *The Poetics of Primitive Accumulation: English Renaissance Culture and the Genealogy of Capital* (Ithaca: Cornell University Press, 1991), 61–75; A. L. Beier, *Masterless Men: The Vagrancy Problem in England, 1560–1640* (New York: Methuen, 1985); Paul Slack, *Poverty and Policy in Tudor and Stuart England* (London: Longman, 1988), 1–16 and 37–60; and William C. Carroll, *Fat King, Lean Beggar: Representations of Poverty in the Age of Shakespeare* (Ithaca: Cornell University Press, 1996).

32. Joyce Oldham Appleby, *Economic Thought and Ideology in Seventeenth-Century England* (Princeton: Princeton University Press, 1978), 42.

33. Poovey, *A History of the Modern Fact*, 72–73.

34. Ibid., 87.

35. Appleby, *Economic Thought*, 45, 47.

36. Poovey, "Accommodating Merchants," 2.

37. Poovey, *A History of the Modern Fact*, 90. See also Richard Helgerson's discussion of merchants in *Forms of Nationhood: The Elizabethan Writing of England* (Chicago: University of Chicago Press, 1992), 149–92.

38. Duncan-Jones, *Shakespeare's Sonnets* (1–45), provides an excellent discussion of the various possible dates of composition, as well as a useful overview of the publishing history.

39. For a history of attempts, see Samuel Schoenbaum, *Shakespeare's Lives*, New Edition (Oxford: Clarendon Press, 1991).

40. De Grazia, "The Scandal," 101–02. See also Christopher Martin, *Policy in Love: Lyric and Public in Ovid, Petrarch, and Shakespeare* (Pittsburgh: Duquesne University Press, 1994): "[t]he abstractions deployed in the procreation series consistently serve a collective function, attempting to fuse addressee and poet to a larger societal purposefulness" (154); and Paul Innes, *Shakespeare and the English Renaissance Sonnet: Verses of Feigning Love* (New York: St. Martin's Press, 1997), 72–206.

41. Greene, "Pitiful Thrivers," 233. For Greene such idealization is a function of both the speaker's bourgeois desperation and, more generally, the workings of language itself. "The [speaker's] bourgeois desire to balance cosmic and human budgets seems to be thwarted by a radical flaw in the universe, in emotion, in value, and in language" (243).

42. See Bourdieu, *The State Nobility: Elite Schools in the Field of Power*, trans. Lauretta C. Clough (Stanford: Stanford University Press, 1996), who remarks that "[w]e cannot understand the symbolic violence of what were once hastily designated as the 'ideological state apparatuses' unless we analyze in detail the relationship between the objective characteristics of the organizations that exercise it and the socially constituted dispositions of the agents upon whom it is exercised" (3).

43. De Grazia, "The Scandal," 102.

44. Ibid., 107.

45. See Louis Althusser, "Ideology and Ideological State Apparatuses (Notes towards an Investigation)," in *Lenin and Philosophy and Other Essays*, trans. Ben Brewster (New York: Monthly Review Press, 1971), 127–86, 127–34.

46. See Hawkes, *Idols of the Marketplace*, 102.

47. See the discussion of usury in the *Sonnets* by Hawkes, *Idols of the Marketplace*, 101–07; and Mischo, "'That use is not forbidden usury,'" who argues that "Shakespeare's appeal for unrestricted circulation, in its rejection of hoarding, appropriates the standard pro-usury arguments marshaled by the mercantile classes in their demand for the freer circulation of capital to finance their ventures and industries" (270). On usury generally see Norman Jones, *God and the Moneylenders: Usury and Law in Early Modern England* (Oxford: Basil Blackwell, 1989); and R. H. Tawney's extensive introduction to Thomas Wilson's 1572 *A Discourse Upon Usury* . . . ed. R. H. Tawney, 1925 (New York: Augustus M. Kelley, 1963), 1–172.

48. See Helgerson, *Forms of Nationhood*, 149–92.

49. Cf. Greene, "Pitiful Thrivers," who argues that in the young man sonnets "we are left with two distinct sources of alleged value, the friend and the poetry, each the basis for a rudimentary economic system, each vulnerable to skepticism. The presence of each system tends to destabilize the other by casting doubt on the kind of value it attempts to establish" (234). Such instability creates "pitiful thrivers," who fail to "bring to a happy conclusion a quest for an adequate economic system which would avoid the 'waste or ruining' and the excessive 'rent' which burden those in [sonnet] 125 who vainly spend themselves" (231).

50. Sedgwick, *Between Men*, 41.

51. Greene, "Pitiful Thrivers," notes that it "is not clear whether *any* of the sonnets is to be read as a spoken address, a dramatic monologue, rather than as a written communication. Many of them refer to themselves as written, refer to paper, ink, pens, and to poetic style. They may occasionally affirm a closeness between poet and friend, but their very existence suggests a distance which has to be crossed. We are never allowed to envision unambiguously the poet in the presence of his friend, as we are in love poems by Wyatt, Sidney, Spenser, and Donne" (235).

52. See the subtle reading of these issues by Arthur Marotti, "Shakespeare's Sonnets as Literary Property," in *Soliciting Interpretation: Literary Theory and Seventeenth-Century English Poetry*, ed. Elizabeth D. Harvey and Katharine Eisaman Maus (Chicago: University of Chicago Press, 1990), 143–73.

53. Cf. Anne Ferry, *The "Inward" Language: Sonnets of Wyatt, Sidney, Shakespeare, Donne* (Chicago: University of Chicago Press, 1983): "Hamlet, whose sighs and tears are not such actions, nevertheless knows that their truth cannot be seen or proved. He therefore declares his sincerity, but offers no demonstration of it. He feels 'that Within' which he does not name. For words, like all outward expression, are radically ambiguous in their capacity to show what is in the heart. Yet within him is a private being which, if known, would denote him truly. Like the speaker in the sonnets, Hamlet therefore casts doubts on the fundamental assumption that what is hidden in the closet of the heart is describable by the commonest sixteenth-century term, *secrets*" (214). The tension between Hamlet's lyrical soliloquy and its position in the narrative of the play is brilliantly manipulated in *William Shakespeare's Hamlet*, dir. Kenneth Branagh, prod. David Baron, 4hr. 2 min., Columbia/Tristar, 1996, videocassette.

54. Greene, "Pitiful Thrivers," 242.

55. Joel Fineman, "Shakespeare's 'Perjured Eye,'" *Representations* 7 (1984): 59–86, 63. Fineman is discussing sonnet 105.

56. Sedgwick, *Between Men*, 44.

57. Fineman, *Shakespeare's Perjured Eye*: "the young man sonnets seem estranged from the laudatory sentiments they assert primarily because they code these sentiments with formal and conceptual duplications that add an equivocating disjunction to the conventional univocities and complementarities of Petrarchan admiration" (242).

58. Murray Krieger, "The Conversion from History to Utopia in Shakespeare's Sonnets," in *Words about Words about Words: Theory, Criticism, and the Literary Text* (Baltimore: The Johns Hopkins University Press, 1988), 242–55, 243.

59. Kerrigan, *The Sonnets and a Lover's Complaint*, 202.

60. Poovey, "Accommodating Merchants," 2.

61. Sedgwick, *Between Men*, 40.

62. See especially the readings of this sonnet by Hawkes, *Idols of the Marketplace*, 111–14; and Leinwand, *Theatre, Finance and Society*, 107–09.

63. Duncan-Jones, *Shakespeare's Sonnets*, 51.

64. My thanks to Tammy Tai for this reading.

7 "THE ENGLISH STRAINE": ABSOLUTISM, CLASS, AND DRAYTON'S *IDEAS*, 1594–1619

1. Drayton's revisions to *Idea* have been traced before, but in largely stylistic, rather than social, terms. See F. Y. St. Clair, "Drayton's First Revision of his Sonnets," *SP* 36 (1939): 40–59; William Thomas Schroeder, "Michael Drayton: A Study of the *Idea* Sonnet Revisions," (Ph.D. diss., Northwestern University, 1958); Jörg Schönert, "Draytons Sonett-Revisionen: Zum Problem des 'Übergangsdichters,'" *Anglia Zeitschrift für Englische Philologie* 85 (1967): 161–83; Walter R. Davis, "'Fantastickly I Sing': Drayton's *Idea* of 1619," *Studies in Philology* 66 (1969): 204–16; and Louise Hutching Westling, *The Evolution of Michael Drayton's* Idea, Salzburg Studies in English Literature 37 (Salzburg: Institut für Englische Sprache und Literatur, 1974). See also Bernard H. Newdigate, *Michael Drayton and His Circle* (Oxford: Shakespeare Head Press, 1941); Oliver Elton, *An Introduction to Michael Drayton* (1895, Spenser Society; reprint, New York: Burt Franklin, 1970); Paul Gerhard Buchloh, *Michael Drayton: Barde und Historiker-Politiker und Prophet* (Neumünster: Karl Wachholtz, 1964); Joan Grundy, *The Spenserian Poets: A Study in Elizabethan and Jacobean Poetry* (London: Edward Arnold, 1969); Richard John Berleth, "In the Field of the Muses: a Reading of Michael Drayton," (Ph.D. diss., Rutgers University 1970); Richard F. Hardin, *Michael Drayton and the Passing of Elizabethan England* (Lawrence/Manhattan/Wichita: University Press of Kansas, 1973); and Ted Brown, "'When First I Ended, Then I First Began': Petrarch's Triumph in Michael Drayton's *Idea*," in *Subjects on the World's Stage: Essays on British Literature of the Middle Ages and the Renaissance*, ed. David Allen and Robert A. White (Newark: University of Delaware Press, 1995), 116–32.

2. In charting the social implications of Drayton's revisions, throughout I am particularly indebted to Leah Marcus' "unediting" of Renaissance literature, especially her renderings of Marlowe and Milton, and to Annabel Patterson's reading of Jonson's *Underwood*. See Leah S. Marcus, *Unediting the Renaissance: Shakespeare, Marlowe, Milton* (London: Routledge, 1996); and Annabel Patterson, *Censorship and Interpretation: The Conditions of Writing and Reading in Early Modern England* (Madison: University of Wisconsin Press, 1984), 120–58.

3. Jonathan Goldberg, *James I and the Politics of Literature: Jonson, Shakespeare, Donne, and Their Contemporaries* (Baltimore: The Johns Hopkins University Press, 1983).

4. Michael McKeon, *The Origins of the English Novel 1600–1740* (Baltimore: The Johns Hopkins University Press, 1987), 178. "Absolutism" marks a terrain of fierce warfare among historians, who alternately see it as a defining term of the seventeenth century or as marginal political position. For an overview of the vast literature, see J. P. Sommerville, *Politics and Ideology in England, 1603–1640* (London: Longman, 1986); Brian P. Levack, "Law and Ideology: The Civil Law and Theories of Absolutism in Elizabethan and Jacobean England," in *The Historical Renaissance: New Essays on Tudor and Stuart Literature and Culture*, ed. Heather Dubrow and Richard Strier (Chicago: University of Chicago Press, 1988), 220–41; Christopher Hill, *A*

Nation of Change and Novelty: Radical Politics, Religion and Literature in Seventeenth-Century England (New York: Routledge, 1990); Linda Levy Peck, "Kingship, Counsel and Law in Early Stuart Britain," in *The Varieties of British Political Thought, 1500–1800*, ed. J. G. A. Pocock, Gordon J. Schochet, and Lois G. Schwoerer (Cambridge: Cambridge University Press, 1993), 80–115; and Glenn Burgess, *Absolute Monarchy and the Stuart Constitution* (New Haven: Yale University Press, 1996).

5. Cf. C. S. Lewis, *English Literature in the Sixteenth Century Excluding Drama* (Oxford: Clarendon Press, 1954): Drayton "began with Drab, constantly relapsed into it, and in his old age, when the Golden period was over, at last produced his perfect Golden work, so pure and fine that no English poet has rivaled it" (531).

6. On the political implications of Drayton's work, see David Norbrook, *Poetry and Politics in the English Renaissance* (London: Routledge and Kegan Paul, 1984), 195–234; Jean R. Brink, *Michael Drayton Revisited* (Boston: Twayne Publisher, 1990); Jane Tylus, "Jacobean Poetry and Lyric Disappointment," in *Soliciting Interpretation: Literary Theory and Seventeenth-Century English Poetry*, ed. Elizabeth D. Harvey and Katharine Eisaman Maus (Chicago: University of Chicago Press, 1990), 174–98; Richard Helgerson, *Forms of Nationhood: The Elizabethan Writing of England* (Chicago: University of Chicago Press, 1992), 105–47 and 193–245; Claire McEachern, *The Poetics of English Nationhood, 1590–1612* (Cambridge: Cambridge University Press, 1996); and Curtis Perry, *The Making of Jacobean Culture: James I and the Renegotiation of Elizabethan Literary Practice* (Cambridge: Cambridge University Press, 1997), 50–80.

7. *Ideas Mirrour*, in J. William Hebel, Kathleen Tillotson, and Bernard Newdigate, eds., *The Works of Michael Drayton*, 5 vols. (Oxford: The Shakespeare Head Press, 1932–41), 1: 98. All quotations of Drayton refer to this edition unless otherwise specified.

8. As Tillotson comments in her introduction to *Ideas Mirrour*, "the name Idea may possibly be taken from de Pontoux's *L'Idée* (1579) – but one need not seek so far for instances of the Platonic 'Idea' as applied to women" (*The Works of Michael Drayton*, 5:13).

9. Sir Philip Sidney, *An Apology for Poetry*, ed. Forrest G. Robinson (Indianapolis: Bobbs-Merrill Educational Publishing, 1970), 16, 81.

10. My understanding of Sidney's paradox in the *Apology* follows the reading by Jacqueline T. Miller, *Poetic License: Authority and Authorship in Medieval and Renaissance Contexts* (Oxford: Oxford University Press, 1986), 75–80.

11. On criticism by Hall and Davies, see Brink, *Michael Drayton Revisited*, 16–17.

12. *The Works of Michael Drayton*, 5: 15.

13. All quotations of the 1599 *Idea* are from Michael Drayton, *Englands Heroicall Epistles. Newly Enlarged. With Idea* (London: N. L.[ing], 1599).

14. My account throughout is indebted to Norbrook, *Poetry and Politics*, 1984, 195–214.

15. Daniel and Constable had, of course, achieved considerable social notoriety. Daniel had worked his way into the circle of the Countess of Pembroke, and Constable had worked his way into James' court in Scotland, contributing the lead dedicatory sonnet to James' *His Maiesties Poeticall Exercises at*

vacant houres (1591). On Daniel's relations with the Countess, see Joan Rees, *Samuel Daniel: A Critical and Biographical Study* (Liverpool: Liverpool University Press, 1964); and H. R. Woudhuysen, *Sir Philip Sidney and the Circulation of Manuscripts 1558–1640* (Oxford: Clarendon Press, 1996), 376–83. On Constable see the introduction to *New Poems by James I of England From a Hitherto Unpublished Manuscript (ADD. 24195) in the British Museum*, ed. Allan F. Westcott (New York: Columbia University Press, 1911), xxxiv–liv; and the introduction to *The Poems of Henry Constable*, ed. Joan Grundy (Liverpool: Liverpool University Press, 1960).

16. On Drayton's patronage see Brink, *Michael Drayton Revisited,* 66–80.

17. Specifically, "To Lucie *Countesse of Bedford.* Sonet 57" was originally the dedication to *Endimion and Phoebe* (1595); "*To the Lady* Anne Harington. Sonet 58" appeared in *Robert Duke of Normandy* (1596); and "To sir [*sic*] Anthony Cooke. Sonet 59" was the dedication to *Ideas Mirrour* (1594).

18. The Countess of Bedford was a principal patron for, among others, Daniel, Jonson, and Donne, and Drayton seems to have taken his failure with her rather hard. In 1606 she is portrayed as Selena in the eighth eclogue in *Poemes lyrick and pastorall.* As Brink suggests, Selena/Lucy is "a faithless patroness who has deserted the faithful Rowland to favor Cerberon, a 'beastly clowne,' figuratively named after the three-headed dog who guards the gates to hell" (*Michael Drayton Revisited*, 18).

19. As Hardin suggests, Drayton may have had to delay publication of the 1594 sequence because of a lack of a patron. His dedication to Anthony Cooke, the "ever-kind Maecenas" from Drayton's native Warwickshire, may actually indicate (and forecast) Drayton's failure in the patronage game (*Michael Drayton*, 19).

20. The *Epistles* themselves enact this tension as witnessed in the critical tradition they have spawned. On one hand, the work is seen as a powerful moment of self-fashioning (see Barbara Ewell, "Unity and the Transformation of Drayton's Poetics in *Englands Heroicall Epistles*: From Mirrored Ideals to 'The Chaos in the Mind'" *MLQ* 44 [1983]: 231–50; Ewell, "From Idea to Act: The New Aesthetic of Drayton's *Englands Heroicall Epistles,*" *JEGP* 82 [1983]: 515–25). But it is also seen as a "general plan" showing "divine Providence guiding England through a troublesome past into a glorious present under Elizabeth" (Hardin, *Michael Drayton*, 48). See also Brink (*Michael Drayton Revisited*, 38–65) who argues that the work was politically volatile because of its unsubtle comments on the issue of royal succession.

21. See the discussion of E. K.'s glosses to Spenser's *The Shepheardes Calendar* in Richard Halpern, *The Poetics of Primitive Accumulation: English Renaissance Culture and the Genealogy of Capital* (Ithaca: Cornell University Press, 1991), 176–214.

22. It is probably worth noting that 1599 was also the year that *Sir John Oldcastle*, the only surviving play to which Drayton contributed, was published. *Oldcastle* has been read of late as a play which offers a social alternative to Shakespeare's obsession with monarchy. Though he does not associate *Oldcastle* with Drayton, see Helgerson's discussion in *Forms of*

Nationhood 195–245; and the introduction to *The Oldcastle Controversy: Sir John Oldcastle, Part I and The Famous Victories of Henry V*, ed. Peter Corbin and Douglas Sedge (Manchester: Manchester University Press, 1991).

23. See Schroeder, "Michael Drayton: A Study"; Davis, "'Fantastickly I Sing'"; and Westling, *The Evolution of Michael Drayton's* Idea.

24. Westling (*The Evolution of Michael Drayton's* Idea, 61–125) traces much of Drayton's changes to the influence of Wyatt, a suggestion that may have important implications for Drayton's positioning of himself in an English, nationalist, Protestant, and oppositional tradition.

25. Goldberg, *James I*, 17. See also Kevin Sharpe, "The King's Writ: Royal Authors and Royal Authority in Early Modern England," in *Culture and Politics in Early Stuart England*, ed. Kevin Sharpe and Peter Lake (Stanford: Stanford University Press, 1993), 117–38.

26. *The Essayes of a Prentise, in the Divine Art of Poesie* (Edinbrugh [*sic*]: Thomas Vautroullier, 1584).

27. See Perry, *The Making of Jacobean Culture*, 17; and Martin Butler, "Ben Jonson and the Limits of Courtly Panegyric," in *Culture and Politics in Early Stuart England*, 91–115.

28. *The Works of Michael Drayton*, 1: 488.

29. *Poems: By Michaell Draiton, Esquire* (London: N. Ling, 1605).

30. Quotations from the 1605 *Idea* are from *Minor Poems of Michael Drayton*, ed. Cyril Brett (Oxford: Clarendon Press, 1907). I have used this edition because, unlike *The Works of Michael Drayton*, Brett retains the spelling and punctuation peculiar to 1605 rather than employing the 1619 Folio. Brett's edition is also extremely useful in that it prints sonnets new to each edition separately.

31. John Huntington, *Ambition, Rank, and Poetry in 1590s England* (Urbana: University of Illinois Press, 2001). See also Grundy, *The Spenserian Poets*, 107–27, on the "heroic" in Drayton's poetry, and her general sense that the "Spenserians are not just lovers of poetry: they are poetry-addicts" (44).

32. Norbrook, *Poetry and Politics*, 217.

33. Draiton, *Poems*, 1605, A2^r.

34. See Bernard Capp, "The Poet and the Bawdy Court: Michael Drayton and the Lodging-House World in Early Stuart London," *Seventeenth Century* 10 (1991): 27–37. In the entertaining court case of 1627 in which Drayton was charged with "suspicion of incontinency with Mary Peters, wife of John Peters" (which was likely an attempt at extortion), Drayton admits in court that even though he was a gentleman "he was worth only 20 nobles in money, debts paid, but assured the court that he was 'worth at least 2000 li. in good parts'" (29).

35. Brink, *Michael Drayton Revisited*, 14.

36. Pierre Bourdieu, "Social Space and Symbolic Space," in *Practical Reason: On the Theory of Action* (Stanford: Stanford University Press, 1998), 11.

37. Goldberg, *James I*, notes that James is "heavily indebted to the plain style poetics of George Gascoigne. . . James begins his poetic career espousing plain style poetics, and if the poem labeled in manuscripts as his earliest is indeed that, he was at first, at his best, an accomplished plain style poet" (20).

38. Davis, "'Fantastickly I Sing,'" 216.

39. Brink, *Michael Drayton Revisited*, 104.
40. Buchloh notes that "In den frühen Eklogen und Sonetten Draytons ist stets die Hoffnung des jungen Dichters dargestellt, während in der Überarbeitung von *Shepherds Garland* in *Pastorals* und in der Überarbeitung von *Ideas Mirrour* in *Idea* das weise, resignierende Alter die Oberhand über die unwissende, stürmische Jugend behält. Besonders deutlich wird diese Haltung in der Ausgabe von 1619." ["In Drayton's early eclogues and sonnets the hopefulness of the young poet is continually represented, while in the revisions of *Shepherds Garland* into *Pastorals* and in the revisions of *Ideas Mirrour* into *Idea* the wise, old man retains the upperhand over the unknowledgeable, tempestuous youth. This attitude becomes especially important in the edition of 1619"] (*Michael Drayton: Barde und Historiker*, 308, n. 149).
41. See Tylus, "Jacobean Poetry and Lyric Disappointment"; Norbrook, *Poetry and Politics*, 207; and Perry, *The Making of Jacobean Culture*, 50–80.
42. See John Watkins, "'Old Bess in the Ruff': Remembering Elizabeth I, 1625–1660," *ELR* 30 (2000): 95–116, who stresses that Stuart invocations of Elizabeth could be used for a multitude of political positions.
43. *Othello* 1.3.143–44, in *The Riverside Shakespeare*, ed. G. Blakemore Evans *et al.* (Boston: Houghton Mifflin, 1974), 1208.
44. See Thomas Cogswell, "The Path to Elizium 'Lately Discovered': Drayton and the Early Stuart Court," *HLQ* 54 (1991): 207–33, who also notes that the "canon of Eliza's seamen had been standard fare for most of James's reign but, as the Anglo-Spanish marriage alliance became imminent in the early 1620s, so too the government sought to retire these militant anti-Spanish memories" (220). Cogswell also observes that in *The Second Part . . . of the Poly-Olbion* (1622) Drayton's celebration of English seamen becomes a link to Elizabethan glory. In the chapter on Essex and Suffolk, Drayton goes on to celebrate Drake, Hawkins, Frobisher, Davies, Filbert, Ralegh, Barlow, Lane, Leigh, Tompson, Cavendish, Dudley, Sherley, and Parker.
45. "And as there [Virginia] Plenty growes/Of Lawrell every where,/APOLLO'S Sacred tree,/You may it see,/A Poets Browes/To crowne, that may sing there" ("To the Virginian Voyage," lines 61–66).
46. Tillotson notes use of it by Spenser, Linche, and Sir David Murray of Gorthie (*The Works of Michael Drayton*, 5:142).
47. Catherine Gray, "Katherine Philips and the Post-Courtly Coterie," *ELR* 32.3 (2002): 426–51, 450.
48. David Norbrook, *Poetry and Politics in the English Renaissance*, Revised Edition (Oxford: Oxford University Press, 2002), 191.
49. David Norbrook, *Writing the English Republic: Poetry, Rhetoric and Politics, 1627–1660* (Cambridge: Cambridge University Press, 1999).
50. See Cogswell, "'The Path to Elizium Lately Discovered,'" who links Drayton with Charles I's personal rule.
51. For a vital overview and unabashed intervention, see James Holstun, *Ehud's Dagger: Class Struggle in the English Revolution* (London: Verso, 2000).

AFTERWORD: ENGENDERING CLASS: DRAYTON, WROTH, MILTON, AND
THE GENESIS OF THE PUBLIC SPHERE

1. Quotations of the 1619 *Idea* are from *The Works of Michael Drayton*, 5 vols.,
   ed. J. William Hebel (Oxford: The Shakespeare Head Press, 1932–41), vol. 2.
2. See for instance Josephine A. Roberts, "Lady Mary Wroth's Sonnets: A
   Labyrinth of the Mind," *Journal of Women's Studies in Literature* 1 (1979):
   319–29; Elaine Beilin, "'The Onely Perfect Vertue': Constancy in Mary
   Wroth's *Pamphilia to Amphilanthus*," *Spenser Studies* 2 (1981): 229–45;
   Josephine A. Roberts, "The Biographical Problem of *Pamphilia to
   Amphilanthus*," *Tulsa Studies in Women's Literature* 1 (1982): 43–53; Mary
   Ellen Lamb, *Gender and Authorship in the Sidney Circle* (Madison: University
   of Wisconsin Press, 1990), 167; Barbara Kiefer Lewalski, *Writing Women in
   Jacobean England* (Cambridge, MA: Harvard University Press, 1993); Gary
   Waller, *The Sidney Family Romance: Mary Wroth, William Herbert, and
   the Early Modern Construction of Gender* (Detroit: Wayne State University
   Press, 1993).
3. See for instance Ann Rosalind Jones, *The Currency of Eros: Women's Love
   Lyric in Europe, 1540–1620* (Bloomington: Indiana University Press, 1990),
   118–54; Jones, "Designing Women: The Self as Spectacle in Mary Wroth and
   Veronica Franco," in *Reading Mary Wroth: Representing Alternatives in
   Early Modern England*, ed. Naomi J. Miller and Gary Waller (Knoxville:
   University of Tennessee Press, 1991), 135–53; Jeffrey Masten, "'Shall I turne
   blabb?': Circulation, Gender, and Subjectivity in Mary Wroth's Sonnets," in
   Reading Mary Wroth, 67–87; Nona Fienberg, "Mary Wroth and the
   Invention of Female Poetic Subjectivity," in *Reading Mary Wroth*, 175–90;
   Naomi J. Miller, *Changing the Subject: Mary Wroth and Figurations of
   Gender in Early Modern England* (Lexington: University Press of Kentucky,
   1996); Heather Dubrow, *Echoes of Desire: English Petrarchism and its
   Counterdiscourses* (Ithaca: Cornell University Press, 1995), 134–61; and
   Rosalind Smith, "Lady Mary Wroth's *Pamphilia to Amphilanthus*: The
   Politics of Withdrawal," *ELR* 30 (2000): 408–31.
4. Miller, *Changing the Subject*, 44.
5. Elizabeth Hanson, "Boredom and Whoredom: Reading Renaissance
   Women's Sonnet Sequences," *The Yale Journal of Criticism* 10 (1997):
   165–91, 177.
6. Smith, "Lady Mary Wroth's *Pamphilia to Amphilanthus*," 420. William
   Kennedy, *The Site of Petrarchism: Early Modern National Sentiment in Italy,
   France, and England* (Baltimore: The Johns Hopkins University Press, 2003),
   172.
7. *The Poems of Lady Mary Wroth*, ed. Josephine A. Roberts (Baton Rouge:
   Louisiana State University Press, 1983), 134. All further quotations of Wroth
   refer to this edition.
8. Smith, "Lady Mary Wroth's *Pamphilia to Amphilanthus*," 430.
9. On *oikos*, see Lorna Hutson, *The Usurer's Daughter: Male Friendship and
   Fictions of Women in Sixteenth-Century England* (London: Routledge, 1994),
   17–51; and Jürgen Habermas, *The Structural Transformation of the Public
   Sphere: An Inquiry into a Category of Bourgeois Society*, trans. Thomas

Burger with the assistance of Frederick Lawrence (Cambridge, MA: MIT Press, 1989), 3, 20. On the intersection of gender and class configurations, see Mary Poovey, *Uneven Developments: The Ideological Work of Gender in Mid-Victorian England* (Chicago: University of Chicago Press, 1988); and Michael McKeon, "Historicizing Patriarchy: The Emergence of Gender Difference in England, 1660–1760," *Eighteenth-Century Studies* 28 (1995): 295–322.

10. Hanson, "Boredom and Whoredom," 183.

11. McKeon, "Historicizing Patriarchy," 313, 298.

12. On Rochester's complex position in the emergence of class, see Sarah Ellenzweig, "Hitherto Propertied: Rochester's Aristocratic Alienation and the Paradox of Class Formation in Restoration England," *ELH* 69.3 (2002): 703–25. On Marvell, see John Rogers' reading of "Nymph Complaining for the Death of Her Faun" in *The Matter of Revolution: Science, Poetry, and Politics in the Age of Milton* (Ithaca: Cornell University Press, 1996), 212–17. On Philips, see Catherine Gray, "Katherine Philips and the Post-Courtly Coterie," *ELR* 32.3 (2002): 426–51.

13. On Milton's debt to a prophetic Sidneyian and Spenserian tradition, see especially David Norbrook, *Poetry and Politics in the English Renaissance*, Revised Edition (Oxford: Oxford University Press, 2002), 224–69.

14. See Milton's sonnet VIII in *John Milton: The Complete Poems*, ed. John Leonard (London: Penguin, 1998), 36. All further quotations of Milton refer to this edition.

15. Christopher Kendrick, *Milton: A Study in Ideology and Form* (New York: Methuen, 1986), 46.

16. See Fineman, *Shakespeare's Perjured Eye*, 45–47.

17. See Kendrick, *Milton*. My debt to Kendrick should be readily apparent, especially when he insists that this subjectivity marks a definite class position: "Milton's radicalism is fairly distinctive . . . because it is apparently one with all that is residual or conservative in his constitution. The form that his purificatory ethic takes, inasmuch as it implies a kind of natural bodily uniqueness that has nothing in common with the strictly compensatory privileging of one's own functions peculiar to the entrenched bourgeois, justifies the epithet of 'aristocratic' so often applied to Milton. He is reviving something resembling 'spontaneous nobility,' and clothing it in saintly garb. So that at this point, monism may be seen as an attempt to reappropriate aristocratic ideology for the hegemonic revolutionary ends of the oppositional class" (38–39).

18. Habermas, *The Structural Transformation of the Public Sphere*, 28. See also Craig Calhoun, "Introduction: Habermas and the Public Sphere," in *Habermas and the Public Sphere*, ed. Craig Calhoun (Cambridge, MA: MIT Press, 1992), 7.

19. What social groups participate in the public sphere has been a source of debate among historians. See the discussion in Harold Mah, "Phantasies of the Public Sphere: Rethinking the Habermas of Historians," *The Journal of Modern History*, 72 (2000): 153–82, which criticizes the reimagination of the public sphere as a space in which any group identity may be politically acted out. Mah especially reacts to essays in *Habermas and the Public Sphere*: Nancy Fraser, "Rethinking the Public Sphere: A Contribution to the Critique

of Actually Existing Democracy," 109–42; Mary P. Ryan, "Gender and Public Access: Women's Politics in Nineteenth-Century America," 259–88; and Geoff Eley, "Nations, Publics, and Political Cultures: Placing Habermas in the Nineteenth Century," 289–339.

20. Mah, "Phantasies of the Public Sphere," 165–66.
21. Habermas, *The Structural Transformation of the Public Sphere*, 7.
22. Ibid., 47, 46.
23. Mah, "Phantasies of the Public Sphere," 168.
24. Carolyn Betensky, "The Prestige of the Oppressed: Symbolic Capital in a Guilt Economy," in *Pierre Bourdieu: Fieldwork in Culture*, ed. Nicholas Brown and Imre Szeman (Lanham, MD: Rowman and Littlefield, 2000), 207–14, 208.
25. Habermas, *The Structural Transformation of the Public Sphere*, 46.
26. "Note to 'Miscellaneous Sonnets,' 1843," in William Wordsworth, *Wordsworth's Poetical Works*, ed. Ernest de Selincourt and Helen Darbishire (Oxford: Clarendon Press, 1952–1959), III. 417; quoted in Stuart Curran, *Poetic Form and British Romanticism* (Oxford: Oxford University Press, 1986): "I had long been well acquainted with [Milton's sonnets], but I was particularly struck on that occasion by the dignified simplicity and majestic harmony that runs through most of them, – in character so different from the Italian, and still more so from Shakespeare's fine Sonnets" (41).

Index

Cambridge Studies in Renaissance Literature and Culture

General Editor
STEPHEN ORGEL
Jackson Eli Reynolds Professor of Humanities, Stanford University